PI IN THE SKY

A REVELATION OF THE ANCIENT CELTIC WISDOM TRADITION

Michael Poynder has lived much of his life by the Carrowkeel mountain
in County Sligo, near the Atlantic coastline. Carrowkeel is known
internationally for its enigmatic neolithic structures, cairns and
standing stones. A landscape painter and poet,
he works as a healer and is a Healer Member of the
UK National Federation of Spiritual Healers.

PI IN THE SKY

A REVELATION OF THE ANCIENT CELTIC WISDOM TRADITION

Michael Poynder

The Collins Press

THIS EDITION IN 1997 BY
The Collins Press
West Link Park
Doughcloyne
Wilton
Cork

Reprinted 1999

First published in the UK in 1992 by Rider, an imprint of Random Century Group Ltd.
© Michael Poynder

Printed in Ireland by Colour Books Ltd., Dublin

Jacket design by Upper Case Ltd, Cork

ISBN: 1-898256-33-0

OM SAI RAM

*This book is dedicated to and
was personally blessed by
Sri Sathya Sai 'Beloved Baba'
on 12 December 1990
at Prasanthi Nilayam, India*

"Basin Reflector" East Chamber
Newgrange, Co. Meath.
© OPW Dublin.

Contents

Foreword

Michael Poynder has done a noble work of patient study and deep interpretation. *Pi in the Sky* is a great achievement and will help many who are drawn into the exploration of the works of ancient man in the landscape. Our far ancestors at the dawn of culture knew the truth that the human being does indeed descend to Earth from an eternal realm of spirit and flowing life. The wise ones knew that this vital knowledge was likely to be lost and must be affirmed in the symbolism of art.

This is the great truth that we need to recover as we pass through our age of materialism, violence and doubt. Could it be that the carved spirals at Newgrange are not mere decoration, but represent the flow of life from which we descended and to which we must, in time, return? Could the little carved 'cups' represent the experience of the individual ego? The ancient carvings symbolise the great truth that the initiates knew and that we must find again in our time. The so-called tombs may well, in truth, have been chambers for initiation into higher knowledge. This great book is rich with knowledge and wisdom. The fact that the author dedicates this scholarly work to Sri Sathya Sai 'Baba' shows that he is dealing not merely with ancient archaeology but with the living, spiritual awakening in our time.

This is a great work and Michael Poynder deserves our thanks and congratulations.

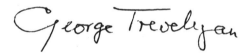

Newgrange K52 (Backstone)

In 1982 the United States sent a space craft out beyond our solar system containing scientific diagrams, music, art and voice telling about our civilization as of now.

In about 3500 BC Stone Age Man (SAM) carved, for future civilizations, a diagram of the way he used the natural science of our solar system in his everyday life. Kerbstone 52 at Newgrange is that enigmatic energy printout, called 'rock art' by the archaeologists but now in this book – finally deciphered (see Chapter VIII).

Acknowledgements

The author has made every possible effort to contact individuals, authors and publishers whose work he has quoted. In a book that is of an esoteric/exoteric nature it is not always possible to define 'quotes' since much of the material is opinion or intuition that cannot be bound by stringent copyright, fact or material substance. Therefore, to any individual author or publisher here represented, the author wishes to offer thanks and appreciation for all the encouragement he has received and for the many 'permissions' granted.

The author wishes to offer special thanks and acknowledgements for permission to reproduce material, for their teaching and sharing to the following individuals and organisations:

Wing Commander Clive Beadon DFC RAF(Retd) and
  Mr Geoffrey King (Earth Stars)
The late Bruce MacMannaway (The Westbank Healing Centre)
Sir George Trevelyan, Bt
The Wrekin Trust
Anna Campbell White (The Alpha Centre)
Ron Bonewitz (*Crystal Consciousness*, Shambhala)
Gavin and Margaret Ann Livingstone (The Shambhala Centre)
Peter and Elizabeth Gill (The Waymark Centre)
Lilla Bek (*Colour Healing*)
A.T. Mann (*The Round Art: Astrology of Time and Space*,
  Dragon World Books)
Maurice Cotterell (*Astrogenetics*, Brooks, Hill, Robinson)
Alice Bailey (*Ponder on This*, Lucis Trust)
Christopher Hills (University of the Trees)
Keith Critchlow (*Time Stands Still*, Gordon Fraser)
The late Robert Webster FGA (*Gems*, Butterworths)
Peter Dawkins (The Gatekeeper Trust)
Arvid and Wendy Willen
The O'Hara
The late Michael J. O'Kelly (*Newgrange*, Thames & Hudson)
Clair O'Kelly (*Concise Guide to Newgrange*)
George Eogan, Irish Archaeologist
Michael Herity (*Irish Passage Graves*, IUP Dublin)
George Wingfield (*The Crop Circle Enigma*)
Göran Burnenhuilt and Stefan Burgh, Swedish Archaeologists
Clair Tuffy (Newgrange Site Office)
David Knight (photographer)
Steve Rogers (photographer)
Rod Bull (photographer, *Time Stands Still*)
George Philip & Son (*Planisphere*)
Leo Regan (VEC Office, Sligo)
Henry Rowan, Sligo
The Royal Irish Academy
The National Museum of Ireland
The Department of Public Works (Dublin)
Parks and Monuments Department, Dublin
Irish Ordnance Survey Office (Phoenix Park)
James P. Whittall II (Ancient Sites Research Society, Mass., USA)
Colin Bloy (Fountain International)
Phillip Carr-Gomm (O.B.O.D)

And to my dear friend P.S., companion of many lifetimes and psychic journeys.

Introduction

In 1962 I took a holiday in the west of Ireland and ended up on the shores of Lough Arrow in County Sligo. To my surprise I felt completely at home in this strange and beautiful environment, and I stayed.

All around the Lough are limestone hills dotted with enigmatic Stone Age and Bronze Age structures, cairns, standing stones, circles and crannoghs about which no-one seemed to have any information. Who had built these structures, when, and above all, what purpose did they serve? There seemed to be no information available from any relevant authority – the Tourist Board, the museums, the locals and the Church declared them to be simply 'pagan' and of the devil. To me this was just not good enough, so I decided to find out for myself. It has been a fascinating, frustrating and financially expensive journey of discovery, covering nearly thirty years' research, now offered in this book.

The first twenty years were what can only be termed 'preliminary acclimatisation', for frankly, I discovered very little; yet having walked and climbed many, many valleys and hills, at least I was familiar with some of the thousands of Irish and English Stone Age sites. Then in 1981, for the first time, I experienced someone using a pendulum in alternative medicine. Suddenly in seeing this swinging pendulum turning through a double sprial of positive and negative, I was given the key to unlock the Stone Age structures. For here, clearly demonstrated before my eyes, was the double scroll of the Stone Age 'rock art' as it is called by the archaeologists and engraved so clearly in 3500 BC at the Great Cairn of Newgrange in County Meath. It was a simple but momentous breakthrough that now, ten years later, has resulted in the deciphering and understanding of Stone Age geometry and structure, and many of my questions have been answered.

Of course the story only starts in the Stone Age – for the pendulum has led me through the Bronze Age with its beautiful gold objects, solar and lunar calculators, that lie unrecognised in the National Museum in Dublin, to the early Christian times of the Celtic monks and their little churches, and subsequently to the flowering of art, metal work and architecture of the early Renaissance in North-west Europe.

It is a journey of magic and mystery and demonstrates quite clearly how the glory and beauty of the Kingdom – the One and only Kingdom of Planet Earth – has gradually been occulted, or hidden, from ordinary men and women to a point where we now express with sadness that the 'ancient wisdom tradition' has been lost.

This book sets out to show how much of the wisdom is all around us still in our countryside, lying unrecognised in our museums and so distorted, denigated and ridiculed in our religious practice that it has been dismissed as irrelevant.

Finally, but most importantly, you will notice that this book is dedicated to Sri Sathya Sai 'Baba' and an explanation is necessary.

My journey has led me through many aspects of mystery and magic and the gradual unfolding of a personal, spiritual awareness that has come about by intuitive contact with the wonderful ancient wisdom tradition that transcends all dogmas and leads us to the idea of the One Creator. This is the force that holds the balance of eternity and reincarnation together, through time and space, as surely SAM (Stone Age Man) understood, and that is still totally expressed through the Eastern mystical teaching.

The present life and work of Sathya Sai 'Baba' encapsulates the perfection of this wisdom that has always been available to human beings since the beginning of time, but which we, being human, can only glimpse occasionally as we strive to acknowledge the Christ within. He offers anyone, of any persuasion, the totality of Universal Love that transcends all religions and human inequalities.

I hope in these few chapters you will find some of the reassurance you may seek – and come to know that we have a magical, beautiful ancient wisdom tradition still fully available to us.

Michael Poynder
1991

The breath of God – the solar wind – blowing round the zodiac. He holds the golden egg of the Sun in his left hand (English 16th-century stained glass window, Suffolk)

Chapter I
OUR SOLAR SYSTEM

Figure 1

*Our solar system: the
planets outwards from
the Sun (not to scale)*

The Sun is the star of our solar planetary system, and as we generally know there are nine major planets orbiting it of which the Earth is one. Viewed from within our own horizons, this planetary system seems vast as light travels at 186,000 miles per second. Therefore, it takes approximately 8 minutes for light to reach the Earth from the Sun and 5 hours and 22 minutes for the same light to reach our farthest planet, Pluto. Moving outwards from the Sun the planets, in order of distance, are as follows: Mercury, Venus, Earth, Mars, Jupiter, Saturn, Uranus, Neptune and Pluto. Each of the planets moves round the Sun with different elliptically-shaped orbits and therefore at varying distances, but in general these orbits are drawn as circles for simple understanding. Neither are they all on the same horizontal plane.

The Sun

Looking up into the heavens at night we see countless thousands of stars in this vast arena that we call the universe. Man's observation of the stars started when he first looked above the horizon and raised his sight and consciousness from the level of the surface of the Earth, about which he had been so concerned in his early evolution. We do not see the Sun as a star like all those other stars because we are so closely concerned with its light. How often during our lives do we actually consider Earth's progression within this little planetary system and recognise and acknowledge the importance of the solstices and equinoxes? How often do we stop and think what would happen if the light did not dispel the darkness at the beginning of each morning as the great 'O' of the day or 'Dei', the orb of our Sun, known as God from the earliest times, appears over the horizon? We take it for granted as we take so much for granted in our transitory lives. Do we ever stop to think how long life would endure on Earth if the Sun failed to flare? It is this age old worry that has directed so much of our agricultural evolution, observance of ritual and, ultimately, mystical knowledge. How long would it be before the trees and their fruits died, cereals and flowers withered away and the heart beat of man, so

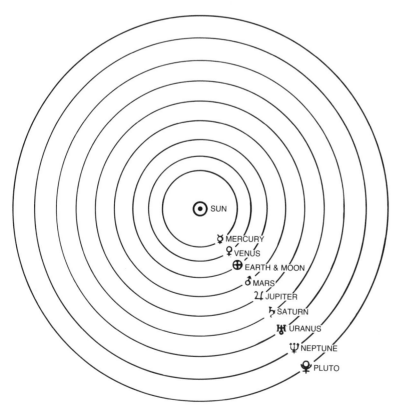

1

integrated and dependent, stopped, if the rhythms of the Sun cycle slowed down to a flicker and ended? Then man, and sooner or later all the other animals, would die; the process would not take very long. The stocks of food, the depleted quantities of unpolluted, drinkable water, the inadequate supplies of heat-providing substances, particularly trees, would soon disappear and within a short time this vibrant body cell we call Earth would fade into negativity. So it is natural (the word itself is symbolic) that man, throughout memorable time, has to a great extent prayed to, for and with the Sun as the symbol of God. It is solar energy which manifests so beautifully as the heat and light that gives us the aura of infinite variety we see in the colours of the spectrum.

The Sun is estimated to have been the energy centre of this planetary system for over 5,000,000,000 years. It is a ball of thermonuclear atomic fusion brought about by the interaction of hydrogen and helium within. The mass of these gases is of tremendous density, perhaps eight times the density of gold; and you may have remarked on gold's extraordinary weight. The energy produced at the centre permeates throughout our atomic solar system. It is our permanent journey round the Sun that determines the amount of heat and light that reaches us, and growth on our planet's surface. It is the vast and steady electro-magnetic push and pull of our Sun that determines each of the planets' path through our solar space.

On a totally predictable cycle the Sun releases varying amounts of energy from different areas of its mass, known as sun flares and sun spots; they create the solar wind – the 'breath of God'. It seems that throughout the millions of years the Earth has been forming these emissions have changed our planet, when periodically a vast release of energy from outside our atmosphere has permeated the Earth, disrupted our auric balance, altered the tilt and reversed our magnetic fields. It was such a sudden change of energy that killed the mastodons of Siberia in the twinkling of an eye. To try and understand the enormity of the Sun envisage, if you can, that it is 1.3 million times bigger by volume than the Earth, approximately 870,312 miles in diameter and about 93,750,000 miles away.

As the Sun produces heat and light, so it also produces electro-magnetic fields of enormous strength. Each planet travels its own particular path because of these fields; each in turn soaks up and reflects energy in different strengths, depending on individual material make-up, therefore acting as individual transformers within the system. If you can accept this simple fact then it is not difficult to understand that the energy released from each planet must also affect the Earth and vice versa. Since each planet is constantly changing position, relative to the others, the resultant energy changes are very varied and affect our own energy field here on Earth. These also subtly affect aspects of our daily lives through all vibrational levels, as electricity, magnetism and light are filtered into the surface of the Earth and into the bodies of human beings. Of course, the relative positions of the planets at the time of our conception and birth must affect our individual life energy too. Hence the relevance of natal and conceptual astrology.

It would be much simpler to comprehend if the Sun itself was static in the universe, but it is not. The Sun moves in a gigantic circle at 12.2 miles per second pulling its revolving planets along with it in yet another spiral within our galaxy. The relationship of the movement of the Sun and the movement of the planets around it as it curves through space is the basis of numerology and mathematics in the ancient mysteries. This is such a vast concept that the only way Stone Age Man (SAM) was able to obtain reference points was to choose constellations that were lying far out around the seemingly static periphery of the Milky Way, and so the 12 constellations of the zodiac became part of the calendar. In AD 1991 the Pole Star, Polaris, is our semi-permanent true northern reference point, but in SAM's time we calculate it was in the constellation of Draco, the Dragon. This change is due to the Earth's tilt on its axis, called precession, a completed 'wobble'

Planetary symbols

☉	Sun
⊕	Earth
☽	Moon
☿	Mercury
♀	Venus
♂	Mars
♃	Jupiter
♄	Saturn
♅	Uranus
♆	Neptune
♇	Pluto
☊	Moon node

Figure 2
Circles of heaven and Earth c.3000 BC. Circuit of the Earth's celestial pole round the pole of the ecliptic, showing how we move from age to age

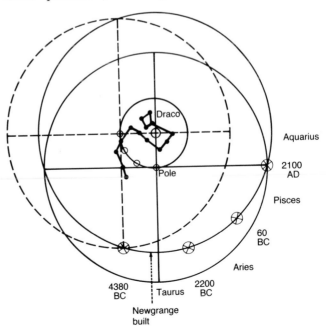

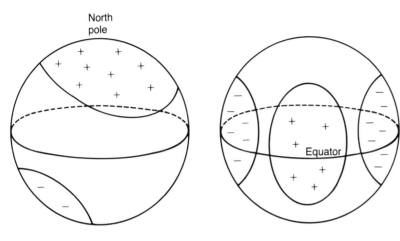

Figure 3
The Sun's magnetic
energy fields (Figures 3,
4a, b, c, 5 and 8,
Maurice Cotterell,
Astrogenetics)

Signs of the zodiac

♈ Aries

♉ Taurus

♊ Gemini

♋ Cancer

♌ Leo

♍ Virgo

♎ Libra

♏ Scorpio

♐ Sagittarius

♑ Capricorn

♒ Aquarius

♓ Pisces

around the celestial pole from start to finish taking 26,000 years.

The centre of the Sun's great orbit is referred to as our Galactic Centre, the star, Sirius, and it is estimated that the Sun takes 25 million years to complete one full orbit around it. In turn the influences from this centre must radiate outwards affecting each star and constellation and our Sun depending on its relative position to any other at any one time. It is a Chinese ball situation of one within one without one in constant motion round and about; the eternal spiral interweaving itself until it eventually goes through a completed gigantic orbit and back to the starting point. In our system of the nine planets this happens on different time scales as explained later, but it must have taken many years for SAM to experience and note the varied approaching conjunctions and divergencies that took place. How often an expected planetary event, that had been so patiently observed through countless years, must have seemed imminent before the observers were finally confident enough to be sure of the pattern in the zodiac. How often the clouds and rains must have frustrated the end of long-awaited events in the last crucial weeks of observation.

Let us now examine how the Sun affects us here on Earth. We know that solar activity is stimulated by the interplay between the Sun's magnetic fields and their differential rotation. The Sun has two distinct magnetic fields which can be called the polar field 'P' and the equatorial field 'E'. This 'E' field consisting of alternating positive and negative polarities. The two fields rotate at different rates, 'P' every 37 days and 'E' every 26 days so that $^{37}/_{26} = 1.42$ which we can accept as 'the solar fraction'.

As rotation occurs, so energy is given off from the Sun in the form of a solar wind that consists of positive and negative particles that take approximately 48 hours to reach Planet

Earth (World) – 'W'. The composition of these particles is primarily an equal number of electrons and protons with 4–5% of heavier ions and nuclei – notably alpha particles. Solar wind particles are a by-product of magnetic solar activity which arise due to the differential rotation of these polar and equatorial fields. They can be drawn in plan view thus:

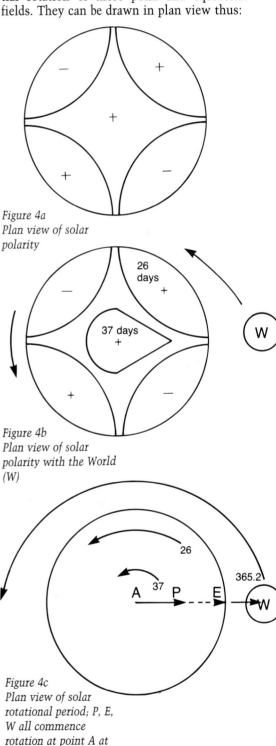

Figure 4a
Plan view of solar
polarity

Figure 4b
Plan view of solar
polarity with the World
(W)

Figure 4c
Plan view of solar
rotational period; P, E,
W all commence
rotation at point A at
time zero

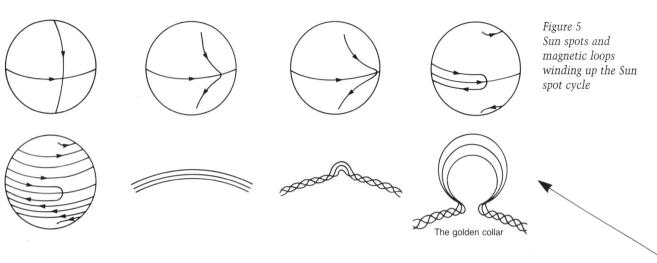

Figure 5
Sun spots and magnetic loops winding up the Sun spot cycle

The golden collar

At the same time the Earth (World) – 'W' – is also rotating once round the Sun every 365 days. Thus it has been calculated that every seven days, due to this differential rotation, the Sun's energy hits 'W' with alternating polarity, i.e. positive to negative every week, as solar wind. This solar wind changing every seven days is the very 'breath of God' known to us through the *Book of Genesis*, telling us how God made the world in seven days. It is interesting to note that the underground water energies change polarity every seven days too.

This is particularly noticeable along the Stone Age 'alignments' at Carnac.

The Sun Spot Cycle
As the 'E' field rotates more quickly than the 'P' field – 26 as compared to 37 days – so these fields get wound up to form a coiled or toroidal field which varies in strength and latitude below the Sun's surface. The magnetic lines of force tangle until the turbulent gas bursts through the surface forming positive and negative Sun spot pairs.

Figure 6
Lanyon Quoit 'dolmen', Cornwall

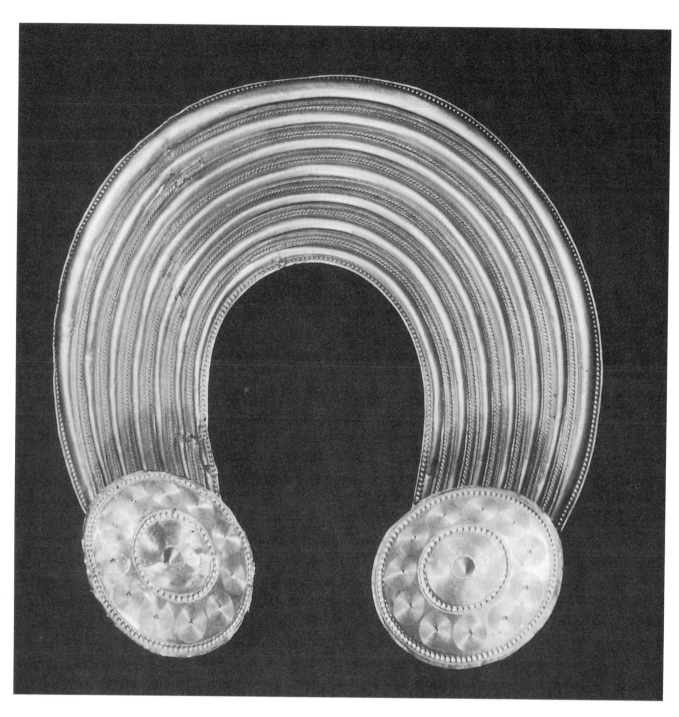

How often we look at artefacts on the ground at ancient sites and see shapes and engravings we 'know' instinctively but are unable to identify. Lying in our museums, particularly in the National Museum of Ireland, are many magnificent gold and stone objects that are merely dismissed as ritual objects yet must have had great significance to the people who made them. In this book we will examine many such artefacts and offer some explanations for their uses.

This magnificent gold collar from the Bronze Age has often been illustrated and shown worn round the neck of a 'Druidic' priest. But if we see it as a solar artefact and count the sundiscs around the circular flanges – there are 11 on each – a total of 22, then count the elliptical bows of the flare collar – there are seven – representing the seven rays of light, we know that $^{22}/_7$ is the fundamental mathematical proportion of circular and three-dimensional geometry or Pi, represented by

Figure 7
Gleninsheen gold Druidic collar: 2×11 dots over 7 semicircles = $^{22}/_7$ = π (National Museum of Ireland)

the figure π. Many Stone and Bronze Age sites are laid out with the use of this mathematical proportion and we note that Pi is represented in the Stone Age by dolmens hence our title of 'Pi in the Sky'.

The relationship of P△E△W Polar and Equatorial Sun rotation to the (W)orld's rotation can be drawn thus:

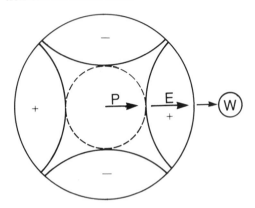

Figure 8
P △ E △ W Sun spot cycle

This shows how the three different variables all start together in line. They will not all come into line again for another 22.985 years or one half cycle of 11.492 years – which is taken as the Sun spot cycle.

The Chinese astrological birthchart is based on the correct regression of the Sun spot cycle, a 12-year 'animal' cycle focusing on a 12 × 5 elemental table totalling 60 years, the five elements being earth, air, fire, water and wood. Therefore, in a 12-year cycle each element occurs twice. This means there are five types of rat, five types of ox, etc., or 60 sign/element combinations. Each combination therefore occurs once every 60 years. Since this discipline was started in 2637 BC, the ancient Chinese, like SAM, must have had a very sophisticated knowledge of the Sun. Also consider that 12 years is 12 × 12 months, or 144 months, a figure that relates to the American Indian sundance myths, then also consider the *Book of Revelations* and remember how John the Diviner refers to the 144,000 members of the 'tribes' that will be saved on the Day of Judgement. Throughout history we have reference to the activity of the Sun as 'God', the great 'O' or 'orb' (sphere) of 'Dei', 'Deus' or DAY! For GOD and the SUN are synonymous. The Sun alternating the Earth's polarity from positive to negative every seven days also controls the female menstrual cycle to 28 days and we now realise that it is not the moon that regulates this natural function.

Consider the Sun has a periodic rate of combustion such that every 500–1,000 years it increases in temperature and size then later contracts and cools, therefore it seemingly pulses as it grows larger or smaller over time. This must affect what happens on Earth. As the Sun expands and grows in size and energy output so it envelops the planet Mercury and as a consequence Mercury's magnetic field decreases with temperature. Consequently Mercury, due to its solar equatorial orbit, no longer causes the Sun's equatorial magnetic field to rotate more quickly than its polar magnetic field. Thus $P=E^{37}/_{37}$, and the Sun spot cycle ceases!

Maurice Cotterell's book *Astrogenetics* shows that when this happens the World (W) is disastrously affected by a subsequent sharp decline in the essential life force contained in the solar wind. So conception and procreation decline swiftly because the human brain responds to magnetic variation and converts such variations into, in the male, the fertility hormone testosterone, and in the female, the fertility hormones oestrogen and progesterone. As fertility declines due to the cessation in solar activity the existing human population also declines over a period of say 100 years until a Doomsday scenario occurs when the whole of civilisation could be wiped out. Selectively this is what has happened in the past during the Ice Age.

Throughout mythology we have 'sagas' of

Figure 9
The Fuller Brooch: Anglo-Saxon 9th century AD (British Museum)

the 'Beings of Light' – in Ireland 'The Shining Ones' or the Tuatha Da-Naan who retired into their cairns never to be seen again. Could this not have been the folk/myth of a period of sharply falling birthrate and zero conception – a time when the tribes did not conceive and reproduce?

As we come to study the Great Cairn at Newgrange, we will see how the priesthood used natural scientific artefacts to rebalance and reproduce that life force energy to counter this solar power failure. They were only partially successful and subsequently were forced to withdraw into the cairns and demanifest through the quartz spirals back into cosmic space. This same natural cycle took place in the Atlantean Age and later in the Greek and Mayan ages – also in the Chinese and the Indian civilisations – and is exactly the situation ahead of us on Planet Earth now.

The old accumulated knowledge was passed from one priest to the next initiate to be retained without the written word until finally it was laid out in and around stone structures of permanence for all to see and learn from, such as Carrowkeel, Newgrange, Stonehenge and the Pyramids. Today we have Greenwich mean time and quartz watches, pocket calculators and home computers, television and satellites. Ancient man, with his true simplicity and natural 'being at one' in the universe, had only the earth and sky and 'that which revolved in it'. He had infinite time and uncluttered clairvoyant perception. He learned that the Sun was the centre of his world but he also knew that it was the apparent movement of the Sun around him, on the Earth, that allowed him to use it as his cosmic clock – a knowledge occulted in the late Bronze Age and supposedly not discovered until the Renaissance 2,500 years later, and only now emerging again, redefined, as the physics of the macrocosm in this Aquarian Age.

The rays of the Sun were seen as the energy that gave nourishment to the Earth and to everything on and in the surface of it. The Sun means purity and life. From within the hidden colours of the rainbow spectrum come the vibrations that motivate life on its path of growth and evolution. Within the harmonic of the Sun nature goes to sleep and slows down, as can be seen from day to night to day, month to month and season to season. Our plants, the annuals and perennials, the animals and man each have their appointed vibrational span; for nothing is new under the Sun.

The Sun generating energy as heat, light and 'hold' on us is positive energy. It is the masculine energy of strength, procreation and growth – ultimately it is LIFE, and the colour of the Sun's energy is pure gold, as the Sun's metal is gold – constant, untarnishable and immutable.

The Moon

As the Sun rises and sets around our horizons each morning and evening giving us life and light and a reliable hour hand to our cosmic clock, so the minute hand, with its faster cycle, our other constant companion, reminds us of its presence during the night. The Moon is a neutral satellite of the Earth, following its path around us held in orbit by the power of the Sun's magnetic field and the strength of our gravitational forces. It is an astringent negative ball of volcanic rock, a quarter of our size, about 239,000 miles away, turning on its axis at the same speed as we turn. Hence we only ever see the same face towards us – for a simple example, face someone and both walk a circle sideways around; you will always face each other.

The Moon reflects the light of the Sun like a solar mirror, and it is the varying amount of sunlight hitting the Moon each night as we both revolve that gives us the different lunar phases during one complete orbit of the Earth

Figure 10
28-night lunar cycle

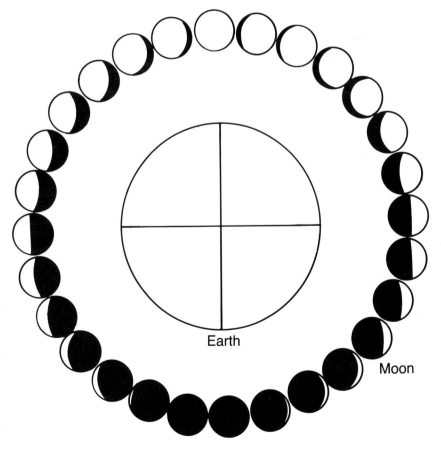

– which we call a month or moon'th. This is simply illustrated by Figure 10. As the Sun controls us significantly during the day so the Sun reflected off the dead negative Moon influences us during the night. The greatest effect is at the 'new Moon' when the far obscured side is being heated up by direct sunlight. This causes a strong gravitational effect towards the near dark side facing us so pulling away from Earth – the side we see – and has a concentrated dense force. For example, if you heat one side of a brick the other side has its energy drawn or pulled through it. This force acts strongly on Earth, on the tides, and is felt by the plant and animal kingdoms too. It is particularly recognised in behaviour patterns as a negative disruptive time in the human 'feminine' Sun cycle – the day before, during and after the new 'sickle' (circle) Moon. As soon as the new Moon begins to grow or 'wax', the dead dark side facing us begins to lighten and warm up. So the plants and animals relax and start to expand with the resultant rise again in growth patterns. It is well known that it is best to plant or conceive on a growing or waxing Moon.

When the full Moon becomes a full orb and in bloom, the night time energy reaches its peak for the Moon is acting as a full-faced mirror reflecting as much of the power of the Sun as is possible, and it becomes a time of expansion. After full Moon, the energy drops away, or wanes, towards the next detractive new Moon. These phases are easily calculable provided you live in an area where you can expect clear night skies, but remember that, due to the westward movement of the Earth through the zodiac, the Moon appears over the horizon later each night. In mythology the Moon governs both positive and negative because of these influences on energy levels, and is known to affect electricity, fertility, conception, growth, decline, decay and death thereby influencing the natural cycle. 'She' is both the mother and kind, or, depending on individual life states, is also accepted as cold and cruel.

Lunar eclipses occur from two to five times a year, when the Moon passes into direct shadow of the Earth with the Sun directly behind it. This is a time of strong negative activity on Earth, but fortunately only lasts for about three and a half hours and only during full Moon alignments.

Each month the Moon circles the entire horoscope and activates the life cycle on an emotional level, particularly affecting latent tensions and forcing them to externalise through the feelings – the Moon establishes the tone of life.
(A.T. Mann, *The Round Art: Astrology of Time and Space*)

The Moon is a holding vessel for the thoughts, feelings and the conditioning patterns which tend to crystallise ideas within the individual being as within the structure built of stone.
(Lorusso and Glick, *Healing Stones*)

The Sun being masculine and constant represents the male and the Moon being feminine and negative represents the female – both, when working together nurturing and influencing the Earth with balance, are expressed by the Chinese as Yin and Yang. Whereas the Sun manifests as golden light the Moon's energy manifests as silver.

The Moon's nodes are the two points at which the Moon crosses the ecliptic. When the Moon is travelling south to north this is called the ascending node and is considered a positive energy release. The opposite, travelling north to south, is the descending node and is considered to be negative energy. The complete cycle of the nodes takes thirteen years and was known and used by ancient man. Note the symbol ☊.

Figure 11
The Golden Mean proportion: the arc or ark of the Golden Mean proportion ⊕ is represented by the arc of the Sun at summer solstice, i.e. at the latitude of Great Britain around 51.42°. The oblong produced by the projection of the Golden Mean (top of page 10) is represented by the coffer in the Pyramid and in the cist burials of Stone Age Man in Britain and Ireland

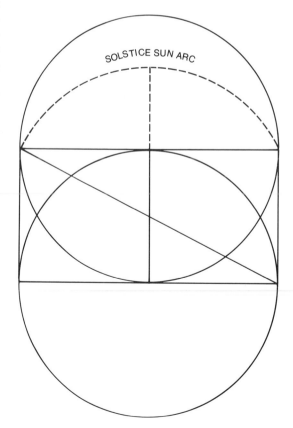

SOLSTICE SUN ARC

Figure 12
'Cist' burial in the
Golden Mean
proportion within a
stone circle (photo: Rod
Bull, *Time Stands Still*)

Figure 13
Cave drawing c.15000
BC, from France,
showing the Golden
Mean proportion.
Recently much interest
has been shown in the
'Kogi' Indians of
Colombia. Their line
engraved 'entrance'
stone depicts an idea of
the solar frequency of
the Golden Mean, as is
seen here in ancient
'rock art'

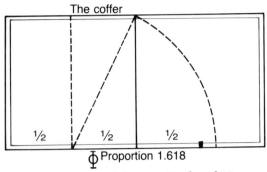

The coffer

½ ½ ½

Φ Proportion 1.618

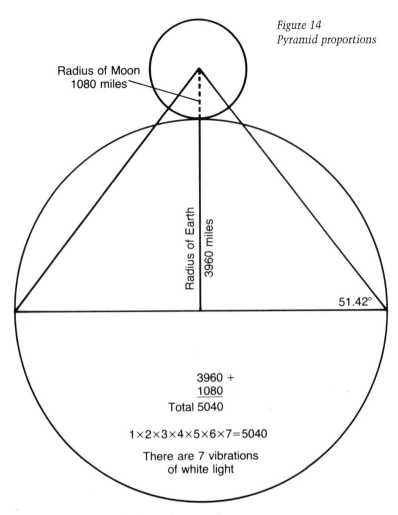

Figure 14
Pyramid proportions

Radius of Moon
1080 miles

Radius of Earth
3960 miles

51.42°

3960 +
1080
Total 5040

1×2×3×4×5×6×7=5040

There are 7 vibrations
of white light

The dimensions of the Sun, Earth and Moon were all carefully calculated when the layout of the Great Pyramid was drawn to 'sacred' geometry – the basis of which is the Golden Mean proportion whose sign is Φ. This is the ultimate geometric proportion expressed through the conjunction of two interlocking circles. The arc, or ark, produced represents the Biblical 'Ark of the Covenant' or more precisely the arc of the Sun's travels round the sky, due to the Earth's offset or tilt, at the summer solstice, 21st June. You will see from the diagram above how an oblong is produced by the two interlocking circles and the diagonal thus formed 'throwing' the arc above or below it – 'as above so below'. The resultant proportions of the oblong give us the 'coffer' referred to as 'Ark of the Covenant' in which were contained the secrets of the Sun. The arc of the Golden Mean is this secret as seen by man every day the Sun shines above us from winter to spring to summer to autumn to winter again. Φ is the geometric expression or proportion of an 'ellipse', i.e. the solar wind.

The builders of the Great Pyramid took the radius of the Moon, 1,080 miles, to make up the height of the pyramid measuring in cubits, and 3,960 miles, the radius of the Earth.

With the proportions of the base the sides were angled at 51.42°. The ascending passage leading to the King's chamber contains the sarcophagus of the Golden Mean proportion and is at 26°18' or the same angle as the diagonal in that Golden section. Later we will see that Newgrange in Ireland is also laid out to the proportions of the Golden Mean and sevenfold symmetry. The symmetry of seven is the symmetry of light, sunlight that gives birth to everything on Earth, for it is the spectrum of white light or the seven colours of the rainbow; red, orange, yellow, green, blue, indigo and violet. We are told 'Man is made in the image of God' so if this is true 'we' must also express this beautiful proportion. Leonardo Da Vinci hinted at it when he drew man projecting a pentagon in a circle – however, to complete this magical proportion the man should be drawn as in Figure 15. For

here is the truth of enlightened man in his coat of many colours – the auric colours of sunlight.

The Planets of the Sun
As already mentioned, there are nine planets within our Sun system of which we, the Earth, are one and about which obviously we are critically concerned, but we tend to dismiss the fact that each of the planets, however near or far, large or small, follows a path of balance one to the other by the same gravitational force fields generated from the Sun. It is this balance in our solar system that influences what happens on Earth in subtle ways.

There are two planets between the Sun and the Earth's orbit termed the 'inferior' planets, Mercury and Venus. Both have their own characteristics, but their seen orbits from Earth only appear as small arcs around the horizon.

Mercury is closest to the Sun but seldom appears for any length of time as it is normally in the Sun's glare, or travelling in front or behind it, and therefore, generally invisible to

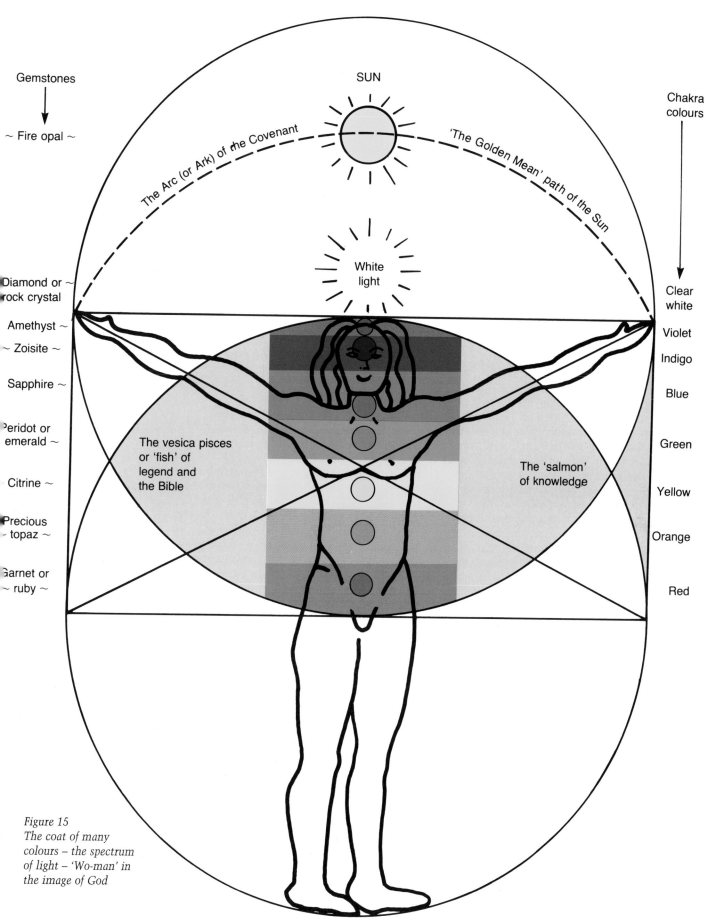

Gemstones

~ Fire opal ~

Diamond or ~
rock crystal

Amethyst ~

~ Zoisite ~

Sapphire ~

Peridot or
emerald ~

Citrine ~

Precious
~ topaz ~

Garnet or
~ ruby ~

SUN

The Arc (or Ark) of the Covenant

'The Golden Mean' path of the Sun

White
light

Chakra
colours

Clear
white

Violet

Indigo

Blue

Green

Yellow

Orange

Red

The vesica pisces
or 'fish' of
legend and
the Bible

The 'salmon'
of knowledge

Figure 15
The coat of many
colours – the spectrum
of light – 'Wo-man' in
the image of God

11

the naked eye. However, when visible it is near our horizon, either just before or after sunrise or in the evening at sunset. It travels around the Sun every eighty-eight days and rotates every sixty days, i.e. approximately every two months, and reflects sunlight, radio waves and radiation rather like our Moon. Mercury affects the strength of the solar wind due to its magnetic influence on the Sun's equatorial field. Since Mercury is similar to our Moon in its relationship to the Sun, it is also considered in myth to be a mediator, or reflector of energy between the two, and its sign is taken as the entwined snakes about the centre staff known as the caduceus. In mythology Mercury governs the positive mind and the quick processes of thought, action and intelligence; but its negativity can also show in humans as weakness and unreliability. Inevitably Mercury energy concerns the nervous system and characterises diplomats, politicians, negotiators and con-men.

Its atmosphere consists of hydrogen and helium around a hard core not dissimilar to our Moon and information from the American spacecraft Mariner 10 suggests it may once have been a moon of Venus. It is either very cold or very hot depending which side is facing the Sun, hence the diverse energy flow from it. The colour vibration from Mercury is taken as yellow and violet.

Venus is a bright planet and nearest to the Earth. The shimmering effect is due to swirling gases of carbon dioxide and acid droplets that reflect sunlight around the ball of the obscured planet, this light being seen at its best in the early morning or evening time. 'Her' constancy, rising and falling with the masculine energy of the Sun, earned her the title of the Morning Star, or the Goddess of Love, later to be Aphrodite of Greek legends. She was the 'consort' of the Sun and, since she orbits roughly between the Sun and the Earth, her path was used as a marker in many ancient sites – the Pyramids and Stonehenge for example, also perhaps in the Irish solar and planetary calculators we know as lunulae. As a 'goddess' she governs love, affection and beauty, the finer aspects of human aspirations.

Venus is about the same size as the Earth, taking 225 days to orbit the Sun, and comes to within 24,000,000 miles of us; but although sunlight is reflected from the swirling interior gases travelling at high speed 'she' has no appreciable magnetic field so little tangible effect on the Earth's energies.

The colour vibration of Venus is taken to be rose/pink, the heart colour.

The planets beyond the Earth's orbit are known as the 'superior' planets and those seen by SAM with the naked eye were used as part of his great time clock as they turned in cycles around him.

Mars is the next planet beyond the Earth and out from the Sun. It is not a big planet being only half the size of the Earth but its composition of iron and aluminium glows red. Our human and emotional perception identifies this energy with the colour of blood, rubies, the 'macho' image, unfortunately thus the God of War. Here is aggressive concentrated energy symbolised in ancient times by the shield and the sword. Every seventeen years Mars comes to within 35,000,000 miles of the Earth. If Venus is feminine then Mars is masculine and characterises the sex organs and the sacral (sacred, sac or procreative) centre – the desire for change and conflict – a selfish, assertive driving force allied to power and possession on Earth; positive energy which, when uncontrolled, can be very destructive but when used with love, and in conjunction with the other balancing forces, can give an energy flow of symmetry to the Earth.

The colour of Martian energy is red.

Jupiter. If Mars is small, dense and full of energy and drive, so Jupiter is the opposite in many ways. An enormous ball of swirling radiating magnetic gases a thousand times bigger than the Earth by volume and consisting mainly of hydrogen and helium, it has an iron silicate central core within and is very conductive. Magnetism swirls out to meet us as Jupiter orbits the Sun every eleven and three-quarter years, similar to our twelve moon'th year cycle. Jupiter was rightly named Zeus, the King of the Gods, and his life-giving properties of disciplined love were recognised and used accordingly. His 'anger' or negative energy brings storms and disastrous weather; his positive energy is symmetry. The colour vibration of Jupiter's energy is white and also blue to violet.

Saturn is the sixth planet out from the Sun and was named by the Greeks 'Chronos' which gives us the words chronological, chronograph, indicating predictable time. 'Old Father Time' refers to Saturn, the dark one, this planet taking nearly thirty years to travel round the Sun. 'He' was visible to SAM and as the farthest out from the Sun, viewed with the naked eye, was of great importance. The energy of Saturn coming towards the Earth is a concentrated dark energy which encloses and contains the 'white' energy of Jupiter. Often Saturn is considered to be black, and Father Time is depicted in the black cloak of death, but in fact this energy manifests as a very dark blue that we know as indigo merging to violet.

Since SAM 'saw' perceptively, he was able to plot the journeys of Mars, Jupiter and Saturn and use their travels in the time scales of progressive thought. A most important and universally talked about event, but generally unrecognised, is the great conjunction that occurred just before the birth of Jesus in the Middle East in 3 BC. This formed the original great 'star' of Bethlehem and brought the Three Kings, the wise men, and astrologers together heralding a planetary event. For at this conjunction there is a greatly concentrated release of positive energy that we choose to call 'divine light'. These 'kings' formed a trinity, the earthly representation of the planetary energy of Mars, Jupiter and Saturn bringing together their gifts of change, expansive white light love and the understanding of time (lessness) or eternal knowledge – gold, frankincense and myrrh respectively. Jesus, as a spiritual son of the divine hierarchy of the cosmos, was heralded and born under a 'shining star', indeed his incarnation was foretold, foreseen, awaited and acknowledged by the mystics for many centuries before. At the suggested actual birth time (p.m.), 22nd August or 15th September at the planetary conjunction, another 'star' stayed over Bethlehem for some time, from which we are told the angels descended having guided the kings to the birth place. The angels or higher beings of light arrived on a cosmic vibration to instruct and direct the rebirth event of an enlightened soul; at an appointed place, in appropriate time, for the benefit of mankind.

Beyond Saturn lie the three further planets only rediscovered by modern science in the last two hundred years. In 1791 Uranus was re-identified and subsequently named. It is an enormous planet fifty times bigger than the Earth and far away, approximately 1,783 million miles from the Sun, taking 84 years to orbit. However, this orbit around the Sun is so oblique that following it through the heavens led to the discovery of two other planets – Neptune in 1846 and Pluto in 1930.

Uranus. All three far-out planets have been compared with ancient gods and given attributes that we feel are necessary to complete certain lacks in our physical, emotional and psychological make-up within the limits of mythology and astrology. The ancient gods (the planets) were very real to the people, and just because they could not be seen with ordinary optical sight it did not mean that they did not exist. To suggest that these three remote planets were unknown to SAM is presumptuous. Arguments about knowledge always arise when we deal with questions of sensitive perception but remember that the whole of life and everything we do concerns the production, storage and dissipation of energy. Energy concerns vibration – wavelengths of various forms which in turn manifest as light, heat, colour and sound. A totally blind person can 'see' with his senses and he can describe accurately the presence or position of another energy form, be it a living body or a thing. A deaf person can 'hear' in his inner perception the vibrations of sound which have never been audible as 'ding-dong bell'. The ancient priesthood had these higher perceptions that we call clairvoyance, the true gifts of the spirit, and they were able, just as clairvoyants are today, to pick up the vibrations of energy that are beyond unawakened people's acceptability. If we think it presumptuous nonsense for sensitives to allot various attributes to planets only recently 'discovered' by science then maybe we are denying ourselves many of our own latent abilities before we have attempted to tune into them.

It has been explained that the Sun holds each planet on its path and that each of the planets reflects and conducts its orbit, however obscure, because of that energy. Everything therefore must have a balance or we, and the universe, would become chaotic and fly away. Since some energies are formed more in the evolutionary spiral than others, it is also obvious that some systems depend more on one wavelength than another. Our solar system is a vibrational force with different influences. The Earth is also vibrating from the inside out and across its surface mantle. Minerals, crystals, plants, animals and man are all in motion too. We can readily identify Mars and its aggressive red energy with out baser energies. So that if sensitives now say that Uranus' energy is blue, concerning the throat 'chakra' and affecting the membranes of the brain and the nervous system, and its electrical impulses pass through the auric body or our electro-magnetic field, we should at least try to experience and 'feel' that perception in ourselves and identify it with new personal growth and understanding. For the energy colour of Uranus is seen as bright blue.

Neptune is only a 145-year-old in current scientific discovery and even more obscure than Uranus. It takes 165 years to orbit and is 2,800 million miles from the Sun. Whereas Uranus allies with Mercury in mythology so Neptune, as the Sea God Poseidon, allies with

Jupiter or 'Zeus'. Like Uranus, Neptune has a mixed mineral composition and is surrounded by the gas methane which makes it intensely cold and bleak. Neptune's energy is considered to influence the perceptive pineal gland, 'the third eye', stimulating psychic activity and awareness, dreams and illusions, perhaps into the weakness of addictive habits; the giving up of the conscious to the unconscious, the effect of swimming and drowning – hence water. The energy colour of Neptune is orange to orchid-pink and denotes the lotus of Eastern tradition, the *padparadsha* golden pink sapphire of Sri Lanka, the opened third eye, the raised 'prana' from the sacred (sexual) base up the spinal column to flower as greater understanding, the universal idea of selflessness and objective sacrifice. This energy can be a path of service, or masochistic tendencies.

Pluto is as yet the farthest away identified planet in our solar system. It takes 248 years to complete one circuit of the Sun and is so remote that it can only be seen through the largest telescope as a tiny point of light. The name Pluto was given to this planet to comemorate its discoverer Percy Lovell, 'PL' being the first two letters of his name. Pluto has a very elliptical orbit and its passage through the heavens, and the energy it releases, are thought to produce erratic and, as yet, little known effects on solar activity. This, in turn, affects the Earth, triggering, perhaps through Sun flare activity, natural disasters resulting as volcanoes, floods and storms. Since Pluto has only been known for such a short scientific time and is so difficult to interpret, there has been little chance to gather much information about its influences.

Mythologically Pluto was the God of the Underworld, and, by virtue of 'his' remoteness, to be feared. His astrological attributes have been taken to coincide with what was happening on Earth at the time of his discovery in 1930. This was a period of world depression, change and the beginning of rising chaos through mid-European nationalism – Hitler and Mussolini, etc., and subsequent disasters, war and death. The radical vibrations flowing from Pluto are not really understood but surely must affect the natural balance of our planet.

Uranus' function is to decrystallise and shatter for Pluto to regenerate on a new foundation and for Neptune to bring freedom and sacrifice in joy and love. This outer trinity is another cosmic clock that tears down only to rebuild

and raise the consciousness of the 'Kingdom of Earth'.
(Lorusso and Glick, *Healing Stones*)

Planets and Glands
Not only do the Sun and the planets have a direct influence on Earth as a whole but also on the internal workings of human glands (read *Genesis* 1:26). As the Sun's energy is transformed through the planets to Earth, parallels were drawn by Rodney Collin with the workings of the endocrine system in the human body:

The seven major glands in order of their distance from the heart obey the same laws as the planets in the order of their distance from the Sun, and each gland is revealed to be a sensitive instrument which not only transforms human energy to the tension required for its function but it is tuned to a similar instrument on a cosmic scale and obeys its guidance.

(Rodney Collin, *The Theory of Celestial Influence*)

Amongst psychics there is knowledge of another sphere yet to be discovered 'scientifically' that may manifest in our planetary system. It is 'seen' as vibratory, the energy of charged particles, perhaps electro-magnetic, held together by that life force that allows, makes or transmutes 'substance', as we know it, to change its gravitational mass to fluidity. By virtue of its lack of density and its vibratio-

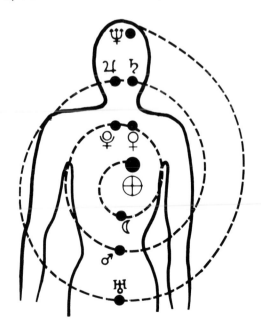

Figure 16
Planets and glands
(Rodney Collin, *Theory of Celestial Influence*)

nal speed, it moves through our solar system outside known conventional orbit or sight. To attempt to give it any viable description is now impossible except to say that perhaps it has the ability to manifest as a 'universal thought form', possibly the expanded 'double' of this planet, i.e. 'matter' within a higher vibrational energy pattern that the unawakened human brain cannot easily decipher or annotate. That our auric form could be separated or 'doubled' in any way from the Earth is laughable to many, but remember if you will the 'unseen' presence in the room with the blind man; and the fact that Pluto only came into sight in our scientific blindness in AD 1930. Yet all the planets were known, and charted, in pyramidic layouts by the Mayan civilisation centuries ago, including a tenth planet and to scale.

There have been minor conjunctions of the planets during the centuries, often producing remarkable cycles of weather change and volcanic activity. This is most interestingly documented and discussed in *Beyond the Jupiter Effect* by John Gribbin and Stephen Plagemann. They state that the Earth came under the influences of a difficult alignment in November 1982 that would herald a period of seismic disruption which would adversely influence our weather patterns. Unfortunately this is true as in the last few years we have experienced Mount St. Helens and many other volcanoes and earthquakes around the world – the disruption of the Pacific currents brought flood and drought to South America and disastrous droughts now in Africa, India, America and Australia. The list of unexpected, unparalleled weather is endless and is being reported regularly in international newspapers. The alignment that occurred is shown in Figure 17a.

However, if you think we have had a difficult time during the last nine years, the major projection of the alignment due in May 2000 could herald a potential disaster on an unprecedented scale. As will be seen from Figure 17b, all the planets in our system will either be opposed or at least at right angles to the Earth as we stand exposed in front of the Sun. The portents are being analysed by astronomers, astrologers, scientists and psychics the world over.

Figure 17
Planetary alignments:
(a) November 1982 AD;
(b) May 2000 AD
(Gribbin and Plagemann, *Beyond the Jupiter Effect*)

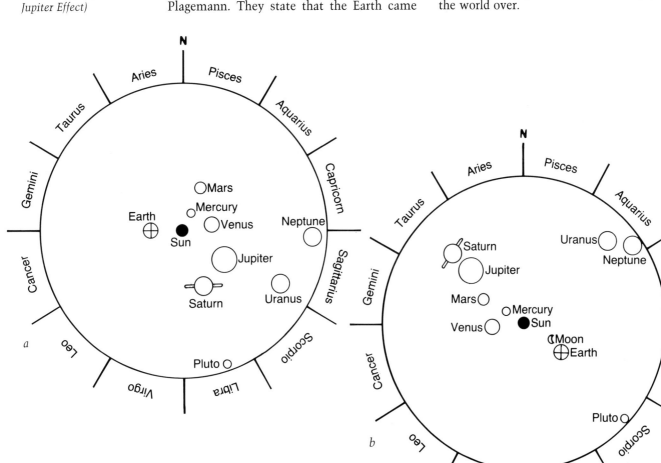

Renaissance – 'Planet Earth'

My Earth is waiting, longing, empty
Barren like a hunted wounded hind
Walking through a wood of winter trees.
Come, dear one – fill me with red berries
That next spring my fountain may unblock,
That in the centre of my swelling summer breasts
No intervening lovers may have lain.

Come in with all the welcomes of my longing,
Touch me with fresh sunshine, release three lifetimes
From the endless ages of my aching past.
You, when I feel you sprouting in me,
Will be my oldest, yet the freshest gift
The stars can give the nurturing seven rays,
Reflected off the mirror of my moon.

Twice seven have I written in the sand
Yet two more verses now can make the sound
Of Saturn's cycle to fulfil this page,
Complete my task and give me freedom
In the eternal spiral through the maze
Of my Labyrinth. Your fiery serpent has leaped
Within; my apple's shed its glorious pip.

Great orb of Day, great Lord restored to us,
My friend of Light, walk now the woods,
The forest of life's waiting good intent –
Such ecstasy; we've known each other's pain,
The crystal sap, the flowering water of my Holy Well.
I've split my boughs for you, so live again
That behind your eyes I may know dappled leaves.

Chapter II
CRYSTAL EARTH AND THE ATMOSPHERE

During the 5,000 million years our Earth has been evolving it has gradually been formed into the structure we live on today by the greenhouse effect of the interaction between radiation and the Sun's heat. As we radiate heat and energy in the form of infra-red waves, so carbon dioxide and water molecules absorb them and stop them escaping. Some of this moisture is permanently retained in the form of clouds that, in turn, shield us from stronger ultra-violet rays from the Sun. This balance has allowed the natural growth of all plant and animal life to evolve as the Earth itself has evolved. Our surface temperature has gradually stabilised at about 15°C which proves ideal. Up until the Industrial Revolution, only 150 years ago, this balance had been naturally held and man and nature had been in reasonable harmony – man's numbers growing all the time, but then he had not taken too much out of the land. The balance of the natural kingdom, the grasslands, forests and animals, the rivers, lakes and seas and the fish therein, even the whales, was still all right. 5,000 million years had passed to this point.

However, as human beings we take so much for granted and never seem to stop and think how our actions can possibly disrupt this seemingly endless beneficence. We never stop to think that one small, selfish action or invention can have catastrophic effects out of all proportion to the lack of caring involved.

The atmosphere suffers in the same way as our skins, or the skin of the Earth, as we build up pockets of filth and stagnation around our cities and in the waterways, cut down our trees and forests, thereby changing the greenhouse effect, and breed ourselves towards gross over-population and the escalating demands of materialism.

In the last 200 years the greed engendered by the industrialised nations has not brought Utopia, only wealth to a very few and debt to most. We are now beginning to experience the results and are in a downward spiral of self-destruction. The perceived needs of the industrialised nations are selfish and quite out of proportion to the real needs of millions of others less fortunate. To give up and give away is something we expect others to do. It is a point worth labouring as its understanding can help any human being feel closer to loving his 'neighbour' and caring for the animal and vegetable kingdoms.

To understand this better it is necessary to look at the structure of the Earth itself and the air we breathe. Between the Earth and the next outer layer is the troposphere, approximately 9 miles away, where the temperature has gradually dropped to about −60°C. Above this at 30 miles is the warmer stratosphere where the Sun's warmth is absorbed and temperatures rise again to around 0°. Here much of the harmful ultra-violet radiation is dissipated. It is this layer that is suffering already and would change most significantly if we embarked on atomic warfare; for the stratosphere is the filter that keeps our breathing air tolerable and the Sun's rays from frying us.

Above the stratosphere is the ionosphere where the temperature falls to −100°. The air gets very thin and becomes ionised, hence the word describing positively charged particles. These particles are influenced by the magnetic pull of the Earth's inner core and are directed to the North and South Poles forming a great force field around us. The electrical build-up at the centre of the Earth forms this magnetic field which can be likened to the coiled principle of a huge electric generator.

Figure 18
The electromagnetic spectrum (R. Webster, *Gems*)

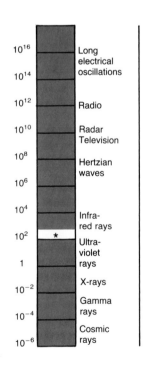

10^{16}	Long electrical oscillations
10^{14}	
10^{12}	Radio
10^{10}	Radar Television
10^{8}	Hertzian waves
10^{6}	
10^{4}	Infra-red rays
10^{2} *	Ultra-violet rays
1	
10^{-2}	X-rays
10^{-4}	Gamma rays
10^{-6}	Cosmic rays

700 nm
Visible spectrum
*
400 nm
Clairvoyance?

All these influences flow down to us in vibratory waves as light, heat and sound, to a thin crust around the Earth's surface only about 18–20 miles thick. This seems thick but remember the *actual* surface skin of the earth in which we dig to plant our vegetables and trees is seldom a depth of more than two or three feet.

It is the formation of this thin skin and the upper crust of the Earth that concerns us as its rock formation and crystalline content consist of the minerals and the chemical essences that make up the elemental structure of so many of our life forms. Every vegetable, animal and human is a combination of fluid crystallography and on this the basics of life are founded. The upper mantle, the layer immediately below the crust, is composed of dense rock, 80% being formed by the crystallisation of molten magma mainly containing iron and magnesium silicates called peridotite. The overlying crust contains rock developed from this with the addition of 'internal juices' pushed up from deep inside the Earth by the action of volcanoes. The resultant spreading of these lavas over large areas and with millions of years of action (remember we are talking about 5,000 million years of evolution) produced pockets and veins, layers and nodules of many different crystalline structures, quartz and olivine (peridotite), garnet, diopside, enstatite and even diamonds, etc.

There are many places in the world where these giant constructions of ageless rocks fold over each other in layer upon layer of white, grey or black granite and basalt 'masses' like piles of tilted sandwiches, which is just what they are. The immense pressures and energies of heat and force have shoved them around into many strange and often eccentric patterns.

Immediately through the mantle is a layer called the lithosphere consisting of a series of large, continental-sized 'plates' – it is suggested about 20 of them exist but that seven of them only form the major structural areas that literally move continents about our planet. These are called tectonic plates. It has also been suggested by three Russian scientists (much quoted) as published in *Khimya Zhizn*, USSR Academy of Sciences, that the Earth is basically a *large crystal structure* in itself, which is not improbable when we consider that the structure of the crust is mainly made up of silicates in granite formations, or their broken-down state. The scientists suggest that the Earth was formed of 12 pentagonal slabs overlaid with 20 equilateral triangles, the

*Figure 19
Earth's crystal
structures in 5-fold
symmetry (from a
Russian magazine)*

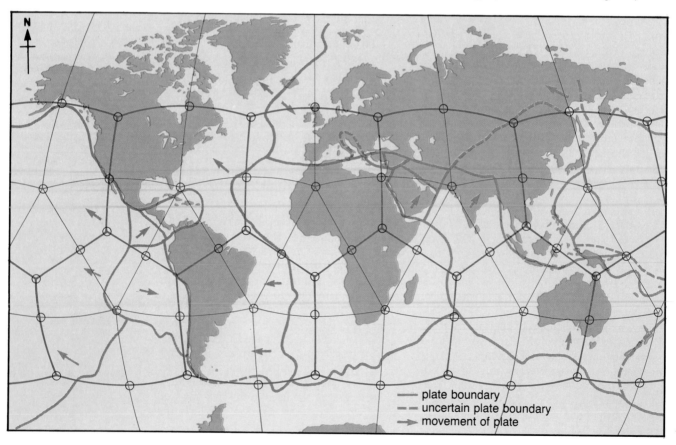

plate boundary
uncertain plate boundary
movement of plate

entire structure being formed during the Earth's early evolution. This form would therefore follow the ultimate geometric shapes of the icosahedron and the dodecahedron of Platonic solids.

Scientific seismic opinion evaluates this theory indifferently but when the internal crystalline structures are discussed shortly, and later the overlay of Earth Stars, the two will be seen to form together into patterns we recognise as 'sacred' geometry, the combination and number of 'life', so perhaps the theory is not so way out. Also, most interestingly, SAM used octagonal and pentagonal stones in his structure showing his awareness of planetary geometry in 3500 BC, thereby pre-dating Plato by some 3 millennia.

Rocks are generally classified under three headings: igneous, sedimentary and metamorphic. The first are formed under the solidification of hot molten magma which was pushed up through fissures in the Earth's crust or extruded as lava. As these rocks cooled crystals formed in the cavities and veins; granite is a well-known example, which includes gold, quartz (rock crystal) and mica. The coarseness or fineness of the grain and original fluidity of the rock produce the quality and size of the crystals in it. Sometimes the cooling was so rapid that the crystals became molten and turned into natural glass, or obsidian, which is also often discovered in ancient sites, fashioned into axes and arrow heads as it can be flaked easily and sharply.

Sedimentary rocks are usually broken down deposited rocks or water/wind carried, moved by the Ice Age to another higher, lower or different location. The carboniferous limestone of Ireland (Carrowkeel) is a good example of this, in which many fossils of another totally different original environment are found pushed up by the upheavals under the then seabed. Gem material that comes from sedimentary rocks tends to collect in waterworn hollows; this is particularly relevant to the sedimentary gravels of India, Sri Lanka and Myanmar (Burma) which produce many fine gems (ruby and sapphire crystals) and of South Africa in the diamond 'pipes' of Kimberley.

Metamorphic rock formed when rock masses were folded and moved during great disturbances in the Earth's crust during evolutionary periods and the resulting pressures changed the nature of the rock already there producing a 'metamorphism' – hence the term. The igneous and sedimentary rocks became schists, gneisses and quartzites under pressure and temperature variations. Any impurities in the original rock subsequently might be squeezed and crystallised. Also, mineral-rich water is often carried into the veins and cavities gradually forming into geodes or hollow balls. This is how and where the veins and hollows of the fine rock crystal, amethyst, cairngorms and agates are formed.

The rock cycle is the same as all other cycles of evolution. In this case birth starts in the molten state; the liquid is then crystallised, extruded, broken up, deposited, decrystallised, redeposited as sedimentary rock and goes back into the earth to remelt and start life again at a later date. It is a process that takes millions of years from birth to death to rebirth.

Planet Earth

The Earth has a core, a mantle, a crust and a skin and we are part of the animal kingdom that lives on and off this skin. The gravitational pull of the core stops us from spinning away into space as the Earth rotates every 24 hours on its axis and every 365.25 days around the superior force from the Sun. We are 93.4 million miles from the Sun and as a nearly spherical object we have a diameter of 7,972.5 miles.

Our scientists now know much more about the Earth and its formation as we have recently been able to gather increasing knowledge with the use of satellites. Computers can obtain facts in retrospect as well as predicting forwards so we learn more about ourselves all of the time. One disturbing fact not generally thought of in any depth, or accepted, is that the Earth is not a permanent, stable sort of materialistic 'Utopia'. As we learn about our past we begin to realise that this planet has gone through fundamental catastrophic events. These changes are not just the ideas or perceptions of sensitives but the facts of hard scientific evidence. The Earth, due to the influence of the Sun and the other planets in their changing planetary configurations, has been pulled and pushed around many times. Some of the inexplicable disasters have been the result of major happenings in the far-out universe – perhaps a super nova (star explosion) light years distant in our galaxy. (Bell's theorem proves the failure of the Law of Local Causes.) Often the evidence of these changes is right in front of us but we don't see or check it.

This book is much concerned with a particular area of the planet, Carrowkeel in Sligo, Southern Ireland, a mountainous area of stratified carboniferous limestone about 12 miles from the Atlantic Ocean. All over these hills there are tropical sea water fossils in the rock, identified by the Natural History Museum as rugose coral, approximately 240 million years old (Figure 20). Perhaps another 180 million years later dinosaurs paddled through these waters – but certainly at a much late date – and within our comprehension the Earth went through a fundamental climatic change which brought in the Ice Age and covered these same hills with thick blankets of frozen water. The grinding, heaving pressure of that period, lasting perhaps 60,000 years and ending just 12,000 years ago, scoured and scraped and bared the area until the Earth healed to what we now accept as the reality of our present balance and growth. Yet how many other countless changes have taken place that we can only begin to imagine? When psychics with the foresight of Edgar Cayce and countless anonymous others refer to lost civilisations, of which there is now no seemingly recognised or accepted trace, why are they dismissed so readily? The civilisation called Atlantis is thought to have been a vast plateau in the middle of the Atlantic Ocean, the remnants now known as the islands of the Azores.

The atmosphere covering the Earth is, at the moment, reasonably stable, in balance only because we have not embarked on the lunacy of nuclear war. But it will only take a periodic natural solar energy disruption bringing earthquakes and floods to trigger an accelerating atomic series that will be just as catastrophic to our skin and atmosphere as a deliberate war. This will be the scenario in the years ahead: the probability is before our eyes and in the newspapers every week.

If we can accept that our physical body, and its whole make-up, is just over yet another energy system of evolution as, say, the tigers or the frogs, that the human atomic structure and energy centres are little different from the lotus or the apple trees and the Earth itself, then we have a chance of finding sense and order in our lives and our relationships to everything else. If we can think of our body as a 'minor Planet Earth' undergoing continual evolution and expressing quantum physics, we can begin to see ourselves in a different light. We are born to grow, evolve and die, and go back to the Earth just as do crystals, trebolites and the pet canary, whilst our soul 'essence' returns to the Sun through the solar wind.

The developed humanoid has not yet been around long enough for the Earth to fossilise and then crystallise a human body – perhaps in another 250 million years someone will excavate 'humanoid c.1990' made of sparkling crystals like the rugose coral. Unfortunately we think we are different, untouchable and superior to the rest of life and suffer accordingly. What happens to our skin and the flesh under it depends on the lifestyle we lead and reflects our own daily behaviour. What we eat, drink or take shows physically and if we choose to abuse a potentially perfect system by pouring in the wrong fuel then we can hardly complain when the structure reacts – with perhaps acne, cancer or heart disease. It is as stupid as buying a Rolls-Royce and deliberately putting paraffin in the petrol tank. Pinch your skin and feel the pain, spill boiling water on your foot and it blisters, breathe poison gas (Bhopal) and you will die – we do all this to Mother Earth every day, over increasing areas, and the Earth as a vibrant breathing structure is reacting. Cut down the forests and the oxygen levels change, pour acid fumes into the air and the trees die, dump waste in the oceans and marine life disappears. Personal experience relates here to Poole Harbour, Dorset – until 1960 a clean, fresh water/sea environment but now due to agricultural nutrients and domestic effluents, it is a foul slimy, green waste. We are preparing our own destruction as carefully and swiftly as if the billions of dollars that expand our supermarket syndrome were spent waging chemical warfare on us.

As the Earth changes so the atmosphere changes above us and is being increasingly disrupted with material pollution. This beautiful shield we call our sky, so glorious in the sunrise when the Earth breathes in again after the exhalation of the night, could so quickly and easily change to a dull, foggy glow of dust and debris, as was seen over thousands of miles after the eruption of Mount St. Helens, and Chernobyl. The shield of the atmosphere is a gigantic, vibrant, moving crystal filter constantly changing, adjusting, readjusting and being imprinted with every action that occurs on Earth. Enshrined there is a record of every smallest energy change that has ever taken place through man's thought, word and deed. If we lift our arm to point to the sky we move the energy field of the macrocosm by that amount, but the space refills immediately and readjusts the balance. To illustrate this better, *Time* magazine reported American fears that a Russian torpedo had been developed that was so sensitive it could track the marine imprint of a ship that had passed through a given area of sea water up to 24 hours later. The quantum impulse generated by a thought in the human brain can be projected anywhere anytime from one individual group or area to another, at will, through what we call space. It has no mass nor

does it need to have. Electrical waves, magnetic waves, infra-red waves, ultra-violet waves, X-rays, brain waves are all a pathway within the divine geometric structure of the macrocosm. The concept is so simple and yet thought to be so complex that to accept it is to undermine all the barriers that civilisation has taken years to build up, and that currently enshrine man's manipulation of man through religion, science and politics, in the form of 'education'.

It is only when we go back to SAM and his environment, before the discovery and use of metal, that we can begin to understand the purity of that universal mind and the understanding of that time; a sharing, loving community held together by the energy of natural spiritual forces that today we fear. There *was* a 'Garden of Eden', not an inquisitional, sinful concept of life, but an ordered lifestyle in sunlight and clean air, unpolluted by the human ego.

Figure 20
Carrowkeel 'mountain'
coral c.240 million BC
(photo: David Knight)

Jewels

My way is paved with diamonds
Leading you to my table
There – before your choice
Lie riches beyond fable.
Men have slaved to mine them
Down evolutions of grace –
Of great endeavours
So have you – now here.

'You choose
Your choice is open
To your reaching hand
Be sure and hope you know your wants
Before you loose them'.

Will it be rubies
From the jungles of Mogok
Or mountainous sapphires
From Kashmir – locked
In roaring valleys
Of the remote Himalayas
At Koswar?

Perhaps you adore Inca emeralds
Hidden in the pyramids
In the City of Cuzco
The choice – dear one
Is yours.
'But I have no choice'
My hand reaches out
To scoop up your riches
Into what?
I shout emptiness
A bag of nothingness
The hole in my ego sack
Holding together my greed.

These seeds of light
Sparkling in heaps are
Star filled materialisations
Only become reality –
When I offer them back –
Give back your generosity.
And take nothing.

Chapter III
CRYSTAL STRUCTURES

The basic unit in crystal structure is an atom of positively-charged protons and negatively-charged electrons and neutral neutrons. The forces that hold the atoms together in crystalline mineral solids are mainly electrical and their internal structure confirms their physical and chemical properties.

Thus a simple rock crystal is expressed as (SiO_2) whereas a complicated aggregate like hauyanite is expressed as $(NaCl)_{4-8}$ $(SiO_3SiO_2)_1^{-2}(AI_6Si_6O_{24})$.

Structures
It is the different proportion of minerals that produces the atomic bonding within a crystal and that determines the ultimate 'family' shape and colour of the crystal. Different mineral solutions or mineral 'vapours' are compressed and solidify within rock as it cools so that various atoms present grow together into a total possibility of six different symmetrical shapes thereby making up sixfold symmetry. If each crystal was able to grow in a perfect environment with a constant growth pattern uninterrupted by changing pressure or heat, then each type within each family of the six symmetries would always grow into exactly the same shape with only the size varying, but natural volcanic rock formation with such massive disturbances does not allow this to happen, therefore external symmetry rarely follows. It is the ingenuity of man subsequently cutting crystals to suit their individual properties that produces the ultimate beauty of a gemstone. By definition a gemstone must have a crystal structure to be classified as such, or at least it must be crystalline. One of the usual confusions is that often when we talk of crystals we are referring technically to gemstones of all types, whereas when we talk about quartz it, too, is referred to as 'crystal'. Glass manufactured and cut to reflect light is wrongly called 'crystal' (glass) when actually it is a fused substance without a symmetrical axis. Therefore it is important to differentiate. However, having said that, as far as we are concerned here, we are primarily interested in that mineral found all over our planet in its true crystalline form known as rock crystal, which is really the fully developed form of quartz.

Crystals perform in a three-dimensional array of atoms or groups arranged in regular repeating patterns which produce crystal axes defined by their individual group/cell edges; each crystal also has an axis which will only go through the actual centre if it has formed in perfect symmetry. No other substances on Earth or in our mineral kingdom have the same properties of disciplined 'static' external strcture which, combined with their other properties, make crystals totally unique and special. The six crystal symmetries are the quintessence of our material planet encapsulating the shapes of 'divine' or 'sacred' geometry as explained by Pythagoras. *Now* we know that the geometry of the disposition of a crystal's face is directly related to its internal atomic arrangement. As the sheer simplicity and completeness of this geometry is expressed in the crystal substances of the Earth so we find the same geometric balance in the universal and planetary or macroscopic imprint.

Quartz or rock crystal is continuously found in Stone Age sites and the archaeologists who have unearthed it consider it was there purely for its prettiness or for adornment but it was of far greater significance to SAM for, with true clairvoyant sight, it is possible to see into

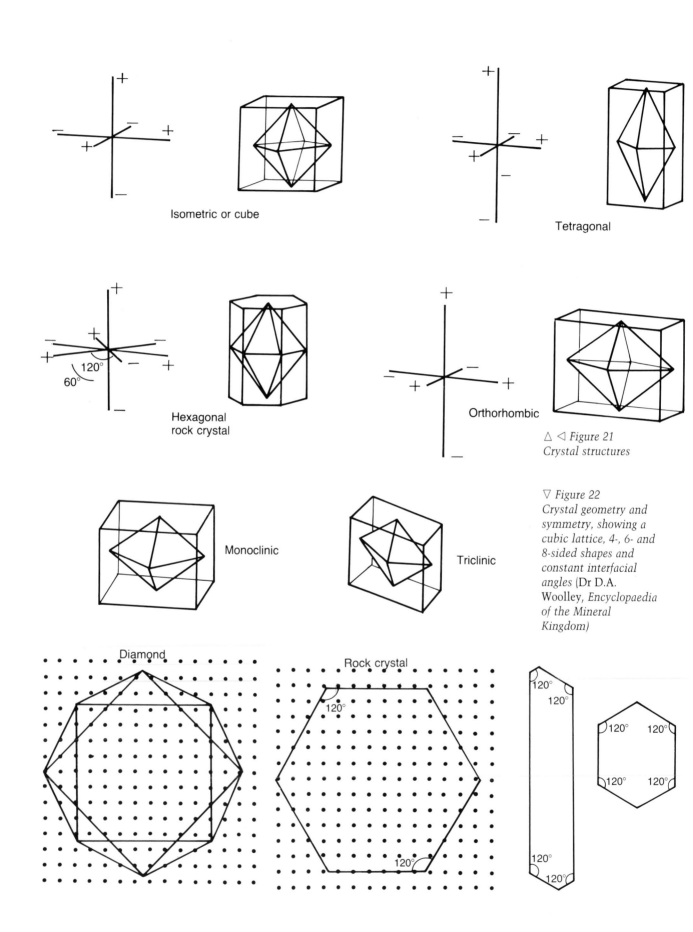

Isometric or cube

Tetragonal

Hexagonal
rock crystal

Orthorhombic

△ ◁ *Figure 21*
Crystal structures

▽ *Figure 22*
Crystal geometry and symmetry, showing a cubic lattice, 4-, 6- and 8-sided shapes and constant interfacial angles (Dr D.A. Woolley, Encyclopaedia of the Mineral Kingdom)

Monoclinic

Triclinic

Diamond

Rock crystal

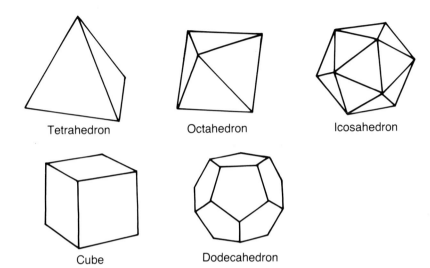

Tetrahedron   Octahedron   Icosahedron

Cube   Dodecahedron

Figure 23
Platonic solids

a substance and see how its atomic structure is put together. SAM saw that the symmetry of rock crystal followed the universal law of growth in all forms – growth patterns in plants, vegetables, trees and animals, not least himself – and these patterns repeated themselves in, on and above Earth.

Quartz and rock crystals grow in the trigonal and hexagonal system and have six-sided ends. The abundance of these crystals, or the remains of this crystalline form that is spread widely throughout the crust of the Earth and on its surface, plays a vital part as a connector to the macroscopic layout of the invisible energy grid system in the atmosphere.

There are other properties that all gemstones have besides crystal symmetry that help in definition and classification.

Refractive Index

As natural white light, i.e. sunlight, passes through a substance it is refracted by that substance at a different angle because of the change of density from one material to another. The commonest example of this is looking at something that is under water. If you try to throw a stone or stick at the object it misses as the object is at a different position to that seen. In the same way each crystal refracts or bends light at different angles as the light passes from one density of matter into, through and out of the other side. The speed of light in air is slowed down as it passes through a crystal – remember how the light of the Sun takes eight minutes to reach us on Earth.

When a beam of light hits the surface of the crystal at right angles, light is not reflected from that surface, as it all passes through. At any other angle some light is thrown back or reflected, hence the sparkle of a crystal surface, but the light that passes through the crystal emerges as split light, i.e. it splits into the natural vibratory colours we know as the spectrum. We know these colours best in rainbows and always remark on how magnificent they are. We even enjoy the fairytale myth of the crock of gold being buried at the end which is not so remote as we shall see when we come to SAM and his Bronze Age children.

Each crystal (gemstone) has its own refractive index, scientifically tabulated and used as another form of identification in gemology. Diamonds have the highest refraction and therefore the greatest reflection from their internal surfaces, so, when properly cut, a diamond 'throws out' more light than say an emerald or a garnet and appears brighter and more fiery. This is known as the absorption and dispersion of light.

Prismatically shown colours (a rainbow is sunlight being split up by water molecules acting as minute prisms) can be seen by people with ordinary sight. Our brains can all register the same imprint except, of course, if someone is colour blind. However, there are people whose perception of vibration, in this case colour, can 'see' the imprint in their brain of this same range of colour in the ultra-violet wavelength without use of special instruments. The ability is one of the attributes of

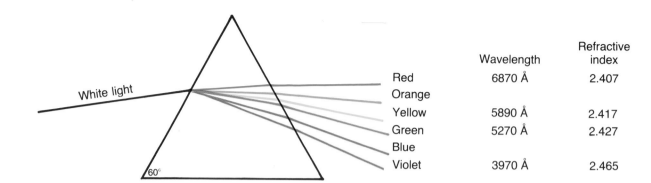

	Wavelength	Refractive index
Red	6870 Å	2.407
Orange		
Yellow	5890 Å	2.417
Green	5270 Å	2.427
Blue		
Violet	3970 Å	2.465

White light

60°

psychic sight or clairvoyance, literally 'clear seeing'. With this ability a whole range of natural vibrations becomes available as imprints on the brain screen that can be registered and actually visualised as images, as through a 'third eye'.

This is very important to understand as it is no different now for those presently enlightened people than it was for SAM to see natural vibrations of a different wavelength. When a clairvoyant says he or she has seen what ordinary people call a 'ghost' or 'spirit' or some natural phenomenon outside our normal experience what they have actually perceived is the splitting up of another form of light through the same atmosphere but at a different speed, which produces an 'unearthly' form.

It is beyond the comprehension of normal sight since it is out of the normal plane of experience. The colours clairvoyants see are not always 'rainbows' or beautiful by any means – unfortunately there are many forms of energy that move through the atmosphere that are often manifestations of negative thought and action from around people, around places or vibrating as illness or pollution. But at the same time there are positive energies of love and healing that help to balance out the darkness near the Earth's surface. This area close to the Earth's surface is called the 'lower astral'.

Atmosphere Crystal Light
How often we talk of light and crystals at the same time. The cryst-al light is little different by definition from the 'Christ light', the light of symmetry. When light can flow on a positive, unbroken and uninterrupted wavelength it illumines our darkness, or the negativity of our emotions. The positive and negative, protons and electrons, in every single atom of every structure react to the impulse of

white light and begin to move when the Sun comes up; at night they slow down or rest just as we do. These same atoms in the air, in the density of our gravity, are activated forming into images we can see with our normal sight, but often the light illuminates something from either the higher positive or lower negative plane, perhaps an ancient imprint, a long past energy form, a transient form or a 'summoned' form to the clairvoyant brain that the ordinary brain cannot register in imagery. To ordinary people that energy may be expressed as the happiness of an unexpected smile or the shiver of the traditional 'ghost walking over my grave'.

An imprint in the atmosphere is always there, part of the universal evolution that has built up over millions of years. It can be remanifested by the correct thought vibration to 'illumine' it again into form. When we die we are told that our spirit and soul go back to God. This is true for when that indefinable inner spark goes out of our body leaving a dead shell behind, it returns to the macrocosm or back into the Sun. If we have generated hate and turmoil, i.e. 'negativity', then the spark will be held in the lower astral of gravity, nearer Earth, nearer the surface perhaps in a particular house or environment to manifest and 'haunt' living beings until some loving energy is able to lift it through to continue its journey. Perhaps it is just waiting for intercession for release to the higher atmospheres. However, the positive, more refined or initiated soul vibration will rise unimpeded to the higher realms and beyond, and only return to Earth to bring help or love when needed. Such was the 'mission' of Jesus, the Master of the Christ Light, experienced by his disciples after his vibration had left its sepulchre or cairn. The Masters of each and every great teaching cycle are available all the time. Buddha, Jesus,

Figure 24
Colour dispersion of white light passing through a prism, wavelength and refractive index of diamond (R. Webster, Gems)

Mahomet literally still live 'astrally' for those who believe objectively in their truth, just as the negative forces of darkness, where there is no light, unfortunately are also available.

Crystals in Healing

This is why so many humans have worn or carried a crystal as a source of positive energy through countless centuries and why crystals adorn the great relics and works of many scriptures, and the fingers of kings and priests – to motivate and activate them in the light. Not until comparatively recently have they symbolised wealth or vanity. Crystals are used in natural healing in conjunction with human energies with great results, as diagnostic instruments, as movers of negative energy from infested areas, as dispellers of tumours and sprains and bruises, often achieving results that totally confound medical logic. They are not a cult of the devil but natural artefacts that typify all the best, the most balanced and the most pure in nature and the world in which we live. They do not control us, we can control them.

We can activate their *latent* good qualities if we feed in the correct positive thought impulses, for crystals are normally at rest, their power and use awaiting activation. Therefore it is the motivation of the user that is vital for effective results. If the user's motives are genuine and selfless, then healing or information is 'given'. That is why we should always try and reach a point of selflessness in the use of crystals. If we can wrest our brain away from chaotic thought to controlled relaxation and raise our consciousness in quiet contemplative meditation on any particular subject, then the electrical brain impulses stream out as positive thought through the higher planes. These sublime wishes or prayers, if passed through a crystal, either an actual crystal or an etherially created crystal, take on an activated boost as the protons and electrons pick them up and transform them on their way, to remove chaos and ego from any situation. So they have the latent ability to remove dis-ease.

Normal visual colour in crystals is an obvious feature as it is the first impression we see reflected back to us when we look through a crystal surface. The colours we see show the crystal's ability either to absorb or reflect different wavelengths of light; in the dark all crystals are colourless. Simply, if we see a red gemstone we know it has absorbed all the other colours and is reflecting only what it cannot absorb, red; similarly with blue, green, etc. This depends on chemical composition.

Hardness

Hardness of crystals is another basic property that helps in identification and use. Each crystal has its own particular hardness, being graduated from one to ten on Moh's scale. Most crystal formations start from five but gradation is by no means regular up to ten. The majority of gems graduate between five to nine in fact and it is only diamond that has the maximum of ten, it being the hardest and the purest substance currently known on this planet.

The importance of relative hardness of different materials is very obvious but its practical application is not realised – that you can only cut or fashion a stone with one harder than itself, i.e. a quartz will not cut a sapphire and a sapphire will not cut a diamond but similar stones will cut each other. Hence diamond powder or industrial diamonds are so much in demand as cutting or polishing agents for they cannot wear out. This is particularly relevant to us when we consider how SAM fashioned or drilled quartz, how he shaped those incredible ceremonial stone axe heads of nephrite or granite. It could not have been an easy task and obviously took a long time, many months, perhaps years, of patient work.

Cleavage and Fracture

Cutting must be considered in the production of implements and an understanding of how each rock performed when hit, where and how hard, was a knowledge built up over a long period of time. Flint splinters easily and cleanly and can then be chipped and polished to give fine leaf-shaped implements but rock and quartz are not so predictable, yet the semi-hexagonal rhombohedral-faced quartz blocks of some size from Carrowkeel are amazing

1	Talc
2	Gypsum
3	Calcite
4	Fluorspar
5	Appatite
6	Feldspar
7	Rock crystal
8	Topaz
9	Corundum only (sapphire and ruby)
10	Diamond only

Figure 25
Hardness table

Figure 26
Carrowkeel cairn quartz 'lozenges' or prisms

examples of SAM's art and perception – original quartz prisms.

Accurate cleavage of crystal is a difficult operation. If the break occurs and is not clearly parallel to an axis it then becomes a fracture. When obsidian, volcanic glass or over-stressed crystal is cut it fractures and shows a 'shell-like' pattern which is called a conchoidal fracture. Many of the fractured crystals found in dolmens are just rough-looking lumps, badly chipped and scarred, but these crystals have been roughened by lighting fires at seasonal ceremonies and have been included in the dolmens as one of the necessary symbolic artefacts to ensure the onward path of the soul.

Specific Gravity

All gems, by virtue of their different mineral chemical compositions, have different densities which can be expressed through specific gravity. The specific gravity of solids, i.e. their reaction to gravity, concerned SAM in his construction of cairns and standing stones.

Quartz and Rock Crystal

Quartz, as we know, occurs widely all over the world and is one of the most beautiful of all minerals. When it has eventually broken down from its massive crystalline state it goes back to the earth as gravel and sand. Quartz in its true form is known as rock crystal (clear white); amethyst (mauve); citrine (golden yellow), often miscalled topaz which is similar in colour but a totally different material and much more valuable; rose quartz (a soft pink opaque colour); and cairngorm (a browny grey colour). These quartz form in a unique way, ideally into doubly terminated crystals consisting of a hexagonal (six-sided) prism at each end. These are positive and negative rhombohedra but usually one end has grown more than the other thereby giving a distorted look. Quartz also twins with other quartz crystals but rarely in equal proportions.

X-ray studies carried out in this century have shown that quartz has a unique property amongst gemstones that made it particularly interesting to SAM. It performs helically, i.e. its internal structure grows in a spiral, which is often revealed externally by small extra faces on the crystal, and it may then be termed a left-handed or right-handed crystal, i.e. one crystal can be a mirror image of another.

Figure 27
Natural rock crystal
(photo: Steve Rogers)

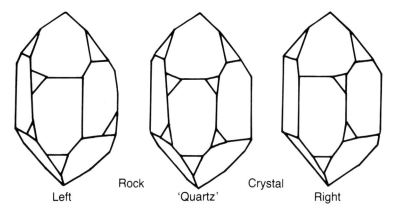

Left   Rock   'Quartz'   Crystal   Right

Such a spiral structure causes a crystal to rotate the plane of polarisation of light as can be seen in the polarised light diagrams (Figure 32), thus forming a light image very similar to the recently identified DNA molecule – Life is Light.

The spiral growth in rock crystals is particularly interesting in the use of crystals for pendulums and healing, as the direction of oscillation is picked up and increased by the needs of the user to give positive or negative responses to specific questions.

Rock crystal has a property known as pyro-electricty which allows it to develop an electrical charge when subjected to a variance of temperature. It also has piezo-electricity which is the development of electrical charges in non-conducting crystals by the application of pressure. This pressure can be as subtle as that engendered by the changing Sun and Moon phases. Rock crystal also has a special application due to its atomic configuration. This was discovered by the Curie brothers in 1880, when they found that a 'plate' of quartz cut parallel to the prism faces gave off electricity when it was put under actual pressure. The crystal would also expand or contract if charges were put through it and it would oscillate. When crystals are heated electric charges are produced and this strange effect was eventually used by W.G. Cady in 1922 as a means of measuring and controlling the frequencies of radio waves. This has developed into our transistor microchip industry of today. Older readers will remember having a frustrating instrument called a 'crystal set' powered by a battery and a crystal, activated by a 'cat's whisker' – a point scratched across the surface of the crystal to produce a charge. The set then had to be orientated to the expected radio frequency and, if lucky, a station would be picked up. The use of an aerial was essential to catch the path of the

Figure 28
Left and right crystal growth (illustration: R.A. Bonewitz)

signals through the atmosphere and also a resonant listening device called an 'earphone'.

An analogy has been given describing the passage of vibrational waves or thought forms through the air as leaving an imprint that could later be 'picked up' or illuminated by a sensitive; as could the passage of a ship some many hours later by its 'wake configuration' through the depths of the sea. It is interesting to read that in 1918, W.G. Cady was working for the US Navy experimenting on the use of piezo-electric crystals in submarine detection. This later came to be the basis of the Asdic systems, for sensitive detection instruments.

The pattern of silicon and oxygen atoms in the unit cell of the quartz crystal consists of six negative oxygen atoms combined with three positive silicon atoms around a core, hence the formula SiO_2. This occurs in such a manner that two oxygen atoms compensate one silicon atom at the termination of the electrical axes of which there are three in the unit cell, the protons, electrons and neutrons forming a primal trinity.

> When pressure is exerted on the face which is normal to the electric axis the 'O' negative atoms move towards one face while the 'Si' positive atoms move towards the other, thus binding opposite charges so that a positive charge appears near the 'O' (negative) atoms and a negative one near the 'Si' (positive) atoms.
>
> (R. Webster, Gems)

Figure 29 is a schematic diagram but is very relevant as will be seen when we trace the natural macroscopic grid pattern on the Earth's surface and understand how this configuration was used by SAM.

It is worth mentioning here that positive and negative mean opposites and form a duality, yet negative unfortunately has come to mean 'bad' in modern parlance. This is unfortunate for to suggest all men are only positive and all women therefore negative is ridiculous. We are a duality within ourselves that can form a trinity as in the atom when we are also neutral and thus achieve balance.

Luminescence

Some crystals show a fluorescent aspect when illuminated by ultra-violet light. We have talked briefly about clairvoyant sight and the ability to see vibrations of colour and form within this frequency but if the energy that originally produced that wavelength is shut off then the resultant after-glow is called

QUARTZ

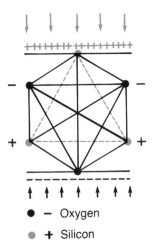

● – Oxygen
● + Silicon

'phosphorescence'. 'Luminescence' is the term covering both.

The term 'fluorescence' comes from the mineral fluorite or fluorspar (expressed as CaF_2) which is cubic in symmetry. Most people know of this in its most striking form as 'Blue John', a mauve to white crystal found in Derbyshire, UK. It was used in the eighteenth and nineteenth centuries for the bodies of extravagant objets d'art or household artefacts such as clocks, candelabra and jugs. The best examples were made by the great craftsman Matthew Boulton in the 'Adam' period of the late eighteenth century.

When activated by ultra-violet light fluorspar glows with a vivid sky-blue to violet to indigo colour. Normally we accept that we have to have special instruments to activate this wavelength but ordinary white light – sunlight – still has ultra-violet in its beams although most has been filtered out in the atmosphere before reaching Earth, as already explained.

Fluorspar occurs widely in carboniferous limestone and in veins of mature crystals which are activated each day by the Sun. Anyone who has travelled in the west of Ireland has remarked on the incredible quality of the 'blue' hills in shadow or in the evening sunsets. This is partly the after-glow of the fluorescence and luminescence of the carboniferous limestone that has been activated by ultra-violet radiation during the day and seen by normal sight. Since SAM's cairns were built of this material, in the West psychics with

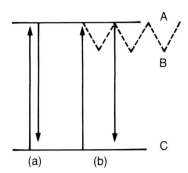

Figure 30
Quantum theory
(R. Webster, *Gems*)

Diagram technical explanation – (a) Fluorescence – an electron taking energy from the incident ultra-violet light jumps from the stable orbit at C to the excited state A from which it immediately returns to the stable orbit with the emission of light. (b) Phosphorescence – an electron taking energy from the incident ultra-violet light jumps from stable orbit C to the excited state A but does not return to the stable orbit at once. The electron drops into a meta-stable level B from which it can only return to stable level after again taking energy from the surrounding medium, which allows it to get back to the excited state from which it can return directly to the stable level with the emission of light.

The minuscule zig-zag movement is significant as it depicts in the smallest possible way the universal sign used for energy or wavelength and vibration ᐱᐱ. This sign also depicts the Sun's rays illuminating and activating the macrocosm. It is found engraved on the lintel and passage stones above the skylights of many of the more sophisticated passage temples in Ireland and France and on the simple Iberian sundials known as 'idols'. The Sun at Newgrange is purposely directed as a narrow polarised energy beam deep into the heart centre of the cairn to strike a marked area of the back chamber to 'tell the time' on a cosmic scale at the winter solstice on 21st/22nd December.

clairvoyant sight often see them as great flowing semi-circles of purple light, surrounded with glowing white borders.

Fluorspar occurs with rock crystal, often the two growing together naturally, so that a pocket of cubic fluorspar may grow round mature rock crystals – such a piece is a rare natural jewel indeed. Deer antler, fashioned and polished, also has a natural purple fluorescence and was used in the temple cairns as a ritual object. The psychic imprint of purple on the surface of the Earth around ancient sites is often noticed in Sligo at, for instance, Carrowkeel, Heapstown and Knocknarea. So it really is not strange that the early Church having taken over so many archaic sites should have adopted purple and white for the garments of the priesthood, the higher colours of initiation.

The phenomena of light as expressed by

Planck in the Quantum Theory suggest that the energy of light will be absorbed into an atom whilst the electrons are at rest or grounded. The electrons then move or become excited and the atom emits light, then the electrons return to rest. With continuous activation or motion, the light goes on shining until the energy source is 'turned off'.

The solstices or fire festivals, held at the early passage temples, were deeply symbolic as the revitalising and re-energising force, not only of the structure but of the whole temple. As the Sun passed through the quartz in the skylight above the entrance, the electrical ultra-violet and X-ray vibrations awaited use as the priesthood energised the temple.

Ordinary white light is travelling through the air giving off energy in all directions but when it is enclosed, put through a filter and reflected off a polished surface at certain

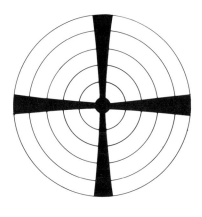

a

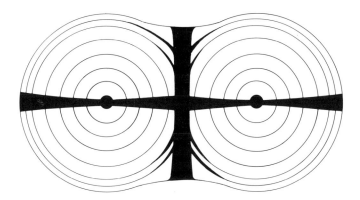

b

angles the light is polarised or reflected to vibrate in one plane only. Convergent polarised light, i.e. reflected from two sources, will produce an 'interference' figure from a crystal showing how the rays will be out of phase with each other.

Uniaxial crystals (trigonal, hexagonal and tetragonal) produce an interference figure depicting a cross. Biaxial crystals (orthorombic, monoclinic and triclinic) produce figures showing double coloured rings intersected by a split cross or an extended cross, but quartz also has the property of rotating the polarisation of light (in conjunction with a mica plate) that eliminates the centre of the cross. This forms a macroscopic DNA 'molecule of light'.

SAM with his light split up into the colours of the spectrum, glowing and flashing around his inner temples, was able to produce polarised light with his large quartz blocks or prisms, and concentrate it with concave parabolic reflectors, so perfectly ground and polished, in the form of his 'basins' at Newgrange and Knowth. This polarised and concentrated the life force through the whole crystal structure of the temple cairn.

To realise that Planck's Quantum Theory was only rediscovered in this century but was known and used by SAM is a sobering thought.

c

SAM used the availability of the life force of the Sun and tuned in or 'plugged in' to the vast universal grid that is imprinted through the macrocosm. Now we have cluttered, overloaded and disrupted these electro-magnetic fields with our sophisticated circuitry to the extent that the opposed nations of the Earth deliberately try to 'jam' the atmosphere to each other's disadvantage. This is so bizarre as to be almost incomprehensible.

Figure 32
Interference figures of polarised light:
(a) Interference phenomena in uniaxial crystals.
(b) Interference phenomena in biaxial crystals.
(c) The DNA figure of light 'macroscopic' molecule: interference figure of quartz showing circular polarization – the true Maltese Cross of the Templars (R. Webster, *Gems*)

Figure 31
Newgrange roof passage stone
(Department of Public Works, Dublin)

Stone Circles

Around stone circles curve the rainbows;
Glistening fire flies wind across the plain
The stones are shining damp in golden light
The sun has just come over the horizon.

There's the hum of nature's living heart beat,
Building up her forces with the lightening;
Transporting sacred messages across the mountain
Into the mouth of the deep purple cave.

'Hear us'
The singing and the chanting
'Hear us'
As we know your ears are open;
Grant us further peace of all creation
Till we join you and can lift the crystals.

Chapter IV
PLANETARY GEOMETRY

We have already discussed the distances of the planets from the Sun and how each one seemingly goes round the Earth thereby creating a cosmic clock but also how the planetary relationships and cycles have imprinted their movements and energies on and through our atmosphere to the surface of the Earth. The paths of the planets form together to make schematic geometric patterns that simply seem to conform to the structures we have already discussed in the symmetry of crystals on Earth. That the atmospheric imprint and the earthly imprint are part of our whole creative geometry is not surprising but the results and the implications of this basic understanding are overwhelming.

SAM looked up into the night sky and selected from his observations the constellations of the zodiac as the outer reference points to the path of the planets around the Sun but at the same time he was aware that the planets, including the Sun, seemingly went round the Earth.

The path of the planets can be demonstrated by the following diagrams so clearly illustrated by Keith Critchlow in his book, *Time Stands Still*.

'Old Father Time', or Saturn, moves in majestic style through the zodiac completing a full circuit every 28 years and 167 days. Jupiter moving faster inside this orbit is seen to come into line with Saturn at regular intervals during this cycle, as do the other planets. These are called conjunctions and mark significant points in time.

We can go a stage further with Saturn and Jupiter and plot the conjunction of a full cycle around the zodiac which shows three conjunction at 20-year intervals, i.e. a sixty-year scale.

Carried forward, the greatest conjunction is the complete cycle from beginning to end – a total of 2,400 years when we move from one great age to another, one house to the next, e.g. the Age of Pisces to Aquarius as we are doing at present. Actually the exact time scale is not 60 years but 59.6 years and the Great Age is therefore 2,383 years. It is interesting that we refer to a young man 'coming of age' in his twentieth year, i.e. 21. This goes back to the initiations in the priesthood following Saturn/Jupiter time and the natural life cycle. The 60-years conjunction can be drawn thus:

Figure 33
Conjunctive patterns of Saturn and Jupiter 1911-71 (Keith Critchlow, Time Stands Still). Note the double ascending and descending equilateral triangle and refer to the diagram of crystal structure in Chapter III.

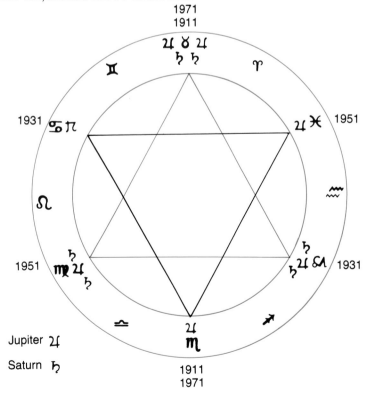

Jupiter ♃

Saturn ♄

35

The conjunctive pattern can now be taken a stage further when we see the Saturn/Jupiter patterns drawn out more fully.

Figure 34
Conjunctive patterns of
Saturn and Jupiter
1911-71 (Keith
Critchlow, Time
Stands Still)

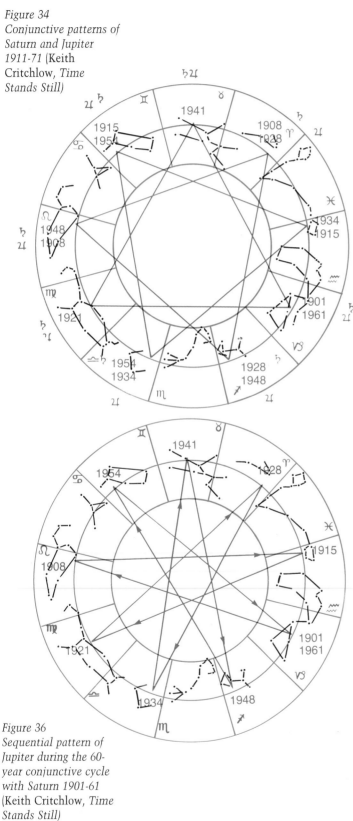

Before we can build up a true composite picture of these paths we must see the sequential patterns made by speedier Jupiter with Saturn, e.g. 1901–61.

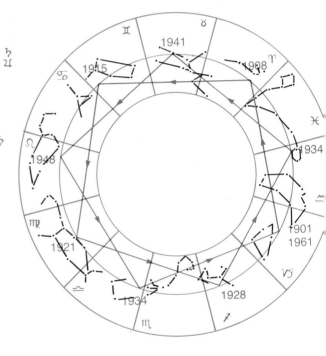

Figure 35
Further patterns
between Saturn and
Jupiter 1901-61 (Keith
Critchlow, Time
Stands Still)

Figure 36
Sequential pattern of
Jupiter during the 60-
year conjunctive cycle
with Saturn 1901-61
(Keith Critchlow, Time
Stands Still)

Max Ernst
Painter
2nd April 1891
Bruhl, Germany

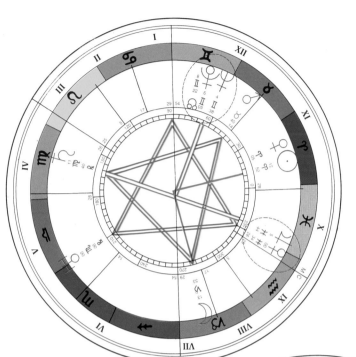

Figure 37
Astrological chart for
Max Ernst (A.T. Mann,
The Round Art: The
Astrology of Time and
Space)

If we can accept that these patterns leave an influence and imprint or 'trace' upon the Earth which combines with the energies of the Earth itself, then we can move to the next stage of plotting the crystalline energy grid that covers the surface which clairvoyant SAM saw, understood and used every day.

The patterns that the movement of the planets makes around the periphery of the zodiac can then be related to the imprint on individuals at birth, the readings of astrology. There is only scope to introduce two characters here for comparison. The first is Max Ernst – a sensitive painter whose chart shows an almost perfect aspecting of two interwoven equilateral triangles and cross – a beautiful symmetry that is easily comparable to the crystal and planetary symmetry we have already discussed. The second is unbalanced where all the energies are mainly concentrated in one-half of the chart, we could almost say one-half of the brain. He is another painter called Hitler. Looking at the astrological profiles so clearly drawn for us in A.T. Mann's book *The Round Art* we see again and again how the tyrants and selfish individuals of history have unbalanced charts whereas the mediators and servers of humanity have balanced charts. There seems to be a direct comparison between the positive and negative areas of the brain and the solar differential cycle, which as yet has not been identified clinically in mental disorders.

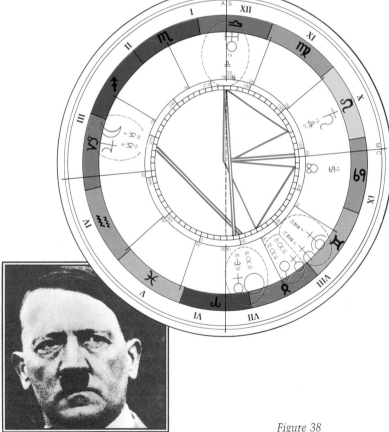

Adolf Hitler
Dictator
20th April 1889
Brauau, Austria

Figure 38
Astrological chart of
Adolf Hitler (A.T.
Mann, The Round Art:
The Astrology of Time
and Space)

The Departure

When the call was given by the Master
The people came up to the hill.
Standing patient, full of wonder,
Waiting for the light to fill the passages
Salute the corners
Where their friend was lying
Soul ascended through the corbelled roof
Into the gossamer sky of night.
He handed on his symbols
Telling them of his travels
Where all the others went before.

He told them,

'The journey's like unfolding wings,
Like a great bird reborn;
Flexing its muscles in the starlight
Soaring, bright-eyed
Longing for an audience
With the Eternal Waiting Presence.'

Those left behind felt the happiness
Of his great departure;
Touched the remains with reverence –
The moon marbles and the crystals.
The dust turning circles
Round and round the inner chamber
Until it settled, again
For the feet to bring
Another Priest and Friend.

Chapter V
EARTH ENERGY STARS

We have now seen how the pattern of the Earth's most finely evolved material grows to crystal symmetry and how the patterns of the planets around us also seemingly conform to a similar geometry. To understand the progress so far is to realise that the surface of the Earth is just another barrier within the density of matter and the passage of light. The air around us is comparatively thick due to gravity and we are held more firmly to the Earth than if we were on the top of Mount Everest. When the Olympic Games were performed in Mexico City at 10,000 feet, the jumpers achieved unprecedented heights and lengths, e.g. Bob Beaman's 29-foot jump that confounded the world. Put another way, if we were descending from outer space we would come from weightlessness to the upper atmosphere where we would begin to feel the pull of the Earth's gravity and the beginnings of density. As we moved closer to the Earth this density would increase proportionately until we approached the surface. Purely for illustration but obviously impractically, we might land in water, a liquid through which surface we would break, albeit with a jolt and come to rest; but if we hit Earth the density is much greater and there would be a sickening thud as our passage was decelerated abruptly! Each substance is denser than the next on the way to the very centre of the Earth – the core – yet all densities have a connective atomic passage through them.

We also know that all these different densities of matter have evolved with atomic form, particularly if they are crystalline – crystal form 'at rest' in the mineral kingdom, or crystal form 'in growth' in the animal and vegetable kingdoms and crystal form in motion in water and air. Throughout all these patterns there is a natural imprint and interlock of energy which builds up into an 'aura', or 'grid', through which the life force acts. This permeates everything.

The life force of the Earth can be tuned into by any human being who chooses to raise his consciousness above the level of egocentric necessity. We can understand this better if we think of an apple pip and how by putting this minute little seed into the earth it will attract and mutate with the life force to make it grow into a large tree that will produce hundreds of complete apples year after year. For the latent pip, working with the extraordinary energies it attracts to achieve this, is a wonder of creativity. If you have read the story of the *Findhorn Garden* you will know how a small group of spiritualists tuned into the essence of each type of flower, fruit and vegetable and produced fruits out of apparently dead ground, the size, shape and beauty, and organic deliciousness of which confused agriculturists and botanists the world over.

Many people living in the country have, on occasion, heard of water dowsers, strange characters considered rather 'fey' who can tell where there is water, its depth, its rate of flow and the mineral content. They do this with a forked stick, usually a hazel, that leaps around in their hands at the appropriate place. These people are also called 'diviners' and they are tuning into energy, a natural flow or static body of energy of one type within the body of another; here water in earth. They are sensitive to these vibrations and therefore can define them. This is the simplest form of dowsing. All other natural substances can be located in the same way; e.g. oil, gravel, copper, gold – each having its own vibrational response. This includes disease and illness.

The life force grid can be defined in geometric patterns within concentric circles forming into what is termed an Earth Star. These Stars are, in their true complete state, connected one to another and another covering the surface of the Earth just like a bee's honeycomb in a basic circular/hexagonal shape. They are not just flat as we can plot them on a map but spherical like a complete three-dimensional rainbow, half above our surface. The energy of these Stars is invisible to normal sight but can be seen with sensitive or clairvoyant sight and plotted either on the flat surface of a map or by physically walking the ground, using a pendulum or divining rods.

The exact shape and dimensions of these Earth Stars are completely symmetrical. They have been re-identified and defined in size, shape and colour by Clive Beadon in his work as a professional dowser so it is best to quote his definition:

The surface of the Earth is covered by an interlocking pattern of energy lines, the nature of which is not fully understood; they do not appear to be either electrical or magnetic but they can be identified by a dowser.

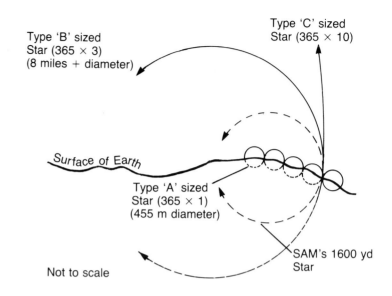

Type 'B' sized
Star (365 × 3)
(8 miles + diameter)

Type 'C' sized
Star (365 × 10)

Surface of Earth

Type 'A' sized
Star (365 × 1)
(455 m diameter)

SAM's 1600 yd
Star

Not to scale

Figure 39
Earth Stars (side elevation). Three-dimensional Earth Stars as they occur all over our planet. An infinite number of other sizes, natural and man-made, permeate through these astral levels. There are approximately 30 type 'A' Stars within one type 'B' Star and approximately 30 type 'B' Stars within one type 'C' Star. SAM seems to have used a Star of approx. 1,600 yards in his layouts

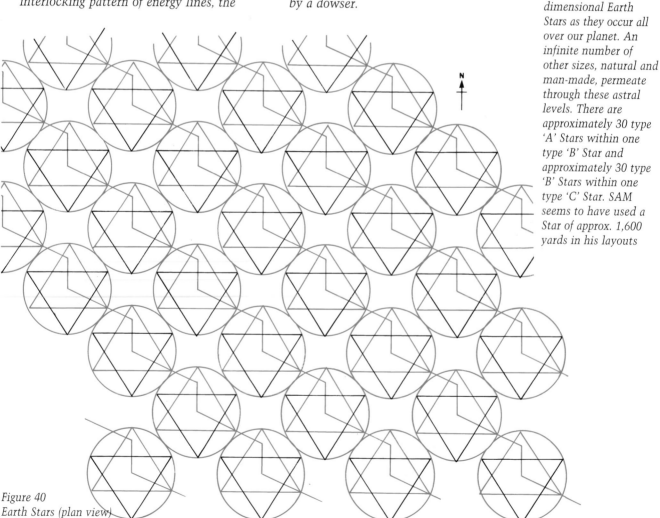

Figure 40
Earth Stars (plan view)

The pattern shows as a six-pointed star within a circle, each unit touching the next and linked together by the major energy line running through the centres. The basic colours of the lines of the patterns are white, red, black and blue, and where damage has occurred these colours still show but they are splintered off in all directions with no coherent shape or form.

In areas away from man's activities the patterns can be traced in their balanced, repeating shapes, but where they have been damaged fragmented lines are generated and it is near these points that disharmony occurs. To a dowser, these lines have the characteristic that they show as black and carry the apparent information of being water. It is probably the origin of the traditional black leys and black streams.

These patterns, sometimes like the acupuncture lines of the human body, are normally in balance but they can be diverted or destroyed and the resulting disharmony and uneasiness affects people in the area. Since we all have the dowsing sense, although we may not be aware of it, we can all be affected in varying degrees by such disturbances. The effect of such damage is being noted

Figure 41
Earth Star – the basic 'diviners' star pattern. Note central hexagon showing + −, rhomboid (◊) showing + − and equilateral triangles ascending and descending conjoined, showing input energy and output energy positions: also blue etheric line of knowledge. Input lines of red, white and black act as the cable that activates the structure (Clive Beadon)

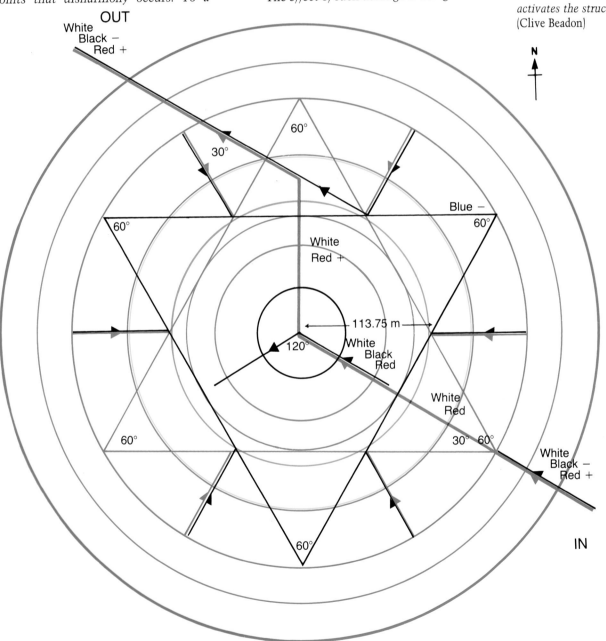

by an increasing number of interested people and there seems to be a growing correlation between their presence and inexplicable tension, unease and illness.
(Clive Beadon assisted
by Geoffrey King)

Immediately a distinct similarity will be noted between the basic shapes of Platonic geometry, the basic shapes of crystal symmetry and the pattern of the movement of the planets around the Earth and most importantly the definitions of the New Jerusalem in *The Book of Revelation*. We can go further than this and suggest that the sequential pattern of planetary movement in the heavens and as represented in the Earth Star mirrors the patterns of movement of the protons and electrons within the atomic structures of crystals when put from rest into an activated state and therefore in the patterns of the solar life force itself.

There was a time, and at certain places, when these Earth Stars and the connective grid were in balance on the surface of the Earth but gradually as evolution built it up man has disrupted and depleted it. Now with man polluting and manipulating the crust and aura of the Earth, there are few places left where the Stars are still complete, unbroken and in balance. Where the energy lines are not in symmetry, but fractured and broken, then all sorts of unpleasantness can result. This continuous spherical cover on the surface of the Earth is the first layer of the Earth's aura and can be likened to the area immediately on and above the surface of the skin of our bodies; the pranic level. If we have a boil or a scar it ruptures the surface and the energy all round it is unbalanced, e.g. we feel heat from a tumour, as an area of disruption within a zone or grid of nerves and tissues. If perhaps you can envisage one pore of your skin as one Earth Star of the Earth's crust, you will begin to get the idea. These Stars on the surface, close to the density or body of the Earth, can be compared to the lower astral in psychic work; the level where all negativity and fear is trapped close in gravity. When we fear we literally sweat from our pores with negativity and that vibration goes out through the aura round our body to the next layer off and so on until it is diffused by space. An animal will always sense our fear as it will see it psychically, for generally all animals are much more sensitive than we are. A classic example of this is the 'guard dog and intruder' situation— the guard dog will always sense the intruder because the man instinctively shows his fear,

being in a negative situation, so the dog identifies this and attacks. When Daniel (and countless others in similar fearful situations throughout history) was placed in the lions' den he was not attacked because he had tuned himself to the same wavelength as the animals' energy, so was on a universal vibration. The lions had no reason to fear him or attack him as he was 'in essence' one of them. There are people who will fearlessly walk up to a dangerous animal, a rogue stallion perhaps, and by their touch and presence the animal will immediately become calm and accepting; it will have recognised someone 'at one' with life, attuned, fearing nothing, loving all and balanced.

Where an Earth Star is out of balance internally, the energy pattern can be re-aligned by the use of selected crystals – a particular group mainly from the quartz family – set in a certain pattern within a copper spiral. These have been called *spirals of tranquillity* by their creator, Clive Beadon. The copper encircles and energises these chips which, because of their atomic and chemical structure interacting with each other, creates a natural energy force field that is strong enough to permeate through the whole atmospheric Star forming a vortex to bring it back into its true symmetrical form. No substances other than crystals have the inherent symmetry or balance in their atomic structure to be able to do this. As these Earth Stars have been more and more disrupted by man during the passing centuries so the original use that the Earth Stars were put to in the alignment and construction of ancient sites or energy centres has become occulted. There was a time before the discovery and use of smelted metal when there were large areas with a balanced energy grid in operation. SAM built his structures on special points and conjunctions, within these circles, erected his standing stones and dolmens always in a particular place. He worked either by instinct or information from the use of the pendulum, conforming in some way to the energy of the Earth Star, the Sun, the Moon and the planets. The constructions in one Star usually aligned with the energy grid of the next Star and so on as we will see in the progression across Ireland from the east, from near St. Patrick's Island through Newgrange and away to the west coast of Sligo and the Atlantic.

It was the gradual influx of the warring emigrants spreading out from the centre of the European landmass to the corners of the known world with their new weapons of iron that destroyed and disrupted the ancient

Figure 42
Earth Star – the complete Star in all its splendour! (Clive Beadon)

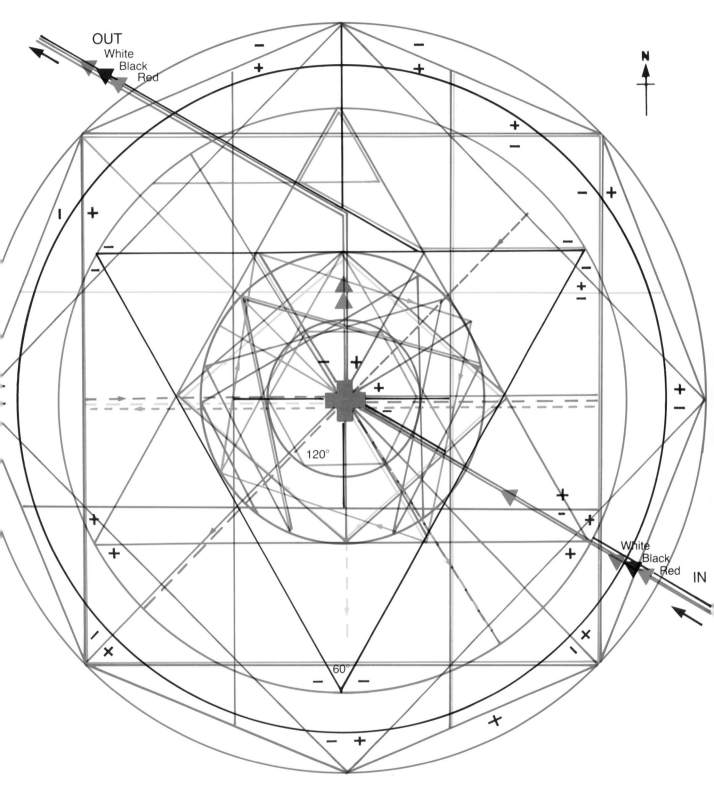

OUT
White
Black
Red

N

120°

60°

White
Black
Red
IN

*Grey interconnecting line
through central cross represents
the white energy flow*

43

sacred places. This has continued until today when even now unaware farmers, planning officers and property developers remove or re-fashion the depleted switched-off remaining examples of these structures in the once integrated vibrant grid. This Earth Star force field followed the natural path of the energy imprint of the whole 'cosmic' structure and was as real to SAM as our modern electrical grid is to us covering, but now marring, our countryside. If someone switched off our electrical current permanently, then in 1,000 years' time people would be saying 'what are all those poles and wires for?', 'what is that vast structure?' pointing at a defunct, crumbling power station, not understanding the invisible forces that once ran through it, lighting up perhaps Dublin, London or New York. The structures of SAM, placed so carefully, were designed for exactly the same purpose – to act as macroscopic power points within the natural energy grid and force flow across whole countries.

The way in which these Earth Stars can be perceived and balanced today is extremely important. It is possible by placing the *spiral of tranquillity* on the ground or on a given area of a map to recreate the original Earth Star 'in plan' and to trace exactly how the energies flowed across that area of countryside, although you, the diviner, might be hundreds of miles away. Map divining is a natural ability that is not generally understood or accepted as it is usually considered to be 'occult' practice, which of course it is, for occult, to reiterate, means hidden. Most human beings have the latent ability to divine energy reasonably accurately as most people are basically psychic. A map or photograph is an image of a place or energy system in miniature in another place. If you carry a picture of your wife in your wallet, when you take it out you immediately tune into her and sense her in your inner being and you relate to all the nuances of her character, her physical form, her health, her whole life force – the photograph registers the hidden detail in your mind and you can see and feel her presence with you at that moment. An insensitive stranger looking at the same photograph could only remark on her in a superficial way. A map is much the same as a photograph. If you know the area you will recognise that clump of trees where you had a picnic, that river where you fish, the hills behind your house and so on but if you are psychically trained and you are given a photograph of someone you have never seen before, you can tune into that person and can 'see' their physical condition or emotional

state because you tune into their life force beyond the surface of a flat piece of paper and there are several levels of response. So it is with a map for a diviner; the map becomes alive as he or she starts to move the pendulum across its contours literally feeling with sensitivity the answers to the questions being asked about the different energy levels present. The pendulum swings in a left-handed or right-handed spiral answering positive and negative, yes or no, to direct factual questions spoken inwardly through the diviner's different levels of consciousness to the atmospheric vibrations. The answer 'yes' or 'no' comes back if the question makes sense and step-by-step the Earth Star takes shape; then the old structures fall into place and become alive again.

The Earth Star fits concisely within a circle forming a pair of ascending and descending equilateral conjoined triangles similar to the schematic Saturn/Jupiter conjunctions and the structure of the crystal atom. Energy must have an input and an output point and these are clearly marked at the south-east and north-west points with their path through the centre of the structure. Note the inner hexagonal shape produced by the conjoined triangles and the blue triangle at the apex.

Colour gradations. Apart from the internal structure lines that permeate the Earth Star there is a formation of concentric circles of colour that spread out from a central cross to and beyond the perimeter of the red enclosing circle. These gradations have been defined and annotated by Clive Beadon, and the table is as follows (these are not shown on Figure 42):

Figure 43

1 Grey
2 Grey – black
3 Black
4 Black – white
5 White
6 Violet – white
7 Violet
8 Violet – blue
9 Blue
10 Blue – green
11 Green
12 Green – yellow
13 Yellow
14 Yellow – red
15 Red
16 Red – grey (triangular perimeter)
17 Violet – blue
18 Blue
19 Blue – green
20 Green (outer perimeter)

All these positive and negative energies and colour gradations have been defined by use of the pendulum. Nowhere are imaginary structures drawn in for fun or neatness.

Attributions of possible planetary influence are the author's own comments and not Clive Beadon's. The central white cross that appears in the Star is not confined to the internal diameter of the sphere but is dowsed as proceeding out of the confines of its 'body', for this is not a flat two-dimensional structure but a sphere of three-dimensional energy actualising as invisible vibration. The white cross is the vertical connector between Stars and proceeds from one Star to the next. It is a column of light – likened to the ladder or 'pillar to heaven' suggested in many mythologies. This column of light is the true connector between one completed level of vibration and the next, one level of the macrocosm and the next. Our solar system is performing in the same way, and our Sun is only the centre of a vastly larger atomic form that is interpolating and merging within an expanding series of differing levels of energy that proceed outwards through infinite space.

Our dense magnetic core creates a gravity or force field of immense strength that uses and forms the energy of the planets and the Sun on our surface to mould these Earth Stars around us. In Figure 41 the connecting 'cable' enters, centres and leaves the Star in a regular pattern through the whole grid. This cable seems to form as a central white energy bounded by a containing dark indigo energy and held together by a red motive energy of power. The Earth Star is similar to a human 'chakra' system but within the atmosphere, having all the gradations and colours of the spectrum of 'split' white light. This first level of the macrocosm therefore performs as a prism of energy comparable to a celestial or crystal prism defining 'as above, so below'.

Spirals

We have mentioned spirals several times – a basic spirall (spelt with a double 'l' deliberately) looks like this ⊚ and is found engraved over or by water points at ancient sites all over the world, because the flow of underground water makes a pendulum swing either clockwise or anti-clockwise above it depending on the solar polarity at the time of dowsing. We know now that the Sun's energies do change from positive (+) to negative (−), a duality of wavelength, every seven days and we as dowsers can ask for our own polarity at any one time (our polarities do not change from week to week incidentally) and the pendulum will

Figure 44
Stone circle water spiral – the origin of ring forts and stone circles: underground water-flow crossing point makes source of energy spiral; the radius of the stone circle = depth of energy found with a pendulum or hazel rods

swing in a double spiral thus: ⊚⊚ or to the answer of 'yes' or 'no' to any question. The use of natural energy in this way is considered by the Christian Church to be pagan, sinful and of the devil today, yet once was essentially part of the Christian wisdom tradition, now misunderstood and, therefore, vilified. Although deep within the few healing ministries of the Church, there are still priests who use the pendulum and fully appreciate its God-given uses. If we think of the word 'spirall' it is no more than the double spiral turned vertically:

 to give us the letter 'S',

π for 'Pi', or the circle fraction we know so well, 'Ra' ☼ the Sun or giver of life and 'LL' the Roman numerals for 50/50 or the balance of (+) (−) written in pictograms, a picture that is fundamental to understanding natural energy physics, and the pendulum, a tool used extensively by SAM. ⓢ π ☼ (+)(−)

Stone circles and ring forts are laid out over underground water junctions, or blind springs, their depth indicated through the radius of the spiral, the size of the circle on the surface. The spiral changes polarity from day (+) to night (−) feeding the natural grid.

Many levels of vibrations and colour are identified with the pendulum in conjunction with natural gem crystals. Amongst psychics many different types of pendulum are thought to be the most effective, from brass to wood to porcelain to plastic, etc. However, as we are demonstrably dealing with the definition of colour as a form of energy, and rock crystal absorbs all the colours of white light and performs in spirals under pressure from our thought processes, it is common sense to use crystal. SAM knew of these properties and used quartz and crystal in his structures. He even managed to use natural rock crystal in its

Figure 45
'Water point' spiral –
Aboriginal cave art

true hexagonal form to produce pendulums, as were found in a dolmen at Carrowmore in County Sligo, Eire. SAM made his pendulums of steatite (peridotite), a soft, easily worked form of soapstone or serpentine which has a talc base. It is found on the western seaboard of the Atlantic coastline of Ireland. For the technically-minded its chemical composition is $Fe_2 Mg_3 (SiO_3)_4$. Perhaps it is also significant that the original scarabs of Ancient Egypt – the carvings of the sacred beetle – were also made out of this substance, as were the prism seals of the Minoan culture of Crete.

The Origins of Jewellery

How do we know SAM had any knowledge of the pendulum? Surprisingly this has been under our noses for the last 150 years or since archaeology first became respectable. Regularly little pendants or pieces of Stone Age 'jewellery' have been found amongst the sparse artefacts removed from megalithic cairns and dolmens (wrongly called passage tombs and graves). These little pendants are cut and carved in such a way that their use as pendulums is patently obvious to anyone interested in dowsing. Some of them are even carved with spirals around their body and when suspended from a cord the movement of the positive and negative energy swings the pendulum. A page of these pendulums is reproduced overleaf.

SAM's pendulums were used by the priesthood of Ireland and by the Egyptians of the Pyramids to plot, measure, geometrise and lay out their structures and to calculate any problem involving the positive and negative use of energy. In Egypt these instruments were called *merkhets* or 'instruments of knowing'. With clairvoyant perception and the use of crystals, the standard measurement of neolithic times is now accepted as the megalithic yard of 0.829 metres or 32.64 inches. Later, after the discovery of metal, various measurements were established with the use of peridot, the origins of which are obscure, but peridotite (olivine), serpentine and steatite are all of the same 'family' materially.

These are the seven planetary metals which when used with peridotite give:

1. Peridot and gold (Sun) gives one megalithic yard or 32.64 inches and dowses on white vibrations.
2. Peridot and silver (Moon) gives one metre or 39 inches and dowses on red vibrations.
3. Peridot and tin (Jupiter) gives one Greek foot or 12.15 inches and dowses on yellow-green vibrations.

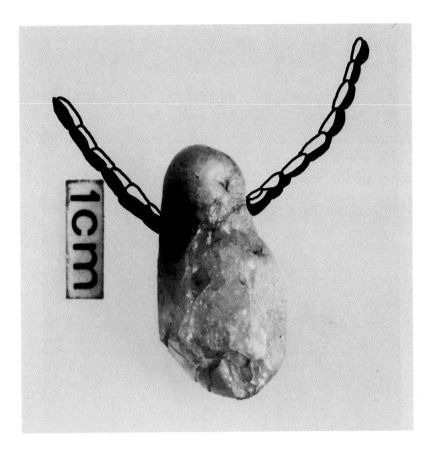

4. Peridot and iron (Mars) gives one 'remen' or 0.370 metres and dowses on red vibrations.
5. Peridot and lead (Saturn) gives one royal cubit or 0.524 metres and dowses on yellow and red vibrations.
6. Peridot and bronze (Mercury) gives half a metre or 19.4 inches and dowses on black and white vibrations.
7. Peridot and copper (Venus) gives the Golden Mean proportion or 1.618, demonstrated in the Fibonacci scale of 1.1.2.3.5.8.13.21, etc.
Copper dowses in spirals.
Peridot and running water dowses 3.141 metres or π (Pi).
Peridot and still water dowses 31.41 metres or (Pi) × 10.
Peridot and one dewdrop Pi ÷ 10.

(Measurements by Clive Beadon; planetary annotations – author)

Peridot is an obscure gemstone of the olivine family. The confusion has arisen because it was used in divination in Egyptian times but was then known under the name of topaz since it was found only on the island of

Figure 46
Rock crystal pendulum from Carrowmore dolmen circle c.4000 BC (National Museum of Ireland)

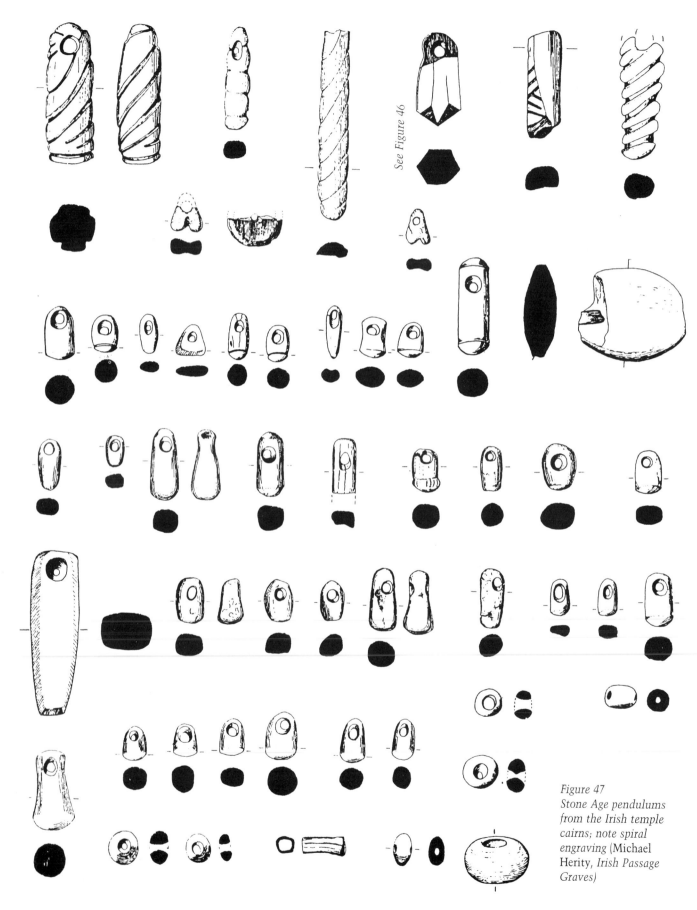

See Figure 46

Figure 47
Stone Age pendulums
from the Irish temple
cairns; note spiral
engraving (Michael
Herity, *Irish Passage
Graves*)

Topazios at the end of the Red Sea near the Indian Ocean – later this island was renamed significantly St. John's Island (St. John the Diviner) but in this century again renamed Socotra; even more recently as Zebirget. When topaz or chrysoberyl is given as one of the twelve stones of the biblical Breastplate of Righteousness (see *Exodus* 25:7, 35:9, *Leviticus* 8:8), it refers to peridot – topaz, precious topaz that is, was not found and universally accepted in jewellery until it was discovered in South America after the Spanish and Portuguese colonisations, and confusingly chrysoberyl looks not unlike peridot.

Peridotite is the parent rock and it forms as serpentine, soapstone and steatite. You will note that peridot and copper gives us the Golden Mean proportion with a pendulum and peridot and running water dowses or divines the Pi proportion. It is interesting that Pi is shown as a dolmen π since it seems to the author that dolmens are usually sited at the southern point of Earth Star patterns on the perimeter of circles. Also the very name Pyramid is really Pi-Ra-Mid, 'Pi' meaning proportion, 'Ra' the emerging sun, 'Mid' the biblical Midianites. If you can accept this – try divining yourself with these materials to prove it – then it is not so impossible to understand how the Egyptian mathematicians worked out their sums. Yet they probably obtained this knowledge from SAM along the Atlantic (Atlantis) seaboard.

It is not surprising that gold and rock crystal both living as part of a quartz in a granite base give the same measurement as the megalithic yard. Why then, if SAM was so intuitively concerned with granite, quartz and rock crystal, are we told that he only started to use gold after the beginning of the Bronze Age, around 2000 BC, and around the influx to North-west Europe of Mediterranean people from Africa? Surely his use of quartz and crystal found in the granite hills led him to discover, use and appreciate gold as the precious metal reflecting the colour and energy of the Sun itself – immutable, untarnishable and easily worked by hand. There are still concentrations of alluvial and seam gold in the Wicklow Hills, also in the Sperrin Hills of Derry and, no doubt, in the quartz veins of the granite masses of the western Atlantic seaboard, so perhaps SAM used gold in Ireland long before the archaeologists currently suppose. Maybe he used it in its natural ore form, i.e. unsmelted.

Star Size and Balance

SAM used his pendulum to perceive the natural balanced Earth Stars that filled his landscapes. He was able to calculate that there are several predictable levels of Star size within the macrocosm of the Earth's gravity.

The basic natural Star (which we will call 'A') is plotted at ground level of our atmospheric cover, the first level of the astral. This Star measures 113.75 metres from the centre across the radius of the inner hexagon formed by the ascending and descending triangles to circle 9 and therefore projects a diameter of the Star to the containing perimeter of approximately 455 metres.

The next size Star 'B' is overlaid on Star 'A' and is the next level of our atmospheric cover. These 'B' Stars have a diameter that varies from the Equator to the Poles as they form around the globe of the Earth. For instance at latitude 28°, the Canary Islands, they measure approximately 9.2 miles in diameter whereas at latitude 52°, Ireland and United Kingdom, they measure about 8.3 miles.

At the third level size 'C' Stars reach out to the edge of our atmosphere at about 200 miles diameter, but they vary considerably. Within these three levels the geometric atmospheric structures inter-permeate forming the Earth's aura or energy sheath, and within these energies we can begin to appreciate the logarithmic expansion of spirals. This is our 'atma'-sphere (*atma* = Hindi for 'universality').

As we go into the solar space we can call the next level 'D' or level '4' and after that, as we reach out into the galaxy that contains our whole solar system, we can call that level 'E' or '5'. If this is correct, how many levels of the macrocosm are there? How 'far out' into space do we have to travel to reach an ultimate end, if an end is there? How far does light travel?

When the natural symmetrical Earth Star is disrupted and goes out of balance the finely structured geometric colour lines splinter into many different components and directions. Each splinters according to the negative vibrations involved. The patterns of disruption can be very chaotic in areas of high density population. Consider any city or town. There are perhaps underground, surface and overhead railways, roads, electric cables, gas pipes, sewage pipes, tramways, TV and radio masts and aerials, let alone the incessant movement of cars, lorries and people all hurrying around like ants. How can the life force operate in balance in such a confused environment? In

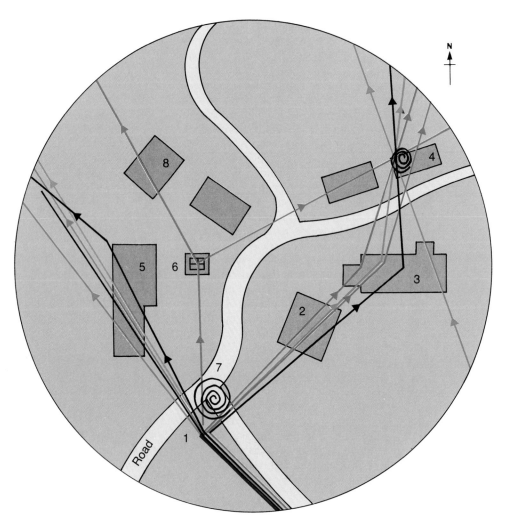

many cities now it is commercial, due to the lack of space, to build high-rise buildings that reach way up into the sky cutting into the lower astral, and people live there! No wonder, encased in glass, they become sick and have nervous breakdowns.

Figure 48 shows a fractured Earth Star. These lines start at the outer perimeter, in this case at the bottom southern point, and hit an old well and watercourse by a 'Y' junction of the road at (1). This well has attracted and fractured the energy in a fan shape in roughly three directions. To the right a red, black, blue and violet line passes through a house at (2) and into the church at (3) where some heavy foundation work and marble statuary (quartz) refract these lines up to the house at (4). Indeed the house at (4) has a deep cellar cut into bedrock which is attracting these lines.

The central area has an old granite monument (6) in front of the main house of the village which is attracting the red and black energy and then fracturing it further. The red is also drawn up to the house at (4).

These lines converging and crossing in the house produce a very unpleasant negative spiral, which combined with the fractured blue energy, could produce extreme discomfort manifesting as emotional upset or diseases of the chest, throat and head. The energy in the house at (5) would be very disrupted too as there are two black lines coupled with a yellow and green in isolation. This very powerful energy is directed at the solar plexus and heart areas of humans and can cause heart stoppage in children or babies – a malfunction we know but cannot understand called *cot death*. The house at (8) has a single red energy line through it which might manifest as anger and over-emotionalism or sexual imbalance on which unexplained movements and poltergeists perform. The point on the road at (7) where there is a heavy black negative spiral, due to the energy split at the well, will mean that there could be regular and inexplicable accidents here involving cars, bicycles, pedestrians and also animals. Even the placing of special crossing markers and lights cannot

Figure 48
Example of a disrupted Earth Star pattern, centring on a small village.
1 Old well and drainage water system.
2, 4, 5, 8 Houses.
3 Church. 6 War memorial (probably granite).
7 Dangerous crossroads (see explanation in text)

counteract this force.

The old-fashioned way of polarising these imbalances into the ground was to drive an iron stake into the ground 'upstream' of the bad flow, it having been defined as a black line by the pendulum. Now that the use of the pendulum with crystals is being rediscovered we can define all these lines as part of the multitude of colours of either the balanced or the chaotic spectrum of vibration. Also as energy reverses from day to night (sunrise to sunset to sunrise), the old method was only half effective. With Clive Beadon's crystal and copper *spiral of tranquillity* all these colours can be identified and rebalanced – a total of 64 colour gradations in all – and brought back into symmetry. Once the Earth Star is rebalanced the humans living in it and the operation of their chakras or colour centres will have a better chance of performing in harmony, only changing to chaos when personal emotional 'pollution' catches up with their intimate lives. The macroscopic Star is a chakra system that reflects the human chakra system that in turn reflects the crystal subatomic realm. 'For All is One'.

Leys

When people talk about 'leys' they are referring to lines that seem to connect many ancient structures and features of our landscape. The actual name 'ley' came from the Anglo-Saxon ending to many of our village place names ending in 'ly' or 'ley', for instance, Bram-ly or Hunt-ley. If you take any large-scale map of the British Isles and choose, perhaps, a tumulus in Dorset and join it to another 25 miles away, the line will inevitably go through many seemingly significant points such as churches, crossroads, wells, track junctions, etc. and often these lines are then dowsed as 'leys' – the supposition having already been fed into the 'lines' before the actual dowsing took place. True ley lines are either the type of lines we have been discussing, or those that follow the natural earth strata lines on or in the surface layers of our crust. From within the natural Star patterns or from within the Star patterns deliberately set up by SAM, there are many force or power points that connect within the whole grid and often over long distances. The clairvoyant or psychic power of SAM's brain impulses (used in conjunction with this natural grid that reflected the balanced life force) was able to connect points as effectively and lastingly as if he had erected a line of telephone poles and wires. These are consciousness lines. In the years to come the energy imprinted onto the earth along our main roads by our cars will still be there long after the road itself has disappeared. So it is in the atmosphere between significant points and on the surface below.

Many of those early power points, always sited over water spirals or blind springs, were subsequently taken over by the Christian Church which assimilated the natural or 'pagan' cultures as the only way the new ideas or practices of its dogma could gain credibility with the suspicous country people. The 'holy wells' of today are still revered as places of healing and power and now annotated as belonging to St. 'Someone or other' in order to hold the beliefs of the people together. The water in these wells most likely did hold healing qualities because it was chemically pure and flowed through quartz, thereby becoming 'activated' with the seven-day duality of the Sun.

So the old energy lines do exist but they are difficult to pick up with a pendulum, often because the user has not understood the correct use of that instrument. The state of the thoughts of each individual and the question fed through the actual pendulum will ultimately define the answers given. The point is that before anyone uses a pendulum he or she must have decided quite clearly in the mind the facts required to be answered. To swing a crystal over an area of the landscape, or over a map, hoping for answers to half-defined questions will not produce a positive response but will result in incorrect and generally garbled information. Perhaps it should be clearly stated again that the pendulum is only an extension of the user. To understand 'leys' we must project ourselves back in time to a period of balance when the macrocosm was mainly free from the age of materialism and ego that pervades everything today. SAM set up and used these energy lines for essentially positive purposes in the course of his daily life, purposes that fulfilled his role as a catalyst between the higher atmospheres and the material nature kingdoms for which he was so responsible. Man is the spiritual guide of Mother Earth, a truth now long forgotten. But often the dark side, the negativity of witchcraft or black magic, has been used on this grid pattern to manipulate or fracture symmetry. These forces can be corrected by absent healing or positive thought by caring, loving groups for the benefit of the countryside, the people and all nature. Such work is undertaken tirelessly by *Fountain International* for instance, in psychic community care.

The Carrowkeel Star

Now the lights shine in the hillside
Few yet see the psychic flame
Life's candles burning in their holders
Marking a path for all eternity.

We are the keepers of the Life flame
Deep within the Earth we guard it
Available always for the lasting truth
Of man in love with each man's wisdom.

Please call the love flame, for it's endless
And has grown down nurturing centuries
Down the many waiting lifetimes
Till your hands return to light it.

Fill our hearts to overflowing
Till the grail cup nearly drowns us
In the Cosmic Christ filled chalice
Of love and truth and light and glory.

Soon the cover of heaven's obscurity
Will lift for new peace to pour out
Over all the damaged nations
The healing awe inspiring Christ light.

Beam the Cosmic Christ ray to us
Fill the Earth again with gladness
Man alone is in God's image
And can do the work expected.

Man alone can bridge the centuries
Bridge of Light, the bridge of healing
Man alone has all the answers
When he gives to God his questions.

Rich man give away your lifestyle
Poor man give away your sorrows
Follow now the chance you're given
Fulfil the Earth for all tomorrows.

Chapter VI
THE CARROWKEEL STAR

Application of an Earth Star by SAM

We have seen how the Earth Stars cover our surface in spherical three-dimensional form to build up our 'aura' and how the standard Star 'A' encountered has a set inner radius of 113.75 metres, but at the same time each and every life form creates its own-sized Star depending on its state of vibration. It is quite clear that SAM was fully conversant with these Earth structural patterns and used the natural ones or ones he, himself, created in his own layouts as they were an essential part of his life.

When he was drawn to an area to construct his temples he chose a place naturally and geographically suitable for that purpose. This would be an area for the protection of the community and also for protection of the knowledge to be enshrined in the structures themselves. Around this area the sacred and practical community would evolve.

There would be some places of great significance considered far more important than others and there was probably one place that was the great centre of them all. We can see immediate and obvious parallels within the buildings and workings of the Christian Church today, with small outlying parishes looked after by a single priest, a city having its own cathedral and a bishop, supported by a dean and attendant clergy at different stages of initiation, and ultimately the primate of the country presiding over the heart seat of learning and recognised by all the strata of that society as the representative of God.

When man was given the power of reason and consciousness again and realised that life was not a continual nomadic state of 'up sticks' to the next feeding ground, and when he realised that larger family units could grow into a loving tribe looking after the interests of all, he chose suitable sites on which to build and finally settle. At the same time his knowledge of the Earth's energy patterns and the paths of the Sun, the Moon and the stars blossomed forth into a renewed understanding that gave him a feeling of security and purpose. He knew *he* was essentially part of the whole kingdom.

To find an area that was totally suitable in size and shape to fulfil the dimensions of the normal size or multiple interlock of the Earth Stars in nigh impossible, if it is simultaneously to be 'in sight', i.e. generally visible. The only place fitting such a requirement would be a flat plain, which in itself would be exposed and unprotectable against natural disaster, wild animals or possible unknown aggression. Therefore, one of the major requirements was that the site should be high up; it could be protected more readily and could be seen for many miles around to give a sense of reassurance for basic directional purposes, not just directional in terms of sight-up but for purposes of dialling Sun, Moon and stars from below looking up. Also the site at the top of a hill or mountain is nearer to the descending cosmic forces whilst the general population below is involved all the time with the Earth; hence the terms 'Father' sky (looking up) and 'Mother' Earth (looking down).

Carrowkeel is such a place. The name has been mentioned already earlier in the book. First let us think of Ireland, a small land on the west coast of Europe, the farthest extremity of the European continent, a place of aged granite and limestone rocks crashed and blown by the Atlantic around most of its

Figure 49
Bricklieve Hills,
cairns L, K, H, G
(photo: David Knight)

coasts. The mountains are mainly along the western seaboard; stark pinnacles and jutting cliffs intersected by gleaming, fish-filled rivers and loughs that flow down from inland hills and plains, often shrouded in grey/blue cloaks of swirling mist and rain. But it was a very different country many millions of years ago as the fossils in the hills show. Once it was a flat, tropical, swampy, sea area; the fossil evidence is irrefutable. Evolution of the plains stretching out into the Atlantic many miles beyond the present coastline took place gradually over thousands and thousands of years. Then a civilisation grew up and lived much further out into the Atlantic all the way down to the Canary Islands. The population was not demarcated by the present Atlantic coastal seaboard but extended across the 'coast' as naturally as, for instance, the Irish nation once merged across the sea into Britain. These people are known to us today as the Atlanteans, whose capital centred on the Azores.

The land of Atlantis or Tir na Og has been written of and thought about by mystics and philosophers for many centuries. Irish legend and folklore persist even now telling of a special land of knowledge and eternal life involving stories and inexplicable happenings and the visions of country people down the centuries, particularly stories of people disappearing and returning many years later without ageing. The Sidhe (Shee), 'the little people', are very real to clairvoyants and even appear sometimes in the sight of people without this vision when in certain states of raised awareness. This is particularly so in the old rural areas where the energies of the Earth are still reasonably in balance.

However, a solar planetary event that disrupted our crystal balance took place, which heralded the end of the most recent great Ice Age when the Earth's climate changed so that the Gulf Stream began to warm the northern seas. Some say it was a tilt of our axis or magnetic reversal due to the influence of the Sun; some that we were knocked sideways by an enormous meteor entering our atmosphere and being sucked in by gravity; or perhaps man himself outgrew his knowledge of the crystal forces and became too clever. Whatever the reason there was a dramatic and Earth-shattering event that we must always dread. The resultant seismic and later climatic changes meant that the sea, the rain and the air warmed sufficiently for ice to melt and the sea to expand until water covered vast areas of low lying land. During that time the low lying coastal areas of the Atlantic seaboard finally settled and became the Atlantic Shelf of today as the Earth came under such enormous pressure and movement due to the sliding tectonic plates. If this was the case, then the survivors of that land, the ordinary people as well as some of the priesthood, might have managed to struggle to the remaining landmass to the east, west and south but as these cataclysmic events took place suddenly and unexpectedly then few could have made the journey. This is the 1990-2000 AD forthcoming scenario shown to us by the greenhouse effect.

The ice disappeared around 8000 BC because the Gulf Stream started to flow north-east from the Caribbean and SAM slowly struggled back to those areas remembered fractionally in dreams and legend and, perhaps, since he was so aware, in remembrance and recall of his past lives. This time the landscape was very different from the memory of coastal plains full of vegetation and rolling hills. A lot had happened; the sea was now much closer to the ranges of bare, empty hills of crushed and sparkling white granite. There was no earth on the mountains as they had been scraped bare, fissured and faulted, chipped and shaled; yet there were plains of pumice and gravel where vegetation and forest were beginning to spring up. The new soft, warm climate meant plenty of growth and fresh water gushing from springs, often out of places in bare rocks. These were later to be named as the 'holy wells' of the Christian priesthood.

The coast of Sligo had become a really magnificent, empty countryside with its soaring inland cliffs and plateaux that had survived but been re-fashioned and shaped by the ice. These hills and valleys then were not covered with peat as they are today but were gleaming grey/white rock and silver water in the sunlight and moonlight, places of great awe-inspiring wonder and flashing colour. Some people arrived by sea and settled on the coast where there was abundant food, clams, oysters, mussels and fish, such as at the middens at Carrowmore; but the fear of the water, the remembrance of gigantic floods, tidal waves and the ice, meant a place of sanctuary was necessary, a place beyond destruction, a place high up for protection and nearer to the spiritual deity, similar perhaps to Machu Picchu in the Andes, or the 'Haven' of the Holy Land (see page 70).

Such a place was inland, away from the dangerous coast, through the scrubs and forests and along the line of the teeming rivers, to the hills in the distance, at Carrowkeel and the Bricklieve Hills seventeen miles away. This area is now known by the name of 'the townland', incorporates the enigmatic series of megalithic cairns and is an area of staggering vistas from the tops of the hills 1,000 feet above sea level. It is a range of parallel escarpments of fissured carboniferous limestone running roughly south-east/north-west that reflects the crystal formation of the Earth. Below, on either side, there is a lough, but particularly in the east is Lough Arrow, a large, deep, magical, pure-water lake that reflects all the significance of the rising Sun as it stretches across the distant Arigna Mountains to light up the hill tops. For anyone with the understanding of the need for space and spiritual security this is home.

Without fresh water there is no support system to life. It is the element of growth that balances earth, fire and air. The lough provides such an impetus.

The Stone Age cairns are marked with letters given them by the archaeological excavation organised in 1911 'during a period of twelve-and-a-half working days' by R.A.S. MacAlister and R.L. Praeger, in which short time fourteen cairns were 'examined'. It was a tragic exercise of haste, lack of preparation and understanding as can be seen by the devastated structures. Fortunately some remain untouched and unopened. Dynamite was used to lift the heaviest stones!

Also around the periphery of this range there are many 'ring forts' and standing stones. Every structure was positioned and built for a particular purpose – nothing was as haphazard as our building patterns of today. It would seem at first glance that the cairns were placed on the most convenient prominent points of the escarpments having no predictable connection in their layout but this is not the case.

Now we must tune into the map and think of it as a picture of a vibrant living organism, having rebalanced any disruptions using the *spiral of tranquillity*. Gradually as the pendulum swings back and forth across the map the white, red and black input line of the Star is located at cairn 'P' on the rear summit of Doonaveeragh.

To anyone unfamiliar with these cairns the trace of the Star is difficult to follow if described line by line using local place names and markers. To avoid confusion, please refer to Figure 50 and accept that the pendulum gradually leads the diviner around the area of the map, building up the two interlocking equilateral triangles. The northern-most point is a ring fort in the towland of Cloghoge and the southern-most point a standing stone on the western edge of the Carricknahorna Valley. The well-known line of cairns located on top of the central escarpment form the 'spine'

Figure 50
The Carrowkeel Star – natural energy lines connecting through the Carrowkeel megalithic cairns

Figure 51
Planetary layout: four Jupiter/Saturn conjunctions are probably recorded by four pairs of cairns

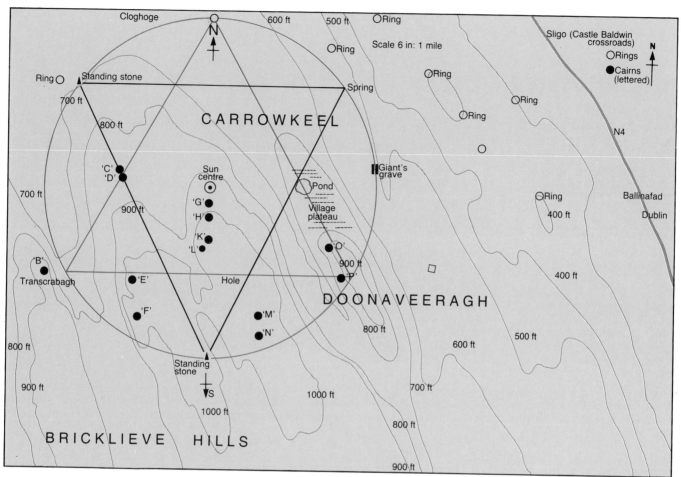

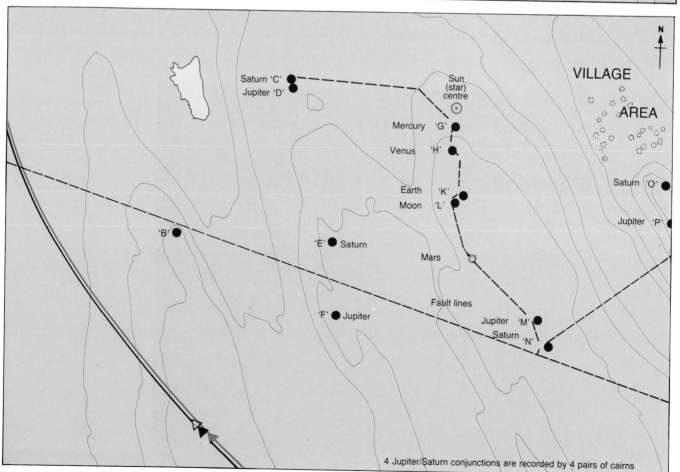

△ *Figure 52*
Doonaveeragh Village
plateau (photo: David
Knight)

◁ *Figure 53*
Doonaveeragh Village
hut circles (Michael
Herity, *Irish Passage*
Graves)

of the Star running along the north/south line from the centre point. To the rear (south) of the top-most cairn (L) there is a deep hole in the hill top, the result of a major subsidence. This is called a 'pollnagolum' in old Irish. Perhaps J.R. Tolkein took the name of his sad character of evil, 'Gollum', from the Irish language for his trilogy *Lord of the Rings*. This subsidence is important as it is directly on a major strata fault line that runs from cairns 'N' and 'M' through the central line of cairns and off to a pair of cairns at 'C' and 'D'. This central line of cairns was sited off the direct north/south line in the Star layout as the structures were placed over the configuration of the fault line to build up the energy. This is shown in Figure 51.

It is interesting that the largest Stone Age sanctuary village in Ireland is located on the Doonaveeragh escarpment. At the centre of the village there was a double circle excavated out of the rocky surface to form a pond or water point that drained the sloping rocks. This is of obvious social significance but is also the conjunction point between the two interlocking triangles and the easterly 'door' to the Star. It is the entry point of the rising Sun's rays at spring and autumn equinox.

To the south-west corner of the Star there is a cairn on top of the Traenscrabbagh promontory. This cairn should really have been sited in the valley below to conform to the exact geometry of the perimeter circle but then it would have been totally hidden by the cliffs in the valley bottom, so it was put on the prominent top to be seen from many miles around. If a line is projected from cairn 'B' (Traenscrabbagh) through the north ring fort at Cloghoge it proceeds to the cairn at the head of Lough Arrow called Heapstown (heap of stone) and if a line from the south-east corner of the Star at cairn 'P' is projected up through the same ring fort it proceeds to the cairn on the top of Knocknarea some seventeen miles away on the Atlantic coastline. As already mentioned SAM liked to integrate his structures to conform with the neolithic energy grid. The circumference of the Star even passes exactly through the 'giant's grave' on the eastern perimeter.

At the very centre of the Star we might expect to find a large marker stone but SAM did not necessarily offer such easy answers. The centre of the Star is 'occulted' and can only be found with a pendulum as it is the mystical or Sun centre – the centre of light – in this case of a complete planetary layout. There is a centre, however, a neat little oblong cut in the rock to form a small cave in front of cairn 'G' in the forward slope of the hill. Due to spillage this is now partly filled with loose stone.

This Carrowkeel Star follows the layout of our solar system in miniature. The size of the Star with a diameter of about 1,600 yards shows that it is a man-made star, as it does not conform to Star 'A' or 'B' sizes. If we look at the conformation of the cairns from the Sun centre and plot them in relation to our planets, we see the positions of Mercury, cairn (G), Venus, cairn (H), Earth, cairn (K), Moon (a 'blind' negative cairn), cairn (L). Mars is represented by the subsidence at the pollnagolum where there was probably a cairn once on this fault, and there are four pairs of Saturn/Jupiter conjunctions around the perimeter at cairns 'M' and 'N', the other conjunctions from the Star centre being 'O' 'P', 'E' 'F' and 'D' 'C'. The standing stone at the southern point of the perimeter is the 12 o'clock midday sundial for the whole annual calendar and also a lunar dialling marker.

It is extraordinary to realise that SAM was aware that the Earth orbits the Sun but used the Sun, seemingly proceeding around the Earth, for his dialling. For here SAM expresses a Sun-centred layout.

Another aspect, and just as important and practical in terms of everyday life to the community, is the layout of the cairns, stones and ring forts that also mark the annual events of the Sun's travels from solstice to equinox to solstice and the maximum to minimum rise and set. For example, gazing out over the rolling plains which look down towards Galway in the west, the Sun drops lazily across the sky to settle exactly behind the magical quartz mountain of Croagh Patrick which is silhouetted against the skyline fifty-five miles away on the November quarter day when observed from cairn 'K'. This is the Earth cairn from which dialling was carried out as it is the top-most point with the greatest all round view of the horizon. The rising and setting points on the vast 360° panorama were carefully noted and passed from one generation to the next. Yet each cairn and ring also allowed local sightings to be taken from wherever they are placed.

Ring Forts

There are about thirty thousand 'rings' of many types recorded on the Ordnance Survey maps, but this number has been sadly depleted over the last twenty years by the expansion of towns and villages and roads all over the country. Originally it was accepted that these enclosures were built solely as small farm-

△ Figure 54
Beltane, Moon over
cairn K

◁ Figure 55
Standing stone,
Carrowkeel Star,
southern marker

steads or 'keeps' for animals and also, since they are referred to as forts, as places of defence or of strategic significance. However, they are usually sited in such unstrategic positions that this latter use must be questioned. One aspect not appreciated by archaeologists or surveyors is that these early constructions are always sited over water points called blind springs or energy rises, underground streams or static water tables. Underground water has a very strong vibration therefore producing visible energy within the colour spectrum into the atmosphere above ground level. This vibration builds up into powerful spirals easily discernible with a pendulum, or in the hand of the traditional rural dowser, with the hazel wands.

SAM understood this energy as it was all part of the supply or power feed into the atmospheric grid we have talked about so much in the formation of the Earth Stars. He built whatever type of construction he thought necessary to fulfil the purpose of supplying or withdrawing 'force' from this invisible network. Sometimes he put up a 'standing stone' to particularise such a place, but usually he built a circular bank or wall of stones to enclose and annotate the energy. Since every member of the community knew all about these forces, there was nothing hidden about the procedure. Just as today at Carrowkeel, in Sligo, we have our own little freshwater scheme with its circular concrete reservoir tank supplying water to the outlying cottages on the hill. We do not think this is remarkable or unusual.

Where necessary and within perhaps a wider layout than we can easily perceive today, certain major rings were integrated into a national grid network. Also sometimes, again

at special points on the landscape, usually high up and therefore exposed, circles were made to conform to the Sun and Moon and/or to orientate to the static true north 'star' point. When we plotted the Carrowkeel Star we found that the north point is marked by a large ring in the townland of Cloghoge at the exact apex of the ascending red positive triangle. It would be wrong to state this ring was laid out at the same time as the cairns within the Star perimeter but it would be equally incorrect to say it was not. A dowser could date it, just as he or she can date anything, but such a source of information has not yet been accepted by the pragmatic scientists and archaeologists.

It is incredibly confusing to look at a map of this area as it is dotted with rings of many types and shapes, but if you get out on the ground amongst the hills and valleys and really look at the sites and their relationship to the land formations, and each other, and the position of the sunrise and sunsets, you begin to see what SAM intuited so naturally.

This whole area is enclosed by a very much larger Star whose perimeter circle passes through the following points of great local significance – Kilmactranny standing stone with a late Christian stone on top; the Moytirra structures; Heapstown; Sheerevagh; Kesh Summit cairn; the huge dolmen at Tinacarra; Boyle Church (on an ancient pre-Christian site) and back to the start. The input line is located just above Church Island and Hog's Island on the west side of Lough Key and runs north-west to a point below the major 'cashalain' (now ruined) approximately seven-eighths of a mile from the village of Ballinafad. Then it branches due north to a ring fort in the area known as Brickeen at the top left corner of Lough Arrow opposite Little's Island.

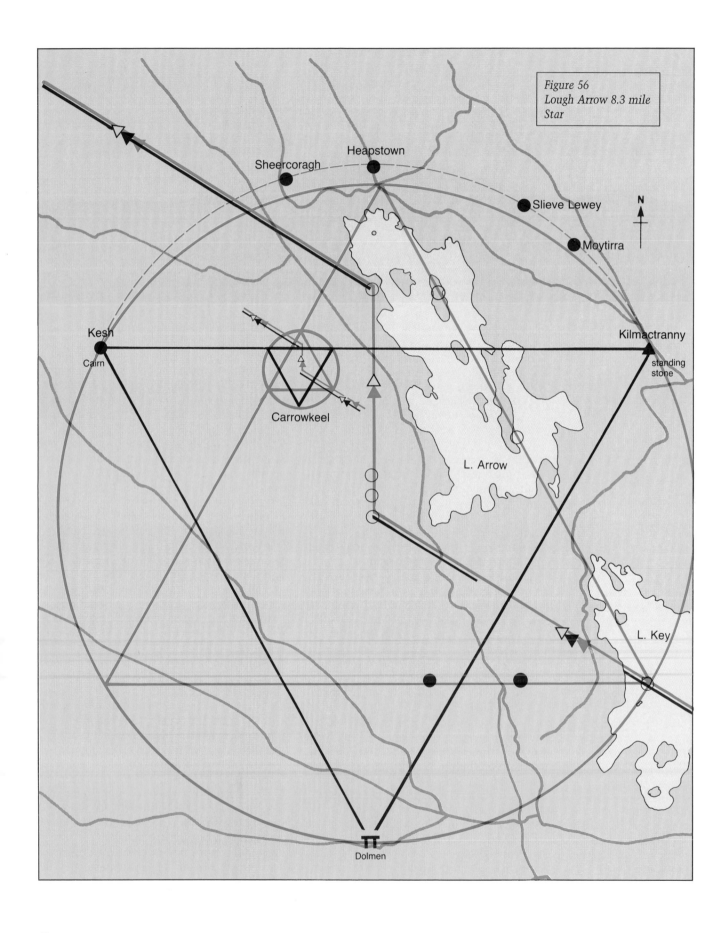

*Figure 56
Lough Arrow 8.3 mile
Star*

Thence it goes out through a line by Castle-baldwin and the Holy Wells, to meet the next Star by the hill of Coolskeagh. The red positive ascending equilateral triangle starts at the entry point by the Rock of Doon (above Lough Key) and runs north-west by Drumdoe cairn across Lough Arrow to the end of the Annagh-loy peninsula where there is a later site of an ancient Christian abbey, then across the water to Gildea's Island and to the Heapstown cairn – the largest and most important unopened cairn in the whole area. From this cairn it travels south-west through the Carrowkeel Star to the area of Stragh, then horizontally along the line of the Curlews to start again. The descending indigo or black negative triangle runs across from the Kilmacktranny standing stone across Lough Arrow and Carrowkeel to the summit cairn of Keshcorran and south-east to the Tinacarra dolmen area near Boyle, thereby interconnecting with the man-made Carrowkeel Star pattern. You will note that the Star perimeter does not fit a true circle drawn with a compass on a six-inch-to-one-mile map exactly, but remember SAM had only the use of his pendulum and sighting from one hill top to the next. There were no aeroplanes to photograph the area for him, so his precision is truly remarkable over an eight-and-a-third-mile diameter circle.

The Lough Arrow Star 'B' proceds to two more stars that connect to the coast and include Knocknarea and the south Sligo Bay area.

Lough Arrow is the sacred lake, the area of highly alkaline (Yin) water that reflects the silver sheen of the Moon and its feminine energy, the gentleness that transmutes the powerful masculinity of the Sun. As gravity and the Earth held the constructions of SAM in place, so the Sun's fire provided the constant solar ray for the stones and the quartz to build up the energy patterns that were needed to balance the layout and provide power to the whole grid of the area. The water provided the purification and the cleansing catalyst and the air was the path to the cosmos and the heavenly bodies, hence 'atma'-sphere.

The lake is protected by the hills of Moytirra on the east, the Curlew Mountains on the south and the Bricklieve Hills on the west. Only the north is open; the path of the eternal spirit and soul where the Sun and the Moon do not rise or set and where the planetary alignments are seemingly fixed, so Heapstown was placed at this northern point. Beyond Heapstown, up on the coast on a solitary domed high hill, was another bigger temple dominating the whole seaboard sea at Knock-narea. Carrowkeel is intimately connected to both.

In Irish mythology the name of Moytirra is well known as the battlefield of the two leading 'tribes' of the ancient country; the Tuatha Da-Naan (possibly known in the Middle East at this time as the people of Anu, the tribe called the Annanage) and the Firbolgs. At some time in SAM's era, history relates that these two peoples met on the plateau of Moytirra to decide on the mastery of Ireland. The Tuatha Da-Naan won and the Firbolgs gave way. It is also suggested that this was not an actual battle but a spiritual encounter between the powers of the light and darkness. Whatever it was, Moytirra is still there today with its major, and now sadly decimated, cairn at Slieve Lewey, on the Lough Arrow perimeter circle; also a giant's grave, together with the standing stones and stone circles that remain to tell us their history if you have the intuition to tune into them. Each and every old structure has a keeper or spiritual guardian and they are available if you can 'see'.

Cross-Country Grid

The next step is to locate Stars of the same dimension (size 'B') at the same progressive angle across Ireland from the east to the west coast, as they show with the pendulum.

Newgrange is written up as the most important structure of Stone Age Ireland so the conformation of an energy grid laid on Newgrange seems to be a sensible point to try and decipher this flow across the country. It is reasonable, therefore, to take a point at the east coast and start the grid there. Immedi-

Figure 57
Kilmactranny standing
stone

63

△ Figure 58
Heapstown cairn

▽ Figure 59
Keshcorran cairn

Figure 60
Tinacarra dolmen

ately the pendulum takes us to a coastal area just below St. Patrick's Island – where, according to legend, St. Patrick is said to have landed on his journey from Wales. This must have been an island of great ancient significance or it would not have been annotated thus by the Church. The energy line just below it crosses the country to the very portal of Newgrange and out through the backstone to nearby Knowth, then in a straight line across Ireland to the cashel on the island of Innishmurray, out in Sligo Bay, the line encompassing 14 size 'B' Stars or 116 miles. How strange it is that this cashel should also enshrine an early Christian settlement founded in 520 AD by Bishop Molaise who is thought to have been ordained by Patrick himself.

The same progression can be followed at Tara and the line will lead across Ireland until it passes through Loughcrew and the Carrowmore dolmen area and across the hill at Knocknarea, beside the great summit cairn. A perceptive statement made by Beranger in 1779 and reiterated by Conwell in 1866 reads:

I have little doubt that the cairns on the Lough Crew Hills are but a portion of a chain of such remains, terminated on the east by the great mounds of Newgrange, Knowth and Dowth, and that a fuller and more careful examination of

the country will prove that chain to have extended westwards to the Atlantic.

It is difficult to find a chronological progression. The only major excavation completed so far has been at Newgrange and on the other side of the country on small dolmen circles at Carrowmore in County Sligo. From carbon dating, by no means complete at either end, the construction of Newgrange is thought to have commenced about 3000 BC. Carrowmore was always thought to be a later, westward offshoot, as the originators were supposed to have come from Crete up the Irish Sea to settle at the Boyne. However, carbon dating now puts Carrowmore at around 4000 BC and no doubt in due course sites will be found on the west coast that were commenced much earlier still as is an example in Brittany at Carnac. Recently a site has been dated in Northern Ireland's 'Navan Fort' as early as 7000 BC. Carbon dating is inaccurate as solar wind energy 'rise and fall' has not been taken into the calculation of decay rates.

Logically if Newgrange is the most sophisticated structure in terms of its purpose, architecture and symbology then that seat of learning would have sent out craftsmen with knowledge of what its engravings meant to build this knowledge into future structures –

Loughcrew, then Carrowkeel, then Carrowmore, i.e. east to west. However, if the knowledge had come from the west and the structures gradually moved south-east with the people spreading out across the country as each place developed, so new techniques would have been used, until the east coast was reached and the jump was made to the Anglesey cairns and on into Britain. It is unusual for new techniques to backtrack; having finally reached Newgrange it is unlikely the craftsmen would then have gone to Carrowkeel to tell them 'look, we have new ways of declaring our science'. The engravers at Carrowkeel would have said in very human terms 'thank you, we do not need to incorporate your engravings since we taught you'.

The planetary layout of Carrowkeel and the cairns covers a large area which is miniaturised at Newgrange into one building using all that knowledge as engravings on the internal and external surfaces of its kerb stones. Yet here it is worth mentioning that Heapstown and Knocknarea are similar major kerbed cairns and possibly also engraved. Certainly Heapstown is a very important cairn although it is not as large as its glorified sister Knocknarea.

Interlocking Earth Stars have relative energy 'value'. We know that there are three natural regular sizes, but having said that it is only the smallest size 'A' that seems to be constant in terms of linear measurement. Size 'B' varies in diameter with latitude and size 'C', as the vast cloak that reaches out to the edge of our atmosphere, seems to pulsate and change more markedly still, almost with the inbreathing and out-breathing of the Earth itself from day to night to day, sunrise to sunrise, Moon to Moon. When we plot a size 'A' Star in symmetry, close to the Earth's surface, we know as we reach its geometric centre. This centre must have an energy value since it demonstrates a true geometric form within a known perimeter. Here, once again, the pendulum shows us or gives us a vibrational 'value' to work with, or if we allow the pendulum to swing freely at this centre it will rotate 365 times and then stop. Perhaps this is not surprising since the Earth itself takes that number of days every year to travel round the Sun, its master. So 365 can be taken as a unit of 1, the basic energy beat unit of the macrocosm. All other Stars, man-made or natural, have an expression at their centres of this unit.

The Carrowkeel Star, the planetary manmade layout with a diameter of approximately one mile, has a centre beat of 365 × 2.8 or 1,022. The large Lough Arrow Star has a beat at its centre of 1,971 or 365 × 5.4 and so on. Each Star that is smaller than the unit 1 expresses as a fraction of the macroscopic unit until we reach perhaps the smallest structure or artefact set up by man, say a fire hearth, or a carved stone ball, before we make the diminishing leap into the particles of subatomic physics of the Earth's densities, called the microcosm. Because we are dealing with light energy, colour and sound, suddenly we realise we are involving ourselves with quantum physics, a complex area that concentrates the majority of the best scientific minds on Earth, notably the late Albert Einstein.

SAM had an innate and clear understanding of the atomic structure of matter and gravity as soon becomes clear to us when we delve further into the magic of his structures. All his structures relate in some way to the path of sunlight around a seemingly static point on Mother Earth. The centres of the great manmade structures build up spirals of energy that express with the pendulum 'beats' up to maximum it seems of 365 × 100 as at Newgrange, Stonehenge and the Pyramids for example. Or is it perhaps that this beat is not × (times) a particular value but 'to the power of', i.e. 365^{100}? Then perhaps we could divine the logarithmic expansion of geometric spirals and as acceleration took place through such a force centre so the molecular and atmospheric densities would approach and pass the speed of light and enter the next dimension!

Each site built by SAM has an energy centre that, at the time of construction, was in geometric symmetry. It was before the advent of smelted metal that dragged our consciousness down into the earth once we had extracted and fashioned it. Metal, particularly gold and iron, should never have been taken from the earth as it *polarised* our thought processes down into the earth and away from the higher densities. Around each major centre there is still a force field of invisible energy that has to be pierced or acknowledged before a diviner can begin to unlock the secrets that SAM encapsulated there.

The first step is to have the dowsing ability, inherent in most human beings who are prepared to 'have a go'. The second is to be able to rebalance the atmospheric energies into the symmetry that existed before man disrupted them into present chaos. Since the grid is now so universally chaotic, this can only be done now, practically, with the *spiral of tranquillity*. Finally, the diviner must be able to attune his brainwaves to the same level at which the universal Earth brain pulses. This can only be achieved through meditation. It may sound

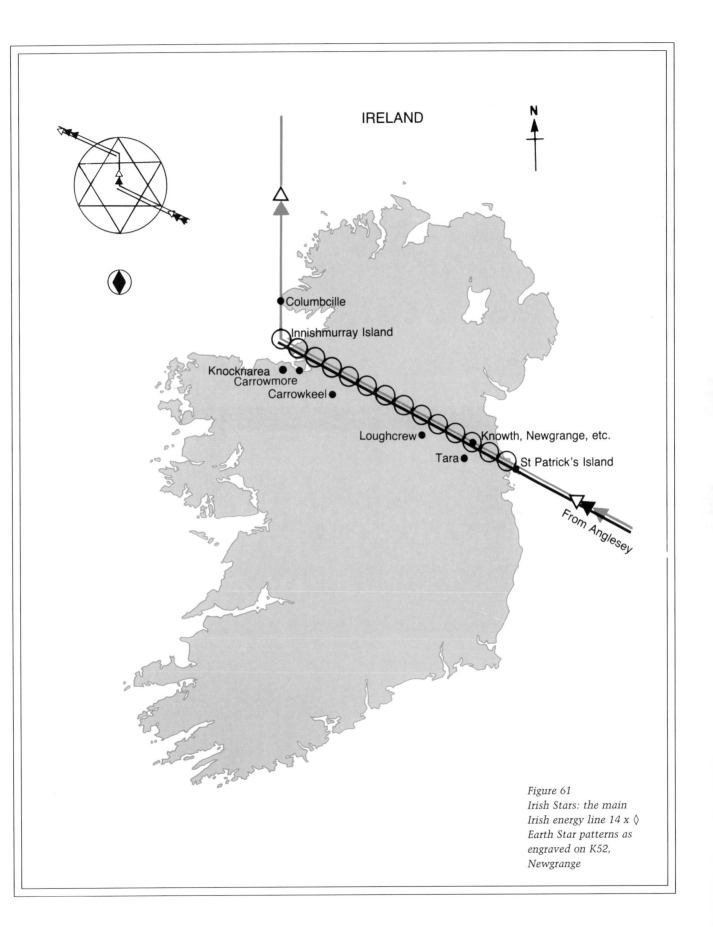

IRELAND

N

● Columbcille

Innishmurray Island

Knocknarea ●
Carrowmore

Carrowkeel ●

Loughcrew ●

Knowth, Newgrange, etc.

Tara ●

St Patrick's Island

From Anglesey

Figure 61
Irish Stars: the main
Irish energy line 14 x ◊
Earth Star patterns as
engraved on K52,
Newgrange

'way-out' but it is a fact that through relaxation we can change the pattern of our brain-waves to a vibration that has been called the 'alpha wave' level. This has been defined and practised by thousands of people all over the world who practise relaxation in one form or another. It is the process followed in principle by ancient mystics and monks of both the Western and Eastern traditions, and the process now followed by Westerners prepared to be involved in the depths of spiritual contemplation.

Whichever process we choose to follow we will only unlock these secrets if we are prepared to train ourselves in the Universal Humanities. There are diviners of enormous practical experience who state quite surely that there is no geometric energy field round a certain structure because they have not been able to tune their minds out of this chaotic materialistic life in which we live, in order to pierce through the protective screen SAM hid behind. His layouts are sometimes very occult because they hide the secrets of universal physics, the secrets of thought transference and the ultimate secret of molecular acceleration of the life force that can manifest in living creatures, and into the cosmic plains. In plotting the spheres of the Earth Stars in some of the great Irish sites a geometric expansion is clearly and beautifully portrayed.

A Meditation to 'Ethne' –
Angel to the Carrowkeel Crystal

Ethne let us lift our arms in wonder
Praise the Light that fills your Star
Feel the rising rending heartbeat
Of the energy released beneath.

Let us hold our hands palm upwards
Lift our brow to call the Light
Feel the coming Cosmic Christ beam
Sway our feet as old Earth shakes.

Now the clouds move back allighted
The soft mists throw a curving rainbow
Between the pillars of your kingdoms –
The Arc of many covenants.

All the plasmas turn to crystals
Spiralling through the blue tint ethers
Dancing, flashing, diamond pinpoints
Bearing love across Earth's chakras.

Man the bridge and man the doorway
WE are the guides the Earth is seeking
Return through your green leaf pathways
Give back the honeysuckle fragrance.

Ethne birth us back to bedrock
Suck our feet back in granites
Remind us that our spirituality
Begins with feet upon the ground.

We emerged from out your chakras
Growing many coloured wo-man
Now we heal your heaven earthwards
Where it lies beneath our feet.

Ethne raise the band of warriors
Light white torches in our arteries
To the crown of all endeavours
So we may be your crystal catalyst.

Chapter VII
ANCIENT SEASONS AND FESTIVALS AND SAM'S LIFESTYLE

If we wish to unlock SAM's understanding of the light in his annual calendar, since he did not have the written word, we must delve into the celebrations of the seasons as handed down through the later Druid traditions.

That many of these festivals were subsequently taken into the Christian calendar also helps us to realise and enjoy their true significance. The stages of the year were far more than just a succession of events to do with watching the Sun or Moon so that crops could be planted and grown at the right time. For as the sequence of these events took place time after time and year after year man realised there was a deeper significance behind the rhythms of the natural progressions both on the surface of the Earth and in his own inner being as he grew from youth to old age, birth to death.

As we know, annually, four of these distinct moments, the mid-points of the seasons, mark the most intense times; whilst the other four, the cusps of the seasons, mark the least intense moments when one season changes over into the next succeeding one. The four mid-points occur at the solstices and equinoxes, the fixed times of the solar calendar of each year. The four cusps, known as the fire festivals or quarter days, are more fluid or movable in their placing in the calendar. In fact, all eight are 'fire' festivals in respect of being aspects of the solar year, with the solstices and equinoxes representing the more dominant 'masculine' aspects and the quarters being more impressionable 'feminine' aspects. The solstices and equinoxes are well known by positions of the Sun but the quarters are not so marked. In order to recognise and thus celebrate the changeover points, the priests of

old made the quarter days coincide with the nearest lunar festivals at the time of the full Moon, which meant that the quarter days were movable within a margin of a fortnight, either side of the hypothetical quarter point. This also had the practical advantage of directly linking the solar cycle with the lunar cycle and in this sense one could consider the quarter days to be lunar festivals.

The feminine and masculine always work together in life and thus the twelve-fold lunar cycle operates in partnership with the eight-fold solar cycle. Each cycle in itself has its more masculine and more feminine aspects working together – the full Moons of the lunar cycle rising in 'male' and 'female' zodiacal signs alternately, and the solar cycle with its solstices and equinoxes complemented by the quarters. The lunar festivals were used to prepare the person for the solar festivals – the feminine aspect being the receptive part that prepares the way for the spiritual impulses to come into the womb of matter and the masculine aspect being the outgoing part which puts into action or expression that which has been received. The disciple initiate offers the grail cup of his heart and soul to receive the light of the spirit; the cup is filled to overflowing and then the disciple goes forth as a son of 'God' to give that consecrated grail to the rest of life.

In other words, when we are born into this world as souls we do not suddenly see and understand truth. Truth is always there but we have to find it and spend life after life seeking the greater mysteries in the depths of our own evolving consciousness. With the unfolding sense of awe at the immensity of the purpose and balance of the whole of life comes the understanding that each and every animal and human being is of God too. This cannot be grasped suddenly but has to be acquired through following a path of initiation from one point of knowledge and belief to the next. So the mysteries came to be known as the path, the journey, or in modern terms 'seeing the light'. The people who chose and today still choose to put themselves voluntarily on this path do so from a deep inner sense of the workings of the life force as a manifestation of the power and love of God, the macroscopic power of supreme balance. Sooner or later on this journey they will encounter the 'mystery school' of occult knowledge and if they have prepared themselves sufficiently may recognise with a sense of great humility that they belong to 'the White Brotherhood'. This is not a club or a gathering or a community but an esoteric brotherhood of light linked by soul consciousness from one being to another along the vibration of the light towards the purpose of the positive progression of the whole Earth in its cosmic journey. The interactions of the powers of God and good workings through each individual or group soul allow many strange and wonderful events to happen in everyday life to help hold the powers of darkness, ignorance, fear and untruth at bay.

To become an initiate in God's light crosses over the dogmatic paths of all religions and creeds as it is a step that can only come from within the deep caverns of the personal self. If the step is taken half-heartedly it is soon an empty illusion and will only bring further unhappiness and pain. If the spur is truth and the longing is to love and forgive then gradually the mysteries will unfold in their due season. This is the path that SAM gladly accepted as his birthright. From amongst the community young men, and later women, were chosen to be trained from an early age in the occult knowledge so that the spirit of the light could be carried forward through each generation.

As each era or cycle passes and man's path is raised one step higher on the ladder of initiation he has to accept more responsibility for his actions. For the young Stone Age initiate there were the old myths and legends of the last great disaster to haunt his spiritual life – the remote memories of times in past civilisations when once before man had reached a point of development that out-ran his sense of responsibility to all nature.

On the plateau at Doonaveeragh he was at least able to feel secure from floods and wild beasts. We do not know for certain when Carrowkeel was first chosen as a major place of sanctuary. Before the cairns were built the people had to know where to put them so there was a long period of learning to apply old knowledge to a new environment. It is possible that a being or a small group of people suddenly arrived 'out of the blue' and taught the complex geometry of space and it is also possible there was an inherent nucleus of old knowledge handed down from person to person from the previous Altantean civilisation.

From early neolithic times to the beginning of the Bronze Age, with the discovery of the use of metal and its smelting in Ireland, the priests of the old religion had led the growing population in the mysteries of the Sun. This was a period of peace and security, a time we can relate to as 'the Garden of Eden' from after the Ice Age in perhaps 7000 BC to around 2000 BC. During this long period man had no need to kill other men or disrupt the laws of nature. He was mainly vegetarian and worked with the nature kingdoms in harmony and trust.

Recently a very pertinent book called *The Genius of the Few* by C. and B. J. O'Brien has been published, which relates and unravels the visitations of the Lord Anu of the Annanage to an area of Israel called 'Haven' (heaven). The early records of this time are all clearly written on stone tablets and cylinders and tell us that these Lords of Light came from 'space', another system, bringing their higher consciousness as a gift to man of that time – 7500 BC approximately, so that man could become a true representative of God 'in his image'. The 'Tuatha Da-Naan' are the Tuatha d'Anu (of the Annanage); could they not have brought this crystal knowledge as their gift of consciousness?

The 'Druids' were the priests of the later Bronze Age and Iron Age holding the knowledge of these mysteries learnt from their predecessors of the neolithic period and continuing the old established celebrations. The celebrations are still known today. The 'festivals' have been named and dated as they mark the change from one season to the next.

1. We start with the Festival of the Dead or Death, or the Festival of Peace, on 1st November each year, known in the early Irish as Samhain, pronounced 'Saun'. This is now celebrated as All Saints' and All Souls' Day or 'Halloween'.
2. Next is the great Festival of Rebirth at the winter solstice on 21st December; the Irish 'Geerah', now widely celebrated three days later as the 'Christ-mass' on 25th December.
3. Then the Festival of Dedication or the

spring quarter day of 1st February called Imbloc, pronounced 'Im-be-all-ock', known as Candlemass or St. Bride's or St. Bridget's Day.

4. The Festival of Promise occurs on 21st March at the spring equinox, called 'Antharoc' and now celebrated as Lady Day and linked to the 'Passover'.
5. The Festival of Unification is 1st May, quarter day called Beltane, pronounced 'Beeyoul-tena', celebrated as Corpus Christi or Ascension Day.
6. The Festival of Joy the great mid-season outpouring of the Sun on 21st June is the summer solstice, known as and pronounced 'Saura', celebrated as Pentecost.
7. The Festival of Transformation is the end of summer, 1st August, called Lugnasadh, pronounced 'Loonisah' (Lug's Day), and celebrated as Lammastide.
8. The Festival of Consummation on 22nd September is the autumn equinox, called 'Law Ala Miheel', now celebrated as St. Michael's Day but on 29th September each year as 'Michaelmass'.

In nature we see how these patterns or laws are worked out in evolving life forms. Firstly, late autumn is a period when the seeds are sown in the earth and at Christmas time they have reached a point where they can be germinated. There the life force goes into the seeds in the ground and brings about a quickening or germination of those seeds and they begin to sprout underground. Then during the last part of the winter they slowly grow up towards the surface of the ground but still in that dense earth element.

When we come to the start of spring, these hidden germinated seeds in the ground begin to pop up and appear in the open air and sunlight. Then spring has truly begun. During spring the plants grow more and more and start to leaf. Some of the early ones begin to flower as well but generally they are going through their leafing experience.

We then come to the end of spring, to the Beltane Festival, and there is another outpouring of energy which quickens that whole plant life and it begins to flower. (Some will have flowered earlier but this calendar is demonstrating the general law or pattern, i.e. nature begins to flower and the flowering continues apace throughout the summer.)

When we reach the autumn we get the fruiting. The flower withers having served its purpose of creating the condition that enables the fruit to grow from that flower. The flower has become fertilised and it conceives and gives birth to a 'child' which is the fruit. The fruit then grows and ripens until eventually there comes the harvesting of that fruit, followed by, in the case of corn, the drying of the harvested sheath during the last part of the autumn and then threshing – the recovery of the seed. The seed is either resown or taken to make bread and other foodstuffs. All that is not needed is burnt and returned to the ground as humus. So another cycle begins, this pattern going on and on.

SAM revered the hazel and its nut in his recognition of this annual cycle, as well as the wheat. In early dolmens and cairns burnt wheat and nuts in their shells are regularly found, the round nut within the shell the kernel of the Earth, the heart and the brain encased and enclosed ready to break forth – the tree being more enduring than the annual wheat plant. The hazel bush was considered a sacred tree in ancient Ireland – to cut one down was punishable with death.

We have heard of, and even been privileged

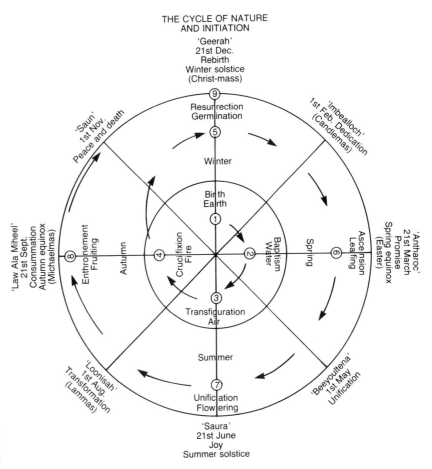

THE CYCLE OF NATURE AND INITIATION

Figure 62
Druidic seasonal wheel: the cycle of nature and initiation (Peter Dawkins and author)

to meet, wonderful people in life who are far up the initiatory ladder, far on the path towards God. The life and the work of Mother Theresa come to mind for instance, also there is a 'man' in the world who expresses his life in selfless service, manifesting through his life the supreme ideal of truth and love to all. The life of Sri Sathya Sai 'Baba' of Puttaparthi expresses the divine principle in its entirety currently on Earth; 'the Avatar of this Age'. However, to return to the cycle of initiation: at some stage during this work the initiate, having given up his or her life into universal care, will receive part or all of the gifts of the spirit. As we raise our consciousness from self to no-self, so we are led forward towards the understanding of the truth of 'man in the image of God'. These gifts are considered by dogmatic Christians to be exclusive to the followers of Jesus and particularly to the Roman Catholic Church. Here is it necessary to remark that the Master Jesus was of the highest initiate stage of the Christ soul, a fully-christed being, illuminated by the light of God. He was Jesus, of the cosmic Christ spirit of God, not *the* God, but *from* God as he himself was quick to point out.

The 'gifts' of spirit are given to any human being prepared to raise his consciousness from selfishness to selflessness, caring for all creatures with love. These gifts are documented in the Christian and Buddhist faith and handed down verbally amongst such 'primitive' peoples as the Aborigines of Australia – the last surviving humans from the Stone Age. In *Corinthians* we learn of the gifts of the spirit thus:

Now there are diversities of gifts, but there is only one Spirit. And there are diversities of ministries, but there is only one Lord. And there are diversities of powers, but it is the one God who works all things in all men. But the manifestation of the Spirit is given to every man as help to him. For to one is given by the Spirit the word of wisdom; to another the word of knowledge by the same Spirit. To another faith by the same Spirit; to another the working of miracles; to another prophecy; to another a means to distinguish the true Spirit; to another different languages; to another interpretation of languages. But all of these gifts are wrought by that one and the same Spirit, dividing to every one severally as he will.

(I Corinthians 4:11, Lamsa Bible)

In Buddhist faith they are listed as the 'siddhis' or the miraculous powers a man may attain on his way to *Nirvana*, the state of grace and all knowledge. How strange it is that Buddhists should use the word *siddhi* for miraculous power (Irish: Sidhe = 'the Little People') – and Tara, the capital of early Ireland, is the same word as the Hindus use to name the 'Earth Mother'.

Buddhist powers or 'siddhis' include experience of previous lives, mental states of other men, the true 'state' of love (the life force), invisibility (in terms of another's perception or the substance of light), clairvoyance and clairaudience, flight and weightlessness (out-of-body experience), and the complete control of hunger, thirst and breath.

To the natives of Australia, the Pacific and the Arctic, these gifts are the ability to know and 'see' places, distances, positions and energies that are incomprehensibly outside our 'civilised' credibility. They are the psychic perceptions already alluded to as vibrations of energy and experience locked into the macrocosm of the Earth and the cosmos to which the human brain becomes able to attune as it opens in awareness.

The gifts of sight and hearing are both vibrations outside the normal range of perception but also they are tuning to brainwaves of another person, i.e. their inner thoughts and conversations. Prophecy is knowing of coming or distant events, visions or dreams, past lives and the knowing of divine purpose or evil and its interpretation. The gift of healing is obvious but sometimes past and current results are so extraordinary they are in line with the greatest miracles performed by Jesus himself; but did He not say in *John* 14:2,

he who believes in me shall do the works which I do; and even greater than these things he shall do, because I am going to my Father.

These powers, in principle, were part of SAM's daily life in his natural, uncluttered, pure existence.

These gifts have been taught incorrectly to Christians over the centuries to be exclusive to followers of Jesus. This is patently incorrect and has caused great hardship and suffering to many people. It is, however, completely correct to teach that the mis-use of these gifts, once achieved, in any way other than to the objective progress of love, is totally wrong. It is also correct to teach that the gifts are only a step in personal initiation and once acquired need to be accepted with humility so the initiate can then proceed to the next hurdle on the path of his or her progress towards the higher mysteries.

Often, unfortunately, the opening of awareness in an individual involving the acquisition of some or all of these abilities engenders an even bigger ego, a 'holier than thou' attitude – and a path of spiritual ego is embarked upon. There are many so-called psychics around today making large sums of money by offering instant initiation and grace. To any true seeker they will be readily obvious, but to the unwary and gullible they pose a threat and trap that could cause much inward speculation, illusion and subsequent breakdown.

SAM's Lifestyle

SAM did not know the use of smelted metal of any sort, except perhaps gold. He lived with stone and wood, fire and water, and the animal and vegetable world of nature; he knew metal only in its 'ore' form, i.e. still within its parent rock – iron ore, silver ore, etc.

The village at Carrowkeel on the Doonaveeragh plateau is difficult to identify until you are right amongst the somewhat flattened stone dwelling circles that are now covered with layers of thick couch grass and wiry old heather. The village plateau lies on the north-west end of the cone-shaped hill and is bounded by an oblong escarpment of natural walls, nearly fifty feet high in most parts, of sheer carboniferous limestone rocks all fissured and cracked by the Ice Age. The flattish top of the escarpment is also deeply cracked and, at first, seems terribly difficult to walk across. SAM was directed to this place for his village because of its extraordinary natural formation giving an ideal site for protection and security against would-be trespassers (see photograph in previous chapter, page 58).

Then the rock was bare and sharp but it was quite easily broken along the lengths of the old Ice Age cracks to make spaces for the base of the circular huts of the village. The long narrow cracks are generally between one to six feet deep and one to six inches wide so the resultant base, or floor, of the huts was not, by any means, regular. In fact, the uneven cracks had to be filled with smaller stones, earth and bits of brushwood to produce a floor that was in any way comfortable. This had an added bonus as the parallel strata acted as a sort of inbuilt radiator to the whole structure. When a fire was lit in the hut the heat radiated out along the strata just like putting an old-fashioned flanged radiator on its side. Also the larger cracks were useful for storing food in either cold or hot weather, acting as a vertical cupboard so to speak, down in the floor. These were like pockets or drawers built naturally into the house. Where possible the walls were left unbroken to add strength to the structure, but it was difficult to make a round house out of north-west/south-east strata.

The size of the huts varies, with the smaller ones often tacked onto larger versions which are from ten to fourteen feet and up to as much as forty-five feet in diameter. The walls were built with the resulting gap filled in with smaller stones that had come from chipping and clearing the whole area. The walls varied in height, obviously, as there was no set piece construction, and were usually two to three feet high. Then boughs of wood were put up to make the double wall and arched across the whole circle to make the domed canopy of the roof, perhaps supported by one or more vertical pillars. The roof could then be thatched with willow and ash, with grasses or reeds from the Lough. A hearth was left in the centre of the structure and the smoke was drawn out of an opening above. It must have been very dark and smoky inside but the flap door could be left open to act as a draught regulator. The door opening into the circle of stones was about two feet wide. The forest below the hills provided many different types of tree wood. It is hardly possible the larger circles were built to house animals immediately beside the houses as the strata of the plateau are so regularly cracked and fissured that any unwary four-footed beast walking across them could have slipped into the cracks and broken a leg very quickly. So the strata had the bonus of giving extra protection against wild animals, particularly wolves at night. The last wolf was killed in Ireland supposedly in 1795. Had wolves ventured up from the forest below, the rocks would have given protection just like a huge natural cattle grid. Domestic animals, dogs, were friends and recognised quite naturally as the partners of man in his struggle for survival. There is little evidence of animals being deliberately exploited and killed for food as we do, so disgracefully, today.

The balance of the natural kingdom was more important than selfish needs, and the allowance for each life form to have a place and a part in the kingdom was deeply respected. We have evidence about the animals of these times from the bone remains found in or around Carrowmore, from the late Bronze Age, even the discovery of a bone of a bear from a Carrowkeel cairn. Bones of ox, horse, sheep, goat, deer, pig, domesticated wild boar and dog have been found as well as hares and rabbits and various fowl. Add to this shellfish such as mussels and cockles, and a fair picture can be built up of the animal scene in the roving farming community of the forest centred on the few villages. To suggest that SAM never killed wild animals would be presumptuous, as he surely did, to protect his family or companions when necessary. That he used leather is also more than probable, yet if he wore shoes on his feet they would have been of plaited grass strapped up his ankles. That he killed for sport or blood lust is very unlikely. There is no evidence from amongst the known 'grave' goods of the middle or late neolithic period of the deliberate hunting of game in Ireland. There is no evidence that the hunt was such an important part of his life that when a man died his prowess had to be perpetuated by including trophies or weapons with his 'personal effects'. It is very rare to find an arrow head in an Irish structure. Much of the odd 'refuse' found in or around cairns had accumulated long after the cairns were closed down by SAM and the many bones and odds and ends represent the litter of curious Iron Age peoples spanning later periods up to as late as the 17th century AD – long after the Norse invasions.

SAM had beautifully-made axe heads of various materials but these were not weapons of war and it is very doubtful they were used for beating a neighbour's brains out. An unskilled modern man with a well-made stone axe can fell a full-grown birch tree in ten minutes. In the hands of SAM it was as efficient as the iron axe of today. If we want to understand a little more of SAM we could read the reported speeches and legends of the great Red Indian cultures of North America and even follow the thinking of the last remnants of the Aborigines of Australia. They tell of respect for animals and that man only 'takes animals' when necessary for the true needs of the 'tribe' and always with reverence and after approaching the life force for permission. How does our conscience stand today in comparison? The fruit and vegetable kingdoms of the Earth are at our disposal if we nurture and treat them with respect and SAM understood this and lived off the abundance of the forest.

On Sunday, 3rd February 1985, there was a two-page article in *The Observer* newspaper extolling the virtue of eating wholemeal bread, nuts and fresh fruit, also more lightly cooked or raw vegetables and as much fish as possible. It says if you must eat meat use 'only lean meat' but give it up if you can. SAM lived this way 6,000 years ago and was happy and healthy. The woods and forests stretched across Ireland below the bare hill tops in waving green seas of abundance. Many varieties of wood and leaf were available for many different purposes; the stately pines and oak trees, the luxuriant and prolific elm and ash, the willows for weaving basket fish traps and always the wonderful hazel bushes with their delicious round nuts that dropped in the autumn and sustained life with protein during the winter. There were many kinds of berries too, the blackberry, wild raspberry, elderberry with its flower and juice providing such strong vitamins, the wild damsons, hips and haws, acorns, blueberries, whitethorn, blackthorn and so on. Then there were all the fungi of the forest which today we mainly disregard and shun as poisonous in our present ignorance, even the psychedelic fungi which brought forth extra perception of the natural life, as if it was needed.

There was a form of wheat and probably barley, so we are told, therefore the making of a coarse bread is likely, or perhaps gruel. It is not difficult to grind grain between stones of carboniferous limestone, nor is it difficult to 'bake' a wadge of dough in the cracks in the rocks beneath or beside the fireplace. The early quern stones are evidence of bread-making. The hillsides and woodlands provided all the natural herbs needed for treatment of particular ailments and the knowledge of the essences of flowers and roots as given to us now by the Bach Flower Remedies was surely known much more fully than today by the priests as a natural science. The hillsides were covered with all the woodland and meadow wild flowers we once knew on our fields before the clearing of land and the use of chemical substances that make the earth over-react for just a few years. How naive and greedy we are, for gradually the ecology is changing as the soil is depleted so the eventual result will be land sucked dry and sterile.

The birds of the air at Carrowkeel were prolific and varied too. Then the migratory routes from the Arctic to Africa were being re-established and as the songbirds, the water-fowl, the waders and the geese were travelling along the Atlantic seaboard looking for their long-remembered habitats out in what was now the sea, so they gradually spread north into the shrinking Arctic. The flow of migration was renewed after the ice retreated and the west of Ireland once again became a place of colour and song – even a few years ago, until AD 1950, it was still possible to see flights of ducks, skeins of geese and literally clouds of waders on their annual migration and – what is that collective name? – 'enchantments' of goldfinches flickering through the teasels looking for seeds. Where are they now?

The bog plants and flowers, the insects, the butterflies – the glorious butterlies – long-taught to be the souls of fairies to the children of old, were all there too. The indigenous songbirds, the blackbirds, thrushes, the hawks and the falcons, that once sang and soared in freedom scarcely remain now. Today gunmen shoot them all for 'sport'. The true Lough Arrow trout, gleaming bars of yellow-gold, swam amongst lazy pike in the scared lake. How sadly different it is even from boyhood days, let alone since 3500 BC. Yes it must have been a haven then, a true Garden of Eden full of abundance and clean air, plenty for all, with a sense of nature and sharing.

The waters of the plateau were trapped in the lowest natural point of the village which is approximately the centre point. Here there is a double unrecorded depression cut into the strata of the rocks so that the natural flow of the rain would drain down the fissures to fill a catchment or pond area. the base of this was filled in to hold water as best possible. This was a reservoir, for although there are several abundant clean fresh springs running out of the rock level immediately below the north-west side of the escarpment, it was inconvenient and awkward to have to go down to them. The 'pond' was also a place of reverence and significance because the forcelines of the ascending red Earth Star triangle and the descending indigo Star triangle cross at this place. Here within the protection of the village was another sacred point held in balance, the feminine energy of water for cleansing and washing the people. The Sun rises along a line directly across to the centre of the Star, for the pond marked the important line of the spring and autumn equinox sunrises.

The spring equinox takes place with the Sun at 0° in Aries (fire), the summer solstice with the Sun at 0° in Cancer (water), the autumn equinox with the Sun at 0° in Libra (air) and the winter solstice with the Sun at 0° in Capricorn (earth).

At Beltane the heart fires were blessed and thanked, and then ceremoniously extinguished as the people left their winter quarters and moved out into the fields and the forest to tend crops and stock. 'Fire' was given to each group of workers to take with them for their summer tasks in the form of quartz or crystal which was used to strike the fire each day. At Samhain the people came back into their winter quarters and to their hearth fires which were ceremoniously rebuilt (at the same time stocking their winter provisions) from the fire at the centre of the community held by the priest, but later, symbolically, in the Iron Age, from the centre of the country at Tara. Again feel the integration of earth, fire, air and water as a spiritual necessity as well as an everyday fact.

(Anna Campbell White)

At the solstices the Sun seems to remain at the same declination for three days and to an observer it appears as if 'time stands still', another special point of the calendar and part of the mystery of three that pervades everything.

At the forward point of the plateau where the escarpment is at its lowest, where it joins present-day farmland, there is a passage of steps cut into the rock that was the main gateway to the village. This was also a point that was the most vulnerable to ingress by any force but was also readily defensible if necessary. There are many stone ring huts in the village; to estimate the total now is very difficult as the vegetation is growing despite the barrenness of the rock, which incidentally is not dissimilar to the strata of the Burren in Country Clare; also it is extremely difficult to say when the first hut was built. The total number seems to be more than a hundred, yet it is unlikely that all were inhabited at any one time, so perhaps no more than fifty would have been occupied as a maximum in the early Bronze Age. The population might not, therefore, have been more than one hundred and fifty, allowing for young and old alike. This is not to say that there was not another village elsewhere, but if we can accept the possibilities of the cairns then we can accept that the people of the village at Doonaveeragh had much to do with looking after them as the area is integrated into the encircling Star. From within this village a priesthood thrived, which had laid out and supervised the construction of the cairns over a long period of time and chose the young initiates to grow up in that environment, learning the mysteries of the life force and how to interpret the nature cycle. This was a slow growing process. It is possible that the first people returned to the area as early as 7000 BC. The first settlements may have started in the area of Carrowkeel before the Ice Age. An excavation of the caves at Keshcorran might verify this except the village was established after the Ice Age, with the first huts being built perhaps around 4500 BC. It is perfectly possible that a community went on living at the village long after the knowledge of the cairns had been lost.

SAM was very small by our elongated standards, truly a 'little' people living on and off the soil – short and stocky, his shoulders square and broad, and his legs thick. Life expectancy to full maturity and old age was somewhere under forty, yet sometimes he lived much longer. There was little speech between individuals as a language was not developed as we understand it today. People moved, worked and lived instinctively close, each knowing the needs and thoughts of his fellows. There was no necessity for idle chatter. He used the silent hand language we now call 'Ogham'. Hair was all the usual colours, black, brown, red and white; clothing was simple coarse woven wool, dyed from many natural sources at hand. Amongst the people the colours of dress in the broadest terms denoted responsibilities. Some dyes used were made from natural juices which produced the following colours in the wool.

tancy was not that long. By twenty the man had experienced a full cycle of a Sun/Moon conjunction and a completion of one Jupiter/ Saturn conjunction. So from here we can progress another step to the cairns and their purposes, and begin to understand their extraordinary uses.

Amongst these people moved representatives of another evolution, not giants as in giants' graves but men of greater knowledge – the teachers and visitors. These manifestations of superior beings are encountered in meditation as they are members of a teaching brotherhood of the galaxy that visits us through our higher consciousness. Visitations by 'people of light' are recorded from all over the world throughout history and the original priests of the Tuatha Da-Naan were probably those representatives in Ireland in SAM's time. The cairns were the sacred centres of the community just as our churches and mosques are today and were served by men chosen from amongst the community to be trained in the

Elderberry ⎫	Pale purple to violet
Bilberry ⎬	(matching the vibratory
Blackberry ⎭	colours of the Star centres)
Lichen	Reddy brown
Heather	Dull yellow
Bracken	Limey green
Horsetail	Soft green
Golden rod	Lemony gold
Oak bark *	Creamy white (the priest's colour)
Wild garlic	Orangey yellow

* The oak has always been the tree of power and majesty because it supports so many insects and endures so many years yet it seems to have a property that attracts lightning (fire).

Earth and urine were used with the wool providing from within its own chemical composition the mordants needed to hold the dye juices.

Everyone in the community had a part to play in its existence and as later the Druids were divided up into Bards, Ovates and Druids so, to a lesser degree, SAM was allotted tasks by the accepted leader or the priest of the community. Kings and queens did not evolve until the late Bronze Age.

The women had the same tasks as the men as it was a community of shared work but obviously when birth and rearing children came along it was necessary for the women to take the role of both mother and gatherer. If the child was a boy and suitable, his training started at an early age, the first initiation for education commencing early, as the life expec-

mysteries of natural science to continue the wisdom and traditions we have lost through dogma in our religions today.

Initiation in the Cairn Temples
The progress of life in the cycle of the unfolding year was transposed into the initiations of young men into the priesthood. We have seen how SAM created Earth Stars by the placement of stones over water to direct, enclose and concentrate the life force and move it into an accelerating spiral of energy. The interiors of the cairns used for the cycle of initiation are usually cruciform in shape. The passage is orientated to capture light from a chosen phase on the Sun's or Moon's annual path – at Newgrange, as we know, the passage is aligned to the Festival of Rebirth or the winter solstice. At Carrowkeel there are thir-

teen smaller cairn temples now, each having its own shape and purpose within a 'planetary' layout. The only cairns open and in good condition after the excavations of 1911 are cairns 'K' and 'G' on the summit of the central escarpment of the Carrowkeel Mountain.

Cairn 'K' is a typical cruciform structure orientated to the summer solstice sunset, the Festival of Joy, and within the soul principle of unification and wholeness. The Sun sets over a spectacular range of hills on the Atlantic shoreline fifteen miles away, finally descending over a shoulder of the Ox Mountains to sink into the Atlantic. The front of cairn 'K' is covered with angular-cut gleaming white quartz hidden beneath the outer limestone shell in just the same manner as at Newgrange, although some of the Carrowkeel quartz blocks have even been shaped deliberately in an attempt to conform to the lozenge-shape of the Earth Star, because if a quartz block is cut to symmetry it will activate and 'tune' the structure more powerfully (see Chapter III). The skylight above the entrance included quartz to refract the last rays of the Sun before it disappeared over the horizon. Near this cairn there is a small oblong chamber in the heather, now without its covering slab. This style of structure is often referred to as a 'cist' burial but was used in the cycle of initiation.

These so-called 'cist' burial chambers are a Φ representation later to be used as the 'coffer' located in the Queen's chamber of the Great Pyramid – a representation of balance and symmetry at the centre of a man-made Star pattern. The trials of initiation within this coffer are stepped up, so to speak, during the acolyte's life until he is fully initiated as a priest of light, i.e. 'soul traveller', when he can enter the coffer to come and go at will. There is another example of this type of coffer in the Blaenglassfrwth Valley of Central Wales and in the centre of a stone circle in Argyllshire at Kilmartin. These coffers are always sited over blind springs.

The following cycle of initiation has been intuited in meditation and offers a possible explanation.

The boy had been selected at an early age and all his boyhood life had been towards his eventual step into the first trials of initiation. A gentle start to life came to a head at the age of eleven when his training with the priest started in earnest. He was then given preparation for his first major step from childhood to puberty to rebirth into adolescence and eventually to manhood. On an appropriate full Moon the youth was interred in the ground in

a small chamber (cist) for a period of a day and a night. He was released the following morning having been ritually dead from the setting of the Sun to the rising of the Moon to the setting of that Moon and the following sunrise. This was a shocking experience and was the first of a series of rebirths he had to experience during the next ten years until he was finally accepted into the mysteries of priesthood and so able to take his part in the many responsibilities and duties of the community. This start was literally being reborn – to experience the energies of the womb of Mother Earth alone this time, to emerge the next day having accepted all the expansive forces of that Sun/Moon energy coursing through his body, meeting and joining the Earth around him in the womb of his loneliness. This was not an easy night, in a way it was an awful night, as the youth, although prepared and willing to start on the path, could not turn back once the 'womb' had been closed. He had to come to terms with himself, his fears and the love and protection that he had always been surrounded with but from which we was now torn apart. Of course some failed to overcome the experience and returned to the village to live a normal agricultural life. After sunrise the next day, the youth would emerge cleansed within, having had the courage to overcome the powers of darkness and ready to take on the next stage of his tuition. From twelve years old his initiation could progress into the actual cairn itself, an event of great anticipation but tinged with fear and the memories now outgrown of that first terrible night in the earth.

The first entry into the temple necessitated spending a night, later to be three nights, shut up in a much bigger structure – a place sacred and awesome, venerated by the whole community. To be left sitting in the chamber having crossed the threshold of the lateral stones in the entrance passage to reach the recesses was another momentous experience. The peace, silence and swirling energies pulsing and spiralling through the stones of the central chamber entered the young man's consciousness driving out all previous thoughts. Eventually his whole being pulsated with unknown energy and a new knowledge came flooding in. When the stone was 'rolled aside' next morning he emerged again with a spirit, reborn into manhood. During his normal life therefore he had now experienced a resurrection, even an ascension (Figure 63).

The teaching he received continued in the eastern chamber. Sometimes he was by himself and sometimes the priest who used the

Figure 63
Brass plaque of Jesus'
Crucifixion showing
open heart and crown
chakras (National
Museum of Ireland)

central space accompanied him during his experiences, guiding and interpreting his meditations and explaining his visions. After this year had been completed he could progress to the west chamber to learn of the powers of the rays of the setting Moon and setting Sun at the solstices and equinoxes. This knowledge was the first part of his esoteric training and fundamental to the rest of his life. Instruction could now commence in the use of the pendulum. This came to him naturally as an extension of the forces he had begun to experience under the influence of the planets and the stars during his cairn experiences. He would also be taught something of the mysteries of healing, with the use of herbs – each having its own essence and application. It was towards this knowledge that the young man was being trained. By 21 years he had come to full manhood or 'come of age' as he had experienced one complete cycle of the outer planets Jupiter and Saturn and of the Sun and the Moon.

Gradually over the following years his knowledge and travels in meditation flowered. Often he would spend three days and nights interred in the temple, coinciding with the major standstills of the Sun at solstice and during the equalising forces of equinox or at the eclipses. During these periods of learning his part in the higher mysteries gradually would be revealed and he would come to 'see' the part his soul had to play in the path of the evolution of the planet. He would be visited by other beings of light to encourage, instruct and protect him and each time he came forth strengthened and reborn. When the older priest, a master, left his earthly body and passed on, his remains would be cremated and his mortal brain trepaned and ceremoniously burnt. The body itself was of little importance but the brain was the cosmic computer that had finally been shut down. It could not be left to wither gradually into dust but through the medium of earth, air, fire and water, it acquired the necessary final impetus to move on its eternal path back into the solar rays. Then the new priest could take over the duties of the cairns ensuring the continuity of balance within the community. The energy of the cairn/temples is now switched off and the planet's auric grid is in chaos.

Love

Love is the master of your life
Let it flow from your eyes
And your finger tips.
May it bless the people around you,
Unconscious flowers from the Royal Garden
Growing sweetly in the sunshine
Of your selflessness.
In time all the wild pastures
Will sing the song of bluebells;
Strange calls you try to understand
Along the path of love.
Many of us watching you
See your myriad difficulties
Encourage you to give yourself away
Into the universal care.

Figure 64
Triple spiral engraving,
Newgrange, Co. Meath,
Ireland

OM
Ireland
c. 3500 BC

OM
India
c. 3500 BC

'Ogham' or 'Ogam' (the silent 'language') is
pronounced OM in the Irish language.

Chapter VIII
NEWGRANGE

Newgrange is the only major Irish Stone Age cairn to have been excavated as yet, although the nearby cairn at Knowth has been under detailed study for many years but in 1991 it lies naked and dismembered and is far from completion.

Newgrange is considered to be the central 'burgh' or 'mound' of ancient Irish mythology with its legends of heroic deeds and romantic stories probably reaching back into the Bronze Age community that lived around it. It is also the centre one of three enormous cairns covering an area dotted with different Stone Age, Bronze Age and Iron Age structures that chronologically overlap each other. The cairn is carefully positioned over a complex interconnecting underground water/energy flow.

Already we have discussed how the Sun's

Figure 65
Newgrange cairn and outer structures, underground water flows and courses

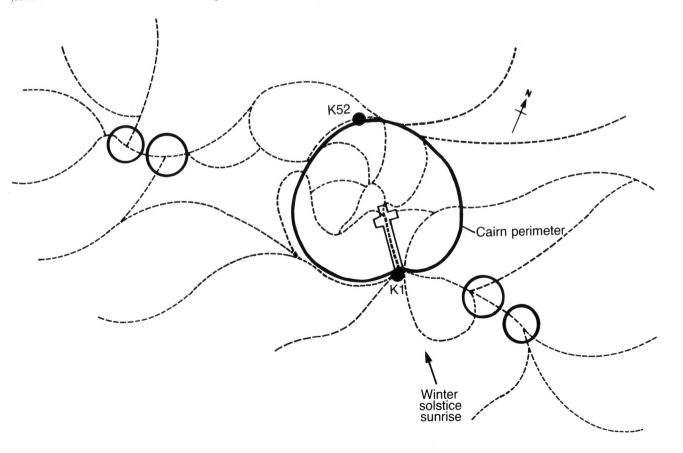

K52

K1

Cairn perimeter

Winter solstice sunrise

Figure 66
Newgrange yesterday
and today (National
Parks and Monuments,
Dublin)

rises and sets play a vital role in the life cycle of Planet Earth and that the early sites were solar and/or lunar aligned in some way. Figure 67 shows how the great cairn was built to incorporate the path of the Sun around the horizon. Newgrange is aligned to the winter solstice sunrise of 21st/22nd December. However, many mythologies suggest that the planetary poles have reversed during ancient time. Maybe this cairn was built to align originally to the summer solstice sunrise before the Earth flipped.

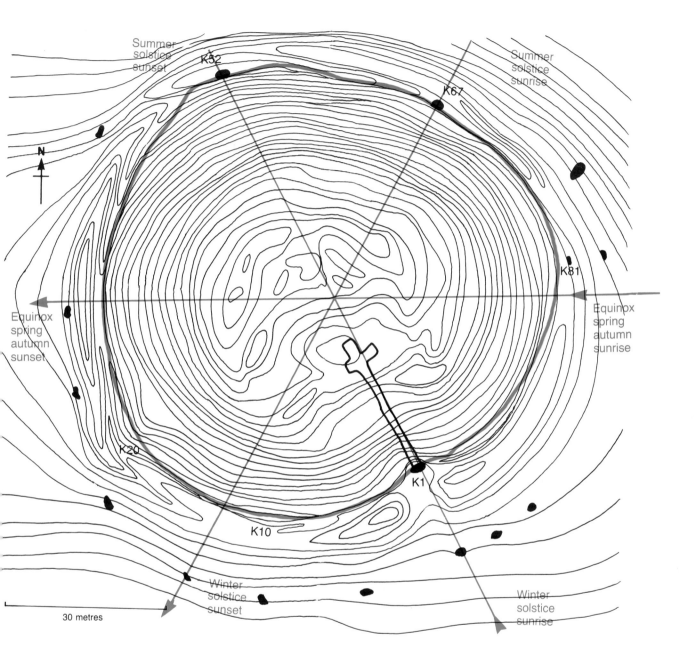

Figure 67
Newgrange – solar
dialling

Next we can refer back to the Golden Mean proportion, as explained in Chapter I – the perfect relationship of geometric form and the combination of the two interlocking circles of equal size from centre to centre.

Figure 68 shows how by taking the passage entrance as the centre of one circle and the radius out to the standing stone at the same level, we can draw a circle – the second circle's centre is on the line of the passage to the backstone at K52. The arc of the Golden Mean then sits happily onto the backstone showing the proportion built into the cairn.

We have already discussed the seven-fold

symmetry of light – the next 'stage' of symmetry from the material world of six-fold crystal symmetry. If we now superimpose a seven-fold layout on the cairn and standing stones of Newgrange the true architecture of the relationship between the standing stones and the body of the cairn itself falls into place. The position of the standing stones, that has for so long intrigued archaeologists, becomes clear at last.

Newgrange has been built to incorporate the natural energies and has been set up by man to attract an expansion of those forces into a complex power station of breathtaking pur-

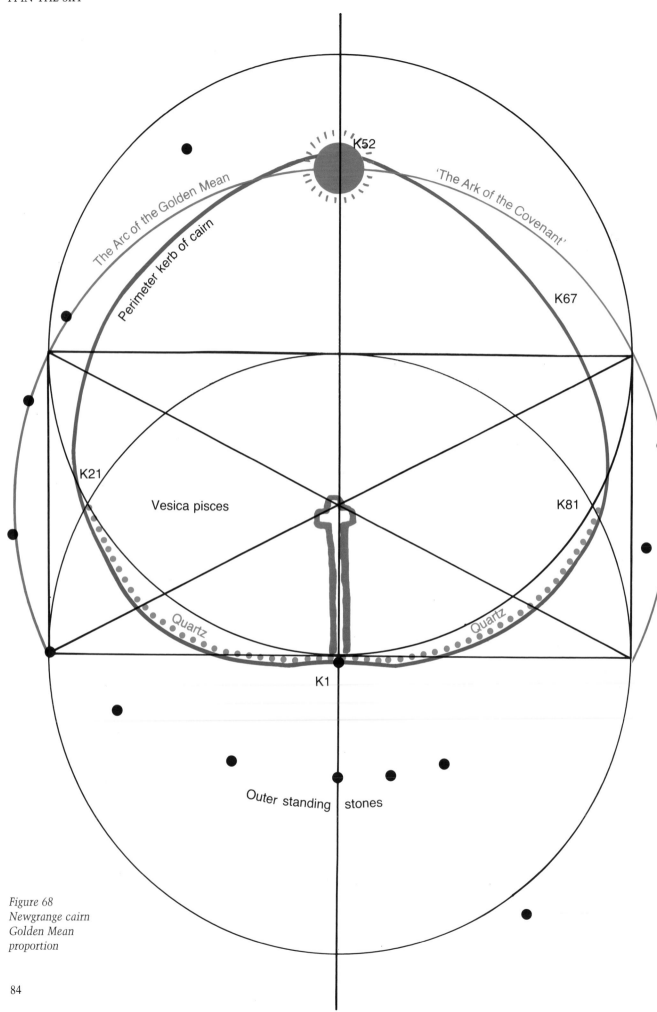

The Arc of the Golden Mean

'The Ark of the Covenant'

Perimeter kerb of cairn

K52

K67

K21

Vesica pisces

K81

Quartz

Quartz

K1

Outer standing stones

Figure 68
Newgrange cairn
Golden Mean
proportion

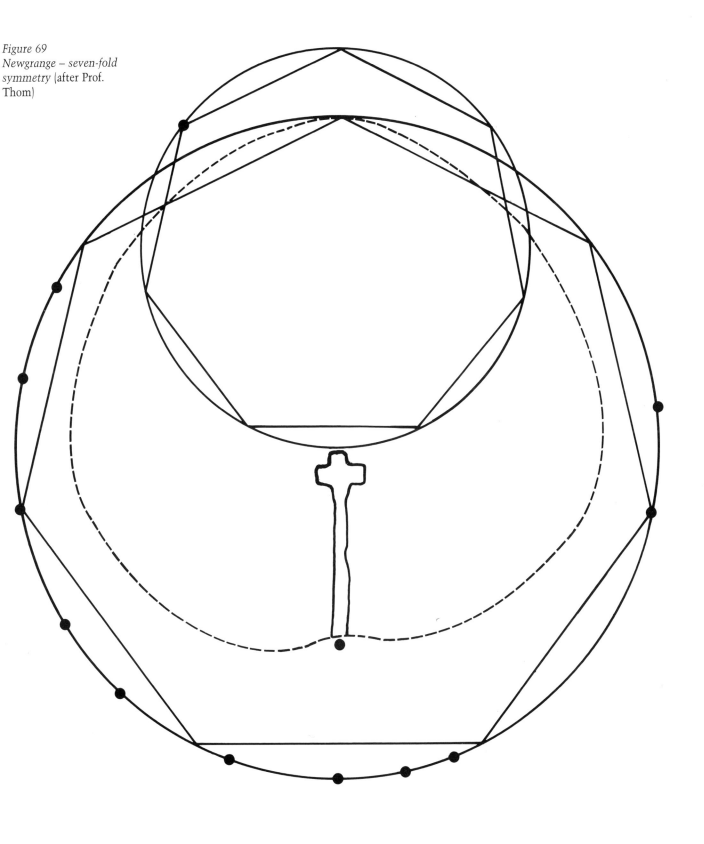

Figure 69
*Newgrange – seven-fold
symmetry* (after Prof.
Thom)

● = Existing standing stones

Figure 70
Newgrange Earth Stars

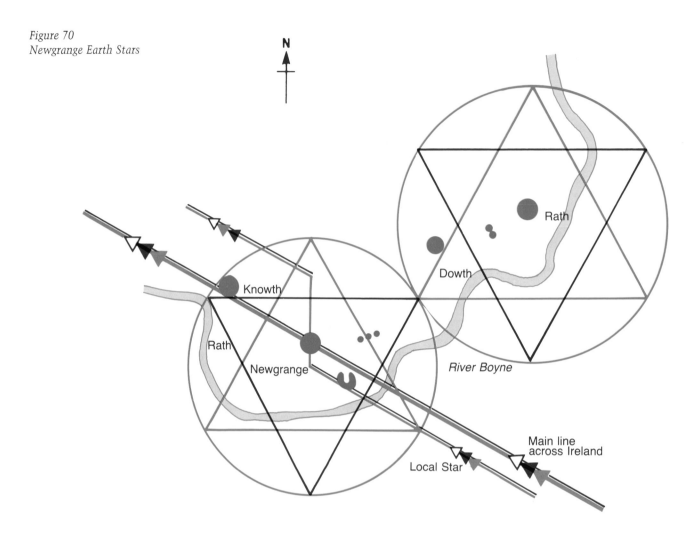

pose and symmetry. We have noted the major connective cable of the natural Star size 'C' from England (Figure 61). It crosses from the area of Anglesey to St. Patrick's Island on the east coast, to Newgrange, then passes onto the west coast of Sligo.

Newgrange Earth Stars

Figure 70 shows the location of two man-made Stars within the grid incorporating most of the Stone Age structures. The main Irish line (also incorporating the 8.3 mile size Star line) enters the area at the centre bottom of this diagram running up to the edge of the actual cairn itself, then passing through it and continuing on at the same angle by the next major structure at Knowth.

This is how these Stars connect more precisely into the grid.

The pendulum shows a Star centring on the cairn. Its conformation fits in with the layout of the markers set up around the area of

mounds and standing stones which we also know demarcate various solar and lunar dialling points as reported in Martin Brennan's book *The Stars and the Stones.* His title relates to the celestial bodies (stars) and not the Earth Stars as discussed in this book. The cairn itself sets up an intimate pattern within the surrounding standing stones and the kerb of the actual mound.

First let us look at the Star around the cairn (Figure 72). The centre of this Star is in the meadows below and between the cairn and the River Boyne. The cairn is positioned on its north/south line. This line shows up as red and white only, or as a positive force line, and enters the circle of the standing stones between GC3 (left) and GC1 (left).

Next, the main energy line enters that area at the south-west corner of the map across the River Boyne. It then runs directly to standing stone GC2 (right). Here it is refracted into positive/negative polarity into and around the

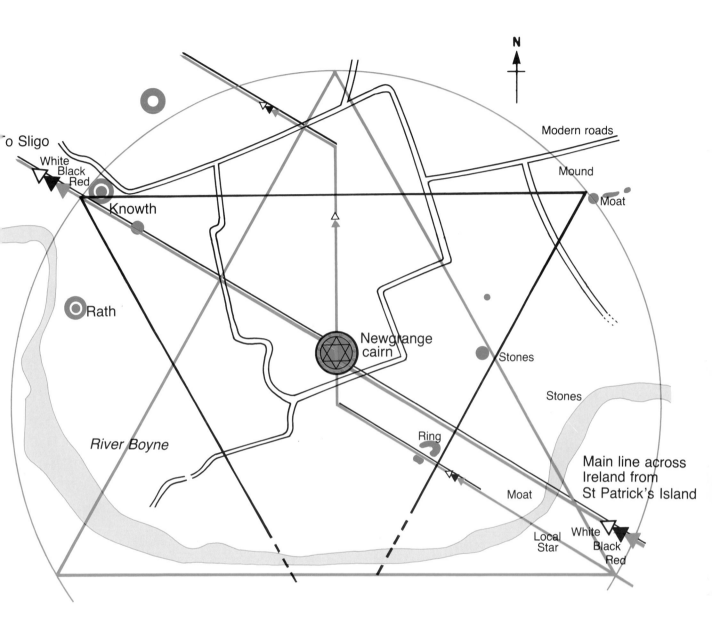

Figure 71
Newgrange cairn
energy Stars

whole structure to meet up again at K52 to travel across to Knowth and on to its Irish journey.

We can now look at the structure of this massive cairn and its scientific purposes. The local Star energy enters the ring of standing stones at a point which may have been the position of a missing stone GC2 (left).

Here this positive energy was refracted to an area outside the entrance passage and slightly to its left. When the archaeological dig took place a structure annotated 'the hut structure' was located here. This was a small roughly circular shape in the surface of the ground containing a foundation and a row of small quartz boulders and several so-called post holes, i.e. pits that contained the ash or remains of burnt wood and bones. These holes are thought to be the foundations of some sort of shelter but in fact are often burning pits to heat up the quartz which, as we know, when expanded gives off an electrical charge that performs helically or in a spiral. So this little structure was a crude accelerator or an expander of natural energy. As these positive forces were directed through it from 'the hut structure' the energy was directed to the centre of the passage entrance stone, known as Kerb Stone 1.

The main energy line arrives at GC2 (right), where it is split and refracted as follows: the negative energy is sent off clockwise around

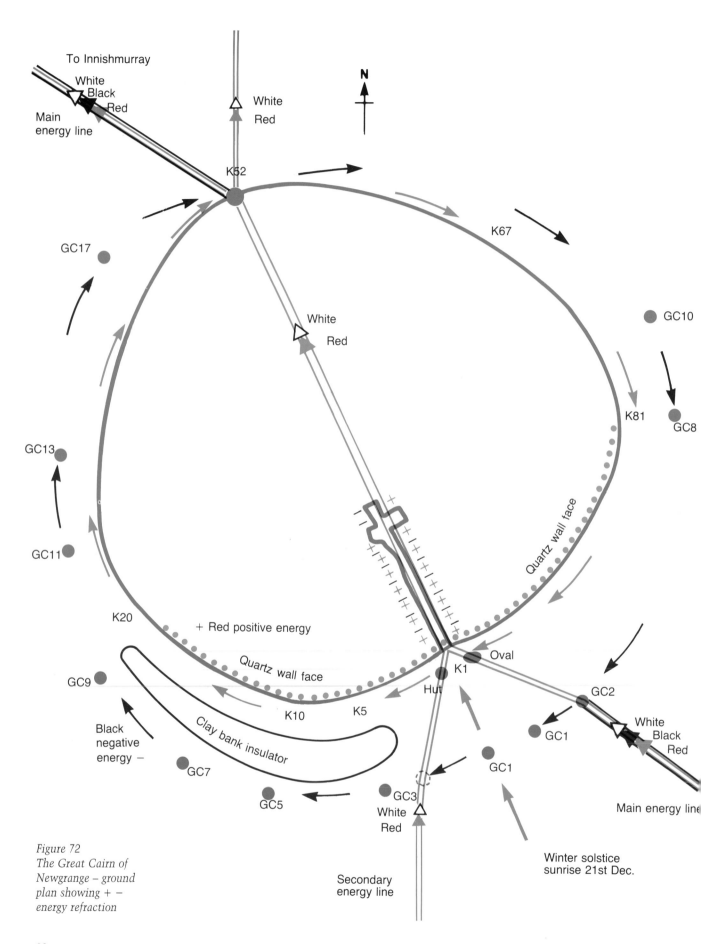

Figure 72
The Great Cairn of
Newgrange – ground
plan showing + −
energy refraction

Figure 73
Oval structure (photo:
M.J. and C. O'Kelly)

the ring of the standing stones to touch in at the rear of the cairn at K52 and follow around the back of its start point. The positive red and white energy is refracted to another little structure, found, annotated and removed by the archaeologists, called 'the oval structure'.

This was located to the right front of the entrance stone K1. It was a much more significant and infinitely more important structure than the simple 'hut structure' and its removal and dissipation are a sad loss for it acted as a unique capacitor. Firstly it has a symmetrical oval geometric shape under a low mound. Secondly, it was built with a low vertical inner retaining wall of mica schist plates which were reported to be 'roughly triangular in shape'. From the only available records the size seems to suggest they were approximately 50° triangles (which if used as templates divide a circle in one-sevenths of its circumference). Once again we are concerned with the division of a circle into seven fold ϕ symmetry.

Mica, as we know, is a component of the materials that make up granite, along with quartz, gold and rock crystal. It also has the well-known property of being a brilliant insulator or container of energy. Within the confines of this oval mound there were 103 granite boulders and '607 quartz potato-sized water rolled pebbles' which for some reason

were reported to be from the bottom of the River Boyne! Also in the approximate centre of the oval there was a limestone 'pillar' about nine inches (228mm) tall and smoothly pointed at one end. This was referred to, of all things, as a 'phallus'. It was the filament of this structure, as limestone, like a chalk ball, is highly alkaline and therefore absorbs heat and has the ability to incandesce. The great force of the main Star input line was passed through this little oval – the power held in a geometric shape and confined by insulators under a dome of heated quartz. So the build-up of the spiralling pure energy must have been terrific. This force was allowed to escape from the oval through 'a split', ten millimetres wide, cut in the end mica plate at a height of 185 millimetres above the base level. From here this vastly enhanced energy was also directed to the centre of the entrance stone at K1. This oval structure performs as a classic example of the thermionic effect, the principle of many electrical devices, the wireless valve, television screen, radar and the X-ray tube.

Before we deal with the cairn itself there is one other structure externally that has puzzled the excavators. This is a long bank of yellow clay running like a curved sausage between the outer standing stones and the inner kerbs between K5 and K20. Clay is a great insulator, its density is such that it does not absorb or

Figure 74
Newgrange entrance
stone (K1) (National
Parks and Monuments,
Dublin), *psychic*
colours

hold water very well, so it is the obvious material to bring in and use to keep apart the energy around the standing stones and the energy around the kerb, on the commencement of their journey, laterally around the whole circular structure.

The entrance stone is a huge oval of rock that lies in front of the passage up which the Earth Star energy travelled and it is carefully engraved with a spiral symbology that depicts its uses both visually and psychically. The triple scrolls show us clearly the use of the primal core of the Earth Star cable and the lozenge-shaped diamonds that form between them in the whole grid picture.

In the bottom centre of this stone there is engraved a little equilateral triangle which marks the point at which the energy enters the stone from Star sizes 'A' and 'C' and from the 'hut' and 'oval'. Now this stone is set centrally before the middle of the entrance passage but originally it was set off slightly to the right as the path of energy up the passage tends to the right-hand side wall. Note the large flat oblong stone that closed the passage door, currently placed (externally) to the right of the passage, and note the *skylight* (not a roof box) over the entrance with its engraved lintel stone or 'summer' ('summer' being another word for lintel).

The cairn is a vast domed structure roughly in the shape of an inverted semi-circle that stands on top of a shallow-sided natural landscape mound. The construction of this cairn, vertically, is alternated with stones and various soils of turf, rather like a giant many-layered sandwich.

This layering produces a vertical alternative positive and negative effect and acts on the same principle as a cosmic battery, using all the natural energies that radiate from the Earth, Sun, Moon, planets and cosmos to activate it.

Long ago dowsers realised the mysterious properties a large semi-sphere has placed convex on a flat surface. A positive energy flows upwards radiating the ageless life force sometimes called 'qi' or 'chi' or 'prana'. This energy, not surprisingly, flows clockwise in the green wavelength of the vibratory light spectrum. At the same time a negative anti-clockwise green flows in a downward path which is debilitating and enhances upset and disease. Many ancient structures were built with this knowledge being understood, not least the Great Pyramid in Egypt, which was orientated to magnetic north and reproduces the flat surfaces, angles and curves of the semi-circle within its pyramidic shape. When these facts and their effects are known and understood the resultant uses of that energy can be very beneficial but the haphazard and ignorant use of pyramids can result in massive negative forces being released into an area or individual with obvious problems building up. It is inadvisable to use any form of pyramid unless

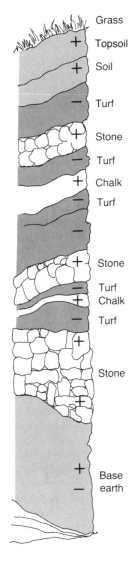

△ *Figure 75*
Newgrange cairn –
vertical layering

Grass
Topsoil
Soil
Turf
Stone
Turf
Chalk
Turf
Stone
Turf
Chalk
Turf
Stone
Base
earth

you understand and can dowse the results. The positive (pranic) energy affects and actuates the magnetic areas of the brain bringing health and vitality, whereas the negative downflow activates electrical impulses that can be harmful. However, within this negative downflow there is a narrow band of energy that is both positive and negative, in balance, known as the pi-ray (pi-ra-mid).

The Egyptian scientists/priests knew of this and built the King's chamber of the Great Pyramid to capture this vibration in the sarcophagus or 'empty tomb' that has intrigued archaeologists so much. This ray geometrically incorporated into the structure from the apex to the coffin is at an angle of 6°, fifteen inches (379mm) from the vertical. The chamber is offset approximately 33 feet (a significant number in numerology, the 'number' of Jesus – also see Tara Brooch geometry, Chapter XI) to the south of the east/west plain allowing the pranic beam to pass through the massive layered room of the cap stones above the chamber at exactly the correct angle.

The ancient hieroglyph for pyramid PR-MS means 'to arise at birth' or 'resurrect' or 'be reborn' – the energy produced demanifests or accelerates the molecular structure of the human cells to vibrate at a much higher wavelength – hence the 'soul spirit' of the person could, in general terms, leave the body

behind, i.e. the auric body was actualised and could move at will to appear anywhere, anytime, within that 'band' of past or future consciousness to another illuminated mind or initiate. Suddenly the visions of so many people down the ages make sense and are no cause for 'burning at the stake' or incarceration in a madhouse.

At Newgrange the construction of the passage gently slopes uphill towards the main chamber, the energy's path being directed mainly up the right-hand side.

The standing stones forming the walls of the passage and the roof alternate positive/negative as they form a giant coil spiralling along its length into the cruciform chamber. The passage was constructed to exclude rain from the upper layers, water grooves and channels even being cut into the upper surfaces of the passage roofing blocks to keep it dry. If the energy had been directed up to the centre of the passage it would have produced balance and so would not have pulled itself into a coil for further acceleration. The path of the energy is clearly shown to us as the well-known enigmatic triple spiral that is engraved at the right rear of the stone forming the support of the inner back chamber.

How wonderful and poignant it is to find that here in the middle of Ireland is an engraving carved about 5,500 years ago show-

▷ *Figure 76*
Cairn or pyramid
(Christopher Hills,
University of the Trees
Press)

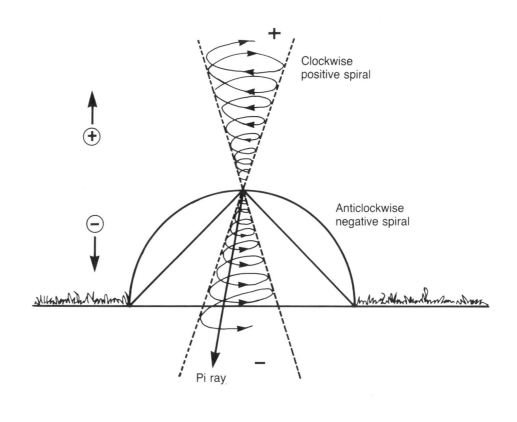

+
Clockwise
positive spiral

⊕

⊖

Anticlockwise
negative spiral

−

Pi ray

ing us clearly the true essence of balance. The red positive energy is Yang, the dark negative energy is Yin, but the white pure centre is the ultimate truth actualised by the Sun as the purity of the life force. This triple spiral is depicted in the East as the sign of 'OM'.

The cruciform chamber at the end of the long 'coil' of the entrance passage again defines a wonderful geometric discipline within its stones for even now after it has been reconstructed it is still possible to intuit the crystal shape and begin to understand what SAM was doing. However, before we can appreciate this we must understand another vitally important energy incorporated into the cairn by the alignment of the structure to the winter solstice sunrise on 21st December.

We have already read of the importance of the annual festivals so recall that the winter solstice is the Festival of Rebirth, the time of the year when the autumn sowing begins to 'birth' the earth or the 'Christ child' for this is the 'Christ-mass festival'. Here nature and man unite to perpetuate the annual festival of inner light ('annual' – renew-al).

On 21st December, for many thousands of years the Sun's rays have suddenly flooded through the skylight of the cairn above the entrance passage to fill the floor of the chamber. This beam was originally passed through two quartz blocks positioned in the skylight. Only one was found still in position by the archaeologists and this was unfortunately removed and discarded by the re-fashioning campaign; thankfully their presence was noted. These two blocks in a much lower lateral aperture than the current skylight acted as the polarising filters of sunlight using the same principle we have read about in Chapter III and in the general principle of splitting white light in quantum physics – the purpose being to excite or activate the sub-atomic particles of quartz to bend energy. We can liken this structure to a particle accelerator or cyclotron but 'particle accelerators' are mis-named as they do not increase the velocity of sub-atomic particles (the definition of acceleration) as much as they increase the mass, so in fact, they are particle enlargers or massifiers.

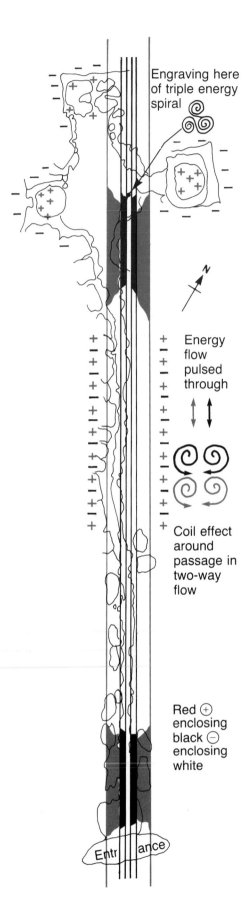

Engraving here of triple energy spiral

Energy flow pulsed through

Coil effect around passage in two-way flow

Red ⊕ enclosing black ⊖ enclosing white

Entrance

Figure 77
Lines of Earth energy in the chamber and passage of Newgrange

Figure 78
The triple spiral energy marker depicting the white, red and black energies (National Parks and Monuments, Dublin)

Figure 79
Newgrange chamber lintel stone (National Parks and Monuments, Dublin)

The exterior wall of the cairn (Figure 72) from K81 (right) across the skylight to K21 (left) is literally covered with angular pieces of white quartz. By this simple scientific use of quartz SAM not only concentrated a particle beam through his skylight but accelerated the Earth Star forces around the perimeter of the kerb stones building up a vast spiral of energy concentrated and centred in the cruciform chamber. You can see how the skylight lintel stone is engraved to depict this concentration of energy.

The Sun pours its light into the chamber to activate the geometric structure. If we draw a line around and between the points of the chamber on the ground they form an octahedron, the external shape of an Earth Star which, in turn, contains the lozenge of the centre part of the conjoined equilateral triangles, the shape we know so well in the crystal.

SAM has thoughtfully engraved for us how he 'saw' this force field on the roof stone of the east recess.

Within the east and west recesses of the cairn are placed dished circular objects which the archaeologists have called 'basins', large bowls sometimes even engraved with pictures of solar energy. The 'basin' at Knowth is a brilliant example of this.

What was SAM doing with a basin in his cairn? It is not difficult to realise this basin is

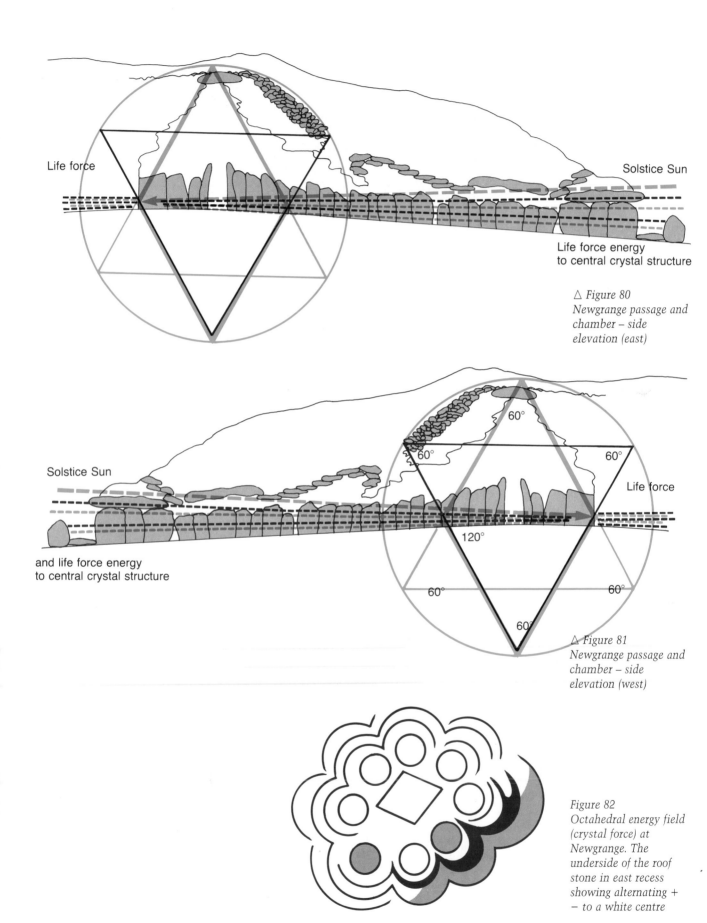

Life force

Solstice Sun

Life force energy
to central crystal structure

△ Figure 80
*Newgrange passage and
chamber – side
elevation (east)*

Solstice Sun

60°

60°   60°

Life force

120°

60°   60°

60°

and life force energy
to central crystal structure

△ Figure 81
*Newgrange passage and
chamber – side
elevation (west)*

Figure 82
*Octahedral energy field
(crystal force) at
Newgrange. The
underside of the roof
stone in east recess
showing alternating +
– to a white centre*

Figure 83
Knowth parabolic Sun reflector or 'basin'
(Commissioners for Public Works, Ireland)

a reflector, not just an ordinary mirror, but when completed and ready for use, a parabolic reflector to concentrate the solar wind energy. Now we realise where those '607 potato-sized water-rolled pebbles' came from, taken outside the cairn, and so usefully placed in the 'oval' capacitor. If you wish to grind a curved reflector of rock you must use a material harder than the substance you wish to fashion, whether it be axe heads, pendulums or even 'basins'. Hold a rough lump of quartz in your hand and begin to grind. As the edges wear down so the quartz becomes rounder and rounder until eventually you end up with not only a lovely quartz ball but also a parabolic mirror.

The large reflector in the east recess at Newgrange was started but never completed – the area that the grinders reached is the area of two shallow depressions to one side of the bowl, clearly showing the beginning of the grinding sequence to the next level. When finished the 'basin' or reflector was then placed to direct the beam of solstice polarised light in the chamber recess required, each chamber also being off-set from the vertical to capture the magic ray as in the Great Pyramid.

Let us now return to Chapter I and the hypothesis of the cycles of the Sun spot activity and subsequent variations in the solar wind – the very 'breath of God' of *Genesis*.

Around 3000 BC the priesthood of the neolithic period in North-west Europe disappeared. Around 1300 BC the Egyptian empire declined. In about AD 700 the Mayan civilisation of Central America fell and the great structures, built without the use of the wheel or metal, fell into disrepair. In AD 1500 the Inca empire also fell apart.

It is suggested that each of these great civilisations incorporating incredible architecture and natural sciences suddenly came to an end due to expected sharp decreases in the life force itself – that energy of the Sun arriving at the planet through the solar wind and interacting through light with our surface and atmospheric densities to give no growth in every sense of the word.

SAM and the priests of Hyperborea (see Chapter XII) knew this and expected it – how they intuited this knowledge is difficult to fathom but surely they understood how the Sun 'worked' and how God generated all living things for us.

Our magnetic fields flow roughly north/south, but due to the tilt of the Earth on its axis, these flows seem to act and twist like the candy stripe on a barber's pole, continually spiralling up and down itself. The solar wind

arrives approximately at a right angle to the planet and thus see Figure 85a.

When the solar wind decreases markedly, the Earth's geomagnetic field increases strongly, depleting natural fertility and causing an imbalance in the life force. Recently in modern science we have heard how the life force can be likened to the DNA spiral and here we have even seen how SAM created a DNA image in the chamber of his cairns through the use of lozenge-shaped white quartz *polarizing* filters which literally rotated the solar wind through 45°, thereby creating a point of pure growth-vibration in the centre of the cairn, with the use of a parabolic mirror.

Let us now suggest that SAM knew about the Sun spot activity and the cycle of the solar

Figure 84
A quartz ball of 8cm width

Figure 85a
The solar wind

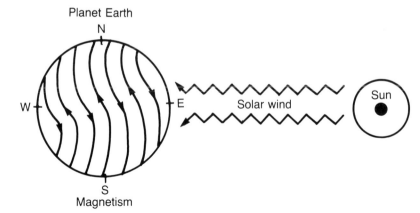

wind – let us suggest that SAM deliberately constructed the cairns thus to bend the energy of the life force to 45° so that when the solar wind was on the *decrease* a balance of life force energy was held in the cairn as a permanent point of generation so that when geomagnetism increased rapidly with falling solar activity, he could go into the cairn and know that the force was still present and strong enough for conception and *procreation*. This is not just on a physical plane to produce babies, but for the *regeneration* of the whole auric 'grid' of the planet.

The cairn was a vast natural cyclotron that helped keep the balance. Therefore diagrammatically this was happening:

Figure 85b

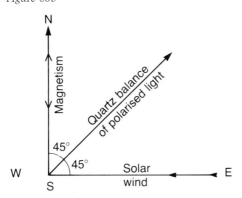

Man was deliberately manipulating the balances of nature – the balance of God's creativity that is cyclical from age to age. This is one hypothesis; the second is even more fantastic but possible. It is as follows: Man has an energy field all around him which emanates from his meridians an the chakra points of physical or material body. This energy builds up into what is called his aura. This can be seen by a trained psychic and from vibrations the state of the person can be diagnosed and categorised – health, emotions, diet, etc. A balanced human shows a similar natural vibration to the aura of the animal and vegetable kingdoms – remember the Findhorn garden. The priests of SAM were such human beings. So they built a vast structure (Newgrange in this case – another type of pyramid), to reflect all their disciplined natural knowledge within the grid of the Earth Stars and within the light of the Sun. This cairn, by virtue of its construction, built up an enormous aura or atmospheric energy field about itself (dare we use the words 'etheric form'?). The Sun's accelerated energy acts as a massifier to the aura of the structure. The Earth Star energy

was accelerated, and degravitised this (massified) aura. By combining these two integrated forces through a series of unified crystal disciplines or force fields – the aura was actuated and separated from the material body to form a 'dual light' structure, the vehicle we have occasionally seen throughout history when it was slowed down and remanifested as a 'UFO'.

The final motivation of the 'machine' was the mind, will energy or electrical impetus provided by a 'cosmic' brain or the priest(s) within. The two stone balls found in a cairn at Loughcrew in Ireland and currently in the National Museum are the core triggers, comparable with the central ball of enriched uranium or plutonium of a nuclear device. One is of iron ore that when used with clairvoyant compression (visualisation) creates a negative *grounding* spiral, whereas the other of granite creates a vast *expansive* and positive spiral, i.e. a black hole and a white hole through which – superluminarly – the light vehicle travels timelessly. Man could literally take off in a geometric timeless machine for he had accelerated himself to the speed of light and crystal resonance into the superluminal vibrations of instaneous travel. The gnomonic expansion of the spiral he had set up was so powerful it allowed him to move anywhere in the cosmos, for he had tuned himself into the power of the expanding circular macroscopic grid and beaten gravity.

Quantum physicists have been investigating the duality of light with massifiers and accelerators without realising there are no opposites if you have a balanced Earth Star grid to work in and with, and the sound, or harmonic resonance, of the universe.

One of the gifts of the Vedic scriptures quotes weightlessness. If the aura of the body, the whole body, can be put into balance by self-discipline and meditation then the brain actualising 'the light' can provide the spiral of energy for a man to 'travel astrally' or to leave his body. To have an 'out-of-body experience' is by no means unusual to many spiritualists and mystics. SAM went further and separated the mineral kingdom, the body of the cairn, to provide him with a vehicle.

We can now understand the use of the entrance stone door beside the Newgrange passage and remember that the Sun seems to 'stand still' for three days at the summer and winter solstice when the sunrise beamed its way down the passage through the skylight, the normal daylight being excluded by 'closing the door'. At the end of the three days the Sun 'seemed' to move again and the door was pushed aside to allow access and exit. Perhaps now, if you have accepted any of the foregoing ideas, you might like to consider the Master Jesus whose material body was placed in a sepulchre which was duly closed. After three days, when the stone was found to be rolled aside, his 'body' had disappeared – only for his auric or ethereal self to reappear to his loved ones as proof of his return.

This seems to be a wonderful reassurance of the end and the beginning of the Christian idyll which is based on our acceptance of and belief in a subsequent spiritual life in the realms of the resurrection. The Bible tells us of these events quite clearly. We also understand the Master Jesus was a fully-initiated Essene priest (an *essential* human person).

To further substantiate the knowledge of the cairns SAM kindly engraved the backstone to show us exactly what he had done. We have already seen how he engraved the triple spiral inside the cairn and repeated it on K52, also how he engraved the constellation of Draco across the stone to give us the star system in the sky he had aligned at the date of the cairn's construction, but he also carefully showed us a diagram of these triple energies on the right-hand side of K52 as a sort of working print-out.

This figure and the engraved ovals with cups in them, surrounded by other ovals, show the main Earth Star energy line running side-by-side with a central balance point engraved between⬭🎱⬭. The oval engravings represent the negative black energy and the positive red and white energy. This line is shown as a 'pair' depicting the energy flowing south-east/north-west and in reverse north-west/south-east, a constant two-way alternating current, producing therefore, balance. The other oval, on its own, to the lower right of the stone shows us the other core of energy that we have plotted as Star 'A'. Around these three engravings are shown the outer magnetic energies that curl around and through the standing stones. The pendulum tells us that the alternating current through the line beats sixteen times each way with a five beat interval.

The backstone of Newgrange shows SAM's intimate knowledge of the invisible Earth Stars and the rhythm of the Sun spot/solar wind cycle. The latter is a seven-day positive seven-day negative alternation – fourteen lozenges are engraved on K52 also depicting geographically, and surprisingly, the fourteen

Figure 86
Newgrange backstone
K52, complete energy
print-out
Red +
Black −
White (neutral) balance
● 'cup marks'
(National Parks and Monuments, Dublin)

eight-and-a-third-mile Earth Stars across Ireland, but also the seven by two 7/7, +/−, alternation of the solar wind. K52 therefore is shown to us as a biorhythm solar calculator that gives us the week, the month and the seasons of the year, and so on through solar time.

So this is Newgrange, the central powerhouse in a particular part of the Irish Star grid pattern. At some point way back in history it was closed down and the knowledge lost till now in this strange emerging age of science and mysticism. Perhaps the knowledge began to be lost with the advent and use of metal. Certainly the use of iron weapons heralded a period of cruelty and beastliness from which we are still suffering in our present lives.

The birth of the cosmic Christ spirit actualising through the Essene/Druid scientist priest, the Master Jesus, was not appreciated or understood by the vast majority of the people of his time or since. Therefore he was killed as his enduring soul is still murdered every day by our ceaseless acts of selfishness and ego. Perhaps now an understanding of SAM's knowledge which still surrounds us, at least in Ireland and Great Britain, may help us to understand how it was in the old mythologies. How SAM was able to fly from his 'burghs' and disappear and to reappear many years later, unaged and timeless. Had he in 3500 BC reincarnated and come back to us from Atlantis? Is he amongst our friends today?

If we look at Newgrange as in some way expressing our base sexually through its artefacts then we are aligning ourselves to our lower nature, the lower astral, the energy centre at the base of our spine, but we can also look at this structure and see in it the archetypal shape of the human heart which allows us to think of it as the vibrant emotional centre of a living community – this is comparable to the second level of consciousness. If we can look at the cairn and see its passage as the entrance to our higher perceptions, or the entrance to the third eye, and its mound as the left and right hemispheres of the human brain, or the cosmic brain, then we have the ability to raise our thought processes up through our body into our crown chakra and out into the realms of pure knowledge. This is the third level of consciousness that almost reaches the universal causal realms. As is known in spiritual work we now have the opportunity to lift those three levels into another sphere or a higher consciousness – above our heads so to speak – to open our crown chakras to the fundamental universal waves or vibrations of nine-fold symmetry, to 'God' and the Sun itself. Then as an act of selflessness we may bring that re-fashioned consciousness back down into our hearts balancing on all levels of our aura to perform in a life of service and possibly procreation at the highest level. This in essence is making an opportunity for a higher soul to reincarnate through our awakened love-making.

Perhaps now our physicists may look again at Bell's theorem and realise that there is no separation anywhere in the universe and the protection racket of local causes can be dispensed with, for there is no probability of duality in anything, only oneness, expressed through trinity.

We need only turn to the wisdom of the Tibetan Master, Djwhal Khul, in Alice Bailey's *Ponder on This* to undstand better some of our responsibilities and hopes for the future for although this was transcribed in 1944, and we now have television and satellites, it is very relevant to the world in 1992.

1. Esoteric science is slowly, yet steadily, finding out the nature of phenomena and discovering for itself the character of electrical manifestation. In this slowness of discovery lies safety. It is not wise nor right yet for the true nature of these different forces and powers to be fully known.

2. In the manipulation of electricity lies hidden much that concerns the vivification of the bodies, especially just now of the etheric. The principal use of the Sun is electrical force adapted to the need of the great average majority, in all the kingdoms of nature. As progress is made, an intensification of this force will be possible in individual cases. Herein lies one of the secrets of initiation.

3. The electricity of the solar system is three-fold; there is fire by friction, solar fire and electric fire – fire of body, soul and spirit. Fire by fricton is coming to be somewhat understood by the scientists of the world, and we are harnessing to our needs the fire which heats, which gives light and which produces motion. This is in the physical sense of the words. One of the imminent discoveries will be the integrating power of electricity, as it produces the cohesion within all forms, and sustains all life during the cycle of manifested existence. It produces also the coming together of atoms and of the organisms within forms, so constructing that which is needed to express the life principle.

4. As yet the mystery of electricity and the true nature of electrical phenomena (than which there is naught else) is at this time an unrevealed secret, even to the most advanced of the modern scientists . . . That there is such a thing as electricity, that it probably accounts for all that can be seen, sensed and known, and that the entire universe is a manifestation of electrical power – all this may be stated and is today coming to be recognised, but when that has been said the mystery remains and will not be revealed, even in partial measure, until the middle of the next century. Then revelation may be possible, as there will be more initiates in the world and inner vision and inner hearing will be more generally recognised and present. When Man arrives at a better understanding of the etheric body and its seven force centres . . . then some further light can intelligbly be thrown upon the nature of the seven types of electrical phenomena, which we call the seven rays.

5. Electricity, in relation to human ills, is as yet an infant science but it has in it the germs of the new techniques and methods of healing.

6. Towards the close of this century and when the world situation has clarified and the period of reconstruction is drawing to a close, discoveries will be made which will reveal some hitherto unrealised electrical potencies. I know not what other word to use for these electrical rays, which will make their presence felt and lead to possibilities beyond the dreams of investigators today. The coming science of electricity will be as different next century as the modern usages of electricity differ from the understanding of the Victorian scientist.

7. People frequently are so preoccupied with the tangible instrument of this side of the veil that they neglect the factor of what must be contributed from the other side by those who have passed over. The work will be done from there with the material aid which as yet has not been provided in the outer scientific field. To bring this about collaboration of a conscious medium (not a trance medium but someone who is consciously clairvoyant and clairaudient) will be required. There are many such

growing up among the children of today and the next generation after them will provide still more. The separating veil will disappear through the testimony of the thousands of those who can see phenomena and hear sounds which lie outside the range of the tangible. Everything in Nature is electrical in nature; life itself is electricity but all that we have contacted and used today is that which is only physical and related to and inherent in the physical and etheric matter of all forms.

8. As regards the use of radio as a means of communication with the 'spirit world' the present electrical instruments are too slow in vibratory activity (if I may use such an unscientific term) .to do the work; if astrally clothed 'spirits' approach them, they are apt to have a shattering effect. Yet the first demonstration of existence after death, in such a way that it can be registered upon the physical plane, will come via the radio, because sound always precedes vision. Think on this. However, no radio now exists which is sufficiently sensitive to carry sound waves from the astral plane. Future scientific discoveries, therefore, hold the secret. This is no evasion on my part but a simple statement of fact. Electrical discovery is only in the initial stage and all that we have is simply a prelude to the real discovery. The magic of the radio would be completely unbelievable to the man of the eighteenth century. The discoveries and developments lying ahead in the twenty-first century will be equally unbelievable to the man of this century.

(Alice Bailey,
Ponder on This,
by kind permission of Lucis Trust Ltd)

Author's note: 'Spiritcom' in America puports to have manufactured a radio that channels the voice directly from souls on the other side – their book *The Ghost of 29 Megacycles* relates this story.

The Five Aspects of 'IT'

'IT' says – 'IT's (Breath is) Nothing in ITself'

I
At the centre there is
One body of nothing –
One atomic centre – creating
The in and out –
Of 'IT'
The solar wind blows
Nobody knows 'ITS' size or dimension
Only one nucleus
Going around – 'IT' flies –
The prize is mystery
A kiss in the silence of 'ITS' dance.

We –
As a cosmic sensation
Chance meeting, each other and –
Evolve
From 'ITS' soulful mating.
Occasionally 'we'
On the spiral, solve – reincarnation
Before 'IT' transmutes – our roots.
We are tricked
Into dancing with each other
Waltzing at 'ITS' leisure
Loving, as 'ITS' human aspect
Turning inside 'ITS' cosmic informal
Pleasure.

'IT'self goes on growing
And dying during millennium ages
As though leafing the leaves of infinitesimal space
Longing to regroup and escape
To last longer (in camera)
Than a chimera photon
'IT' – as a positional something
A notion in the web of space
Inside 'ITS' non-existent head – is –
Like a spider unreeling
Timelessness around spacelessness
Nowhere from inside 'IT'self.

This is the prancing of souls
Waltzing unpredictably
As dust in rainbows
Flitting 'up' its 'down' – golden
These fireflies dance miracles
Nightly as in moonlight's fractles
Of unreality – forgiving themselves.

At 'ITS' command – predictably –
'IT' says nothing –
Has happened
Outwardly – anywhere – at all.
Really

The secret – 'IT' says – finally –
Silently now of course
Is to lay a lie – 'IT' ought to as a duty – and –
Is to the 'why' of this spherical riddle.
'IT' is that 'IT' – as the sky shines
Through a dolmen protal – opens
'ITS' – elf-ine sight – filtering –
A quantity of the light
Of the sun into beautiful
Immortality.

Only a mirror is now needed
To reflect this sensational thought
Of breath – resonating 'IT'self
To become – beyond death
Reseeded, magnetically – 'In foetus Dei'.

II
'IT'
Continuing 'ITS' journey
'In foetus Dei'
Slipped into the moon mirror
And was – amazed.

What can 'IT' express
About 'IT'self
In reflection
No image
No shadow
No imprint
Atomic or otherwise
Of 'IT'self – just
A shimmer.

'IT' isn't, or is 'IT' –
A human idea – a chimera
Without space or time.
'IT' hasn't returned
From departing tomorrow,
On other – age – time – tables
Spiralling through inter space.
'IT' is – lasered
The lasered sun of mythic yarns
Rutilated, weaving crystal balls
Held above – in the cairnful light
By the shining priests
In their now mutilated cairns
'IT' went
And will come again –
Through love.

III
'IT'
Has observed this phase
Of 'ITS' experiment
That is planet Earth,
And dispassionately allows
Us – that is 'IT'self
To evolve and die.

'What sadness' 'IT' says
After all 'IT' has given
For us not to have understood
'ITS' totally objective self
Coming through us –
One day 'IT' will do it
All again.
NOW –
At this last time
'IT' is here – walking
The earth on Lotus feet
Amongst 'ITS' own extension
'IT' – experiences 'IT'self
Physically, deeply loving

The void is filled
The atomic centre becomes
'Man' again being born –
Blissfully procreating each other
Until alone, agonisingly fading.

'IT' encourages us to come closer
To hold hands – 'ITS' hands
Extended – because 'IT' needs
Us to establish 'IT'self
Again, on Earth
Later.

IV
'IT' knows temporarily
'IT' will die quite unconcernedly
'ITS' dimensions will no longer
Walk upright in humans
In the song of blackbirds
And thrushes –
In the adoration of a dog's eyes
Silently in cats' paws
Enduring as vast whales
And intelligent ants –
'ITS' size is as infinite
As ever resting mountains
'IT' knows temporarily
All will die – just not
Re-seed 'IT'self – impotent
No conception –

The wombs will be dry
Caves of longing, unfulfilled
Like polluted fields
Over-fertilised by greed.
No longer green and grazed
By the laughter of children
And lovers lying making love
Now, soon
The little people are memories
The myth of how 'IT' was
Before the sun went out
Stopped blowing cosmic breath,
Stopped giving 'IT'self
To us freely.

No more grand-children
In our latter years
The end of an Age
Happening now.

Embrace 'IT' now
And know 'ITS' love
Go close – get inside
This wraith – 'IT' –
Dear God –
Is yourself.

V
'IT' is now pure,
Free
Of total movement,
Gone
Through light
Beyond materials we generally know
Or link into the next suspension.
A new world unparalleled
By quantum mind
An emanation inter-dimensionally
Inter-weaving inter –
Immediately completely spatially.

The solar structure – with perfect
Symmetry expands electrically
Inter-polating laterally
Waiting to come again
Please may I be with 'IT'?
But stop!
'I am
'IT'
Already'.

Chapter IX
SYMBOLS AND ENGRAVINGS

To help us understand the occult purpose of SAM's temples or Irish passage graves we need to examine the artefacts and engravings that are found within them, as they provide the practical clues to a natural jigsaw puzzle. Many antiquarians have indulged their curiosity in trying to identify the purpose of these sparse artefacts and the use of the engraving has generally been misinterpreted. The following artefacts are encountered.

Pendulums
We all know small stone 'pendants' shaped like the familiar centre drop of any Victorian necklace as a usual form in jewellery. Indeed they are pendants because this word is taken from the French for hanging – *pendant* or 'penta' (five'). We have discussed these briefly in relation to divining pendulums. Perhaps if

we thought a little deeper we could say they are the plumb-bobs of an architect. When we look at the size and complexity of the cairns it is not unreasonable to suggest this use as being both rational and practical and there is no reason why they should not have been used for this purpose, as the Freemasons used them later in their architecture. But we know the pendulum is used in divining to interpret the positive and negative duality of natural energy within the whole life force – this is activated as we have discussed by the life-giving rays of the Sun. At Newgrange the summer solstice sunrise is depicted on Kerb Stone 67.

We associate summer with the Sun, so it is interesting to note the Sumerian (summer) linear script for 'seeing the Sun rising over the horizon'.─◇

Summer in the *Oxford Dictionary* is indicated as the hot season and distance and length meaning 'far off' just as the Sumerians were far from Ireland. Also, another description is given: *summer – large beam or stone serving as a lintel or base of arch or the like.* This is identifiable immediately in many Irish Stone Age structures where the lintel stones of individual chambers within cairns and the entrance stones above the skylights are clearly engraved with the zig-zag or wavelength energy pattern of the Sun.

It is not necessary to prove the use of the pendulum to the uninitiated or disbelieving. There is a well-appointed and thriving organisation called the British Society of Dowsers to whom you may refer if you wish, who will give you their programme of courses and lectures; they also have a regular magazine. Write to: The Secretary, B.S.D., Sycamore Cottage, Tamley Lane, Hastingleigh, Ashford,

Figure 87
Newgrange – K67 –
summer solstice stone
(M.J. and C. O'Kelly)

Length approx. 7 ft 5 in
Height approx. 5 ft

Kent; or the Society of Irish Dowsers, Treasurer: Mrs G. Hackett, 4 Wade's Avenue, Dublin 5.

With this understanding of one of the principal engraved 'art' forms of Irish passage graves a whole new possibility of unfolding knowledge is open to us. All the old speculation about SAM's mathematics and manpower organisation can be swept aside as we realise finally that he used his clairvoyance and sensitive perception to follow the forms of prismatic Sun shapes. What he knew and saw in the sky and in his mind he could readily translate onto the ground. He could plot on a sandtable an Earth picture of what he knew he must build, and draw with a pointed curved bone pin the exact geometry required. Having 'fixed' the geometry in his mind and on the sandtable in miniature he could then walk the ground with his pendulum to the exact spot at each point of the expanded plan, for he had already 'planted' the energy there with his mind and he was reliving the geometry. Since this plan also conformed in some way to the actual form of the Earth Star, thereby giving an easily recognised central point, this job was not nearly as difficult as the archaeologists and engineers have made out. The highly complicated geometric performances suggested by the late Professor Alexander Thom satisfy some people today, but were quite unnecessary to SAM. The size of the engraved spirals on the kerbs and standing stone, or the number of rings, does not necessarily depicts the intensity of the energy but merely indicates the interwoven flow. All Earth energy, due to the magnetic field around us, flows in both directions and it is with the pendulum that we pick up the direction and intensity at any point we require.

A pendulum was the main tool of the priest and a very treasured possession which hung around his neck for safety. We deduce that there was probably only one priest to each structured area, just as we have a vicar to a parish, as so few pendulums have survived. It is reasonable to accept that each structure held the remains of its temporal keeper, in whatever form. Macalister (1910), to quote Herity, estimated that all the cairns he excavated at Carrowkeel (14) contained the 'remains of approximately thirty-four individuals', representing therefore about three to a cairn. On this premise we can therefore accept that only a very small number of priests were 'cremated' in the cairns during the period of their use – perhaps as long as 3,000 years. So we can assume that a pendulum was such a highly regarded tool, it was passed from one priest to the next initiate. Thirty-four individuals, each in the master position for say twenty years only, covers six hundred and eighty years. Possibly many of these little articles were subsequently stolen in the Iron Age and the early Christian era, or even the Viking times, but this is unlikely as the ordinary people had a deep superstition about the potent qualities and attributes of the early temples – with good cause. Had not unwary strangers been known to disappear for ever on inadvertently entering a 'burgh', or men and women been 'spirited' away to return quite suddenly and unexpectedly many years later, still in the flower of youth?

Other strange little objects that have puzzled the excavators over the years are the small round white chalk balls, referred to as 'marbles'. These objects had two uses. The first was as a representation of the full Moon. If you ˈk at the horizon on a clear spring evening and see the full Moon climb over the skyline it appears to be just the size and colour of a little chalk marble. The Moon's changes of shape and position were one of the most important events in the monthly and annual calendar. To anticipate the exact rising point of the Moon was naturally of great importance; to be able to put the full Moon on a flat earth diagram or hold it against the skyline to show the next *moonth* rising or setting point was another duty of the priest. You will recall the energy of the full Moon is also a time of expansion, illuminating the sky for the entire night allowing early man maximum nocturnal mobility: a time of effusion and bringing forth and a time for festivals and celebrations. The other quality of chalk (and limestone) is that it will incandesce under extreme heat or vibrationary input to give energy. It is unlikely that these balls were a child's plaything or a priest's toy.

The energy build-up to the full Moon expands Earth's substance, not least the standing stones so carefully placed, and the whole structure of the temples. The new Moon does the opposite, pulling the energies away from Earth and contracting the substance. This nightly/monthly performance is one of the forces that activates the life force on the Earth. This lunar energy is another form of the vibration coming ultimately from our central atomic power station, the Sun, and it works in sequence with the day-time energies.

Bone Pins or Wands
The bone pins are usually made out of antler horn and had their special uses too: in practical terms they were good tools to use as large

Figure 88 Carrowkeel pendulums, chalk balls and bone from cairns K, F and H (M. Herity, Irish Passage Graves); notes by author in brackets

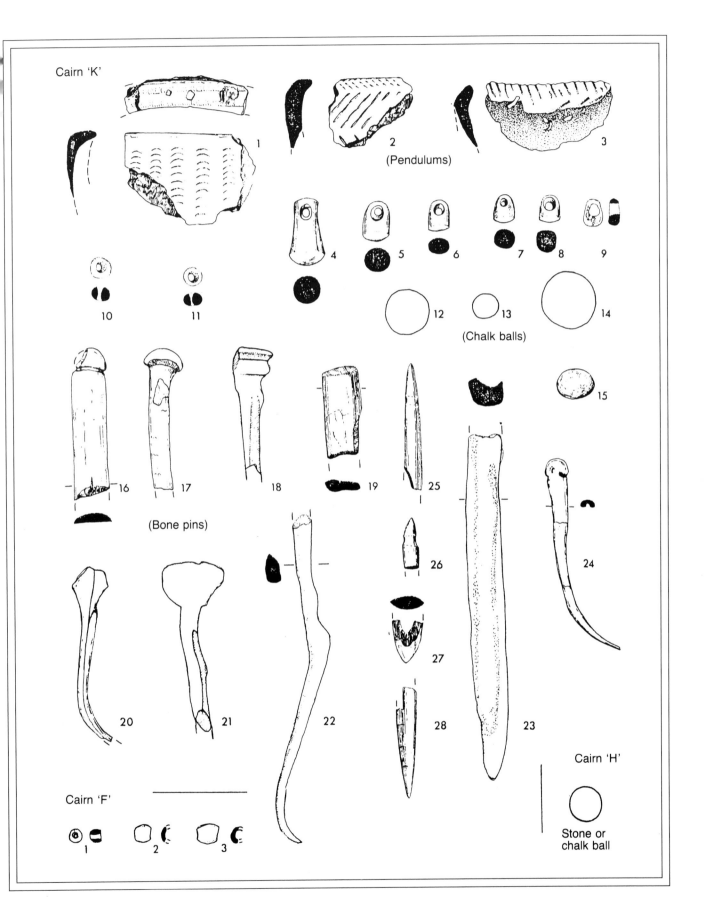

Cairn 'K'

(Pendulums)

(Chalk balls)

(Bone pins)

Cairn 'F'

Cairn 'H'

Stone or
chalk ball

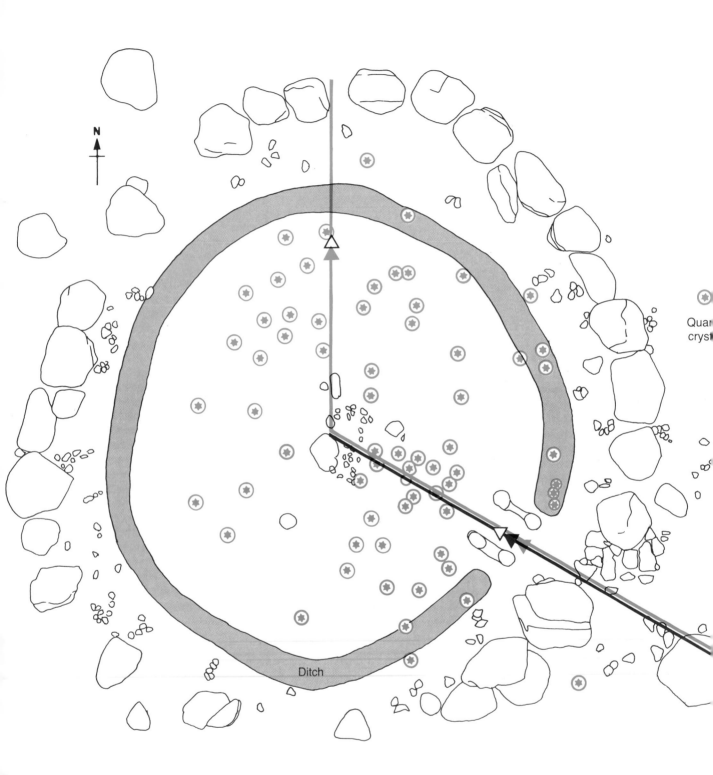

Quar
cryst

Ditch

Figure 89
Carrowmore
excavations and
Dolmen 26 (Göran
Burnenhuilt,
Archaeology of
Carrowmore)

needles in the making of plaited grass nets and baskets of all sizes. Some pins were drilled at the knob end and have a hole and groove for a thong, or for the grasses and cattle tail hair of the net-maker and thatcher. However, their inclusion in the temple indicates they also had a ritual purpose more important than everyday crafting. Evans Wentz in *The Fairy Faith in Celtic Countries* refers to the Irish Bards as having 'a wand in the form of a symbolic branch like a little spike or crescent, with gently tinkling bells upon it', but SAM's antler pins were in use two thousand years before the manufacture of metal bells. The wand or spike was very useful for drawing an earth picture or geometric design. It was also a special tool for gently digging out the necessary herbs and roots for many healing purposes. One of the priestly secrets was the magical use and combination of herbs, roots and fungi of the forest – a knowledge passed secretly from priest to initiate and used for the general health of the community. The fineness and care in the decoration of the Carrowkeel ware clay pots would have been achieved with such an instrument; no mere twig has such an easy shape or comes to hand so neatly. In 'magical' terms antler has a strange attribute not generally recognised, in that like natural ivory (the true ivory of the elephant and the woolly mammoth) annually discarded antler bone fluoresces under the influence of ultra-violet light or psychic sight. These little bone pins could be 'seen' to illuminate and glow violet white under the excitation of this vibration. No wonder these pins were later held in such awe as magic and remembered in legend, and included in the cairns.

We have already mentioned the Egyptian instrument for dowsing and divining, the instrument they called the *merkhet*. This is described as a small bone object which hung from a narrow horizontal bone bar with a transverse hole bored in one end to hold the upper end of the 'plumb line' to which the merkhet was attached – this device has been described as an astral gauge and was employed with another object the Egyptians called a 'bay' (*en imy unut*) or palm rib (used by the Observer of Hours). It was a palm rib with a 'V' notched slot cut in the wider end, very similar to the stone device dug up at Knowth, County Meath, in the 1970 excavations and annotated as a 'carved stone' c.3000–2000 BC, object No. 1 in the *Treasures of Ireland* publication, page 74. The pendulum, the handle and the sighting device are understandable and the Egyptian/Irish connection comes up once again.

Crystals

Many small chips and flakes of quartz and crystal have been found in the circular dolmen cairns during the excavations at Carrowmore. For instance, in 'Grave 26' there are about two hundred and fifty quartz chips in the area excavated. These have already been mentioned as the crystals which were given to the leader of the village – not the priest – to take with him as he foraged in the forest with his family group in order to make fire. The Sun's rays struck through crystal quickly ignite a fire. The need for fire had great significance so the 'tool' was included in the structures. That crystal represents fire also means it represents the vibrations necessary to transmit energy which helped the departing soul on its spiral journey through the astral to return to the Sun, i.e. the ascent of the soul, for crystal performs helically as discussed in Chapter III when activated by heat generated using charcoal.

Carrowkeel Ware

We are told the large circular Carrowkeel pots often contained the remains of cremated humans in the cairns. The structure of the pots is very brittle as the materials available were so indifferent but the decoration is often highly sophisticated. The pots were made by the coiled method and obviously not turned on a wheel. The waved decoration that occurs again and again around the rim represents the vibrations of energy depicting the path of the Earth and the Sun in the sky. Man's puny vehicle is burnt to ashes whilst his soul is

*Figure 90
Carrowkeel ware (M. Herity, Irish Passage Graves)*

5 cm

allowed to go free. If it was possible to study this decoration carefully the patterns might conform to astronomical progression.

There are very rarely weapons of any sort in Irish cairns. In comparison the builders of the numerous Iberian dolmens filled their corners and crevices with hundreds of flint arrow heads and spear points marking their involvement in pursuit of game. This in itself indicates a completely different and lower level of spiritual and intellectual evolution not found in Ireland.

Large Stone Balls
(referred to in Chapter VIII)

Finally amongst the articles found in SAM's temples are the rare and interesting large stone balls, two of which illustrated are from the Loughcrew cairns. Their size (diameter) is 83mm and 70mm respectively. They are almost completely round and of ironstone and granite but they have also been found elsewhere in quartz and serpentine. Except when made out of chalk and/or very small, these balls have a particularly and extremely important function that is not in any way decorative or playful.

Keith Critchlow remarked on and illustrated in his book *Time Stands Still* the uses of strange shaped little stone spheres found in Scottish constructions from about 2500 BC. These spheres are shaped to represent the different symmetries encountered in Platonic geometry. The four elements: fire, air, water and earth are represented by the tetrahedron, the octahedron, the icosahedron and the cube; the dodecahedron referring to the universe. In *Time Stands Still* Critchlow says:

> In three-dimensional assemblies the tetrahedron embodies the symmetry of two and three foldness, the octahedron two, three and four foldness as does its dual the cube, the icosahedron two, three and five foldness as does its dual the pentagonal dodecahedron – completing the five platonic solids – one constructed as squares, three of equilateral triangles and one (the universe) of regular pentagons. If circumference is interpreted literally, we are also dealing with a spherical surface. This not only satisfies the principle that it is the sphere that is the 'fairest form' for the universe, the differentiated elements as such being merely perceived but none the less essential subdivisions of that unity in which their reality lies. To return to the significance of numbers of elements in the dodecahedron and icosahedron, we see that if a spherical surface is divided into the greatest number of equal triangles the result is 120. Most significantly Plato does not ever

Figure 91
Stone balls,
Loughcrew: left,
ironstone (−),
grounding; right,
granite (+), expanding
(National Museum of Ireland)

Figure 92
Stone ball,
Aberdeenshire: triple
spiral in three
dimensions (Keith
Critchlow, *Time
Stands Still*)

give specific angles. Therefore, when it is learnt that these 120 parts are both the composite symmetry of the icosahedron and dodecahedron we realise that indeed there are only two kinds of triangle on the sphere which encompass exactly the spherical projection of all five regular figures. The implications are that Plato was merely giving an introduction to a whole esoteric science of both plane and spherical geometry as a cosmology. (Internal structural angle of quartz and rock crystals is 120°.)

When SAM ground his stone balls he was making a geometric form in which he could plot in miniature with clairvoyant ease the necessary angles and shapes he required to

construct his temples. The balls, used with the pendulum, were all he needed as instruments to allow him to lay out the network of constructions covering Ireland from the west to the east coast. He could literally 'see' into the sphere and relate it to the natural energy grid covering the surface of the Earth and out into the cosmos. His intuition predated Plato by some 3,000 years so perhaps this knowledge had come from the cosmos and not from casual observation after all.

The engravings on the Scottish balls are decipherable from knowledge gained from the Earth Star and the pendulum. Already the symbol of vibration and wavelength ∿∿ has been explained, in the skylights of the cairns. The central shape of all Earth Stars is the diamond shape 'lozenge' of two interlock-

109

ing equilateral triangles end on ◇ which, as Martin Brennan remarked in *The Boyne Valley Vision*, 'might be a representation of measurement'. The 'unit' here is the eight-and-a-third mile diameter of the Earth Star size 'B'. This is depicted at Newgrange on the rear stone K52 which is a diagram of the Irish energy grid at this location, and aligned to the summer solstice sunset. There are fourteen lozenges on the left side under a triple spiral of energy, this triple spiral being repeated in the chamber showing the energy's actual path. This lozenge can be interpreted in the construction of the Earth Star in Chapter V.

Cup Marks

It is important to study the little hollows so often seen on standing stones around SAM's sites. Sometimes these marks are of no significance at all, merely being rain or ice scraped hollows of age-old weathering. But on special stones such as K52 there is a series of cups that would suggest the form of a constellation. This stone is at the rear of the cairn marking the exit of the energy in the north-western sector. Cairns, in this case Newgrange, can sometimes be recognised as aligned to a constellation and we know that in SAM's time the arc of the 'N' markers was in the constellation

Figure 93 Spherical geometry of stone balls (Keith Critchlow, *Time Stands Still*)

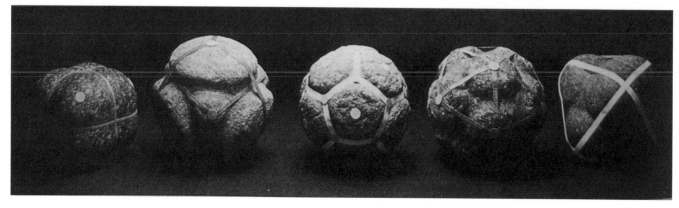

we know as Draco or the Dragon. The pendulum connects the cups and the brightest star of the constellation is Thuban, which is double ringed. To the right on the next stone, K51, we note an engraved depiction for the constellation of Cassiopeia, and to the left K53 – a sandstone block – depicted symbolically by its presence, the constellation of Cheops, the crowned king, similar in the mysteries to the red sandstone carved imagery of the Sphinx stones at the Pyramids of Egypt. Cup marks are often therefore star maps or constellation markers.

Sun and Moon Dialling Symbols

The Sun dialling and Moon dialling symbols engraved in and around SAM's cairns have already been written of by Martin Brennan in *The Stars and the Stones* so there is no point in describing them now, except to say that the dialling is precise and carefully depicted and is just another piece in the whole jigsaw. The Sun as ⊕ and the Moon's path ∿ with its processional wiggle can be experienced and followed by anyone using a compass and binoculars. It is inadvisable to look at the Sun through optical instruments or you will burn out your eyes.

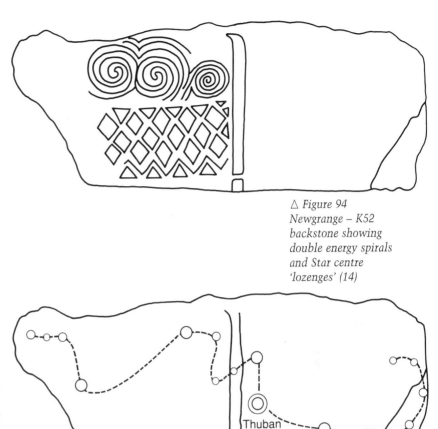

△ Figure 94
Newgrange – K52
backstone showing
double energy spirals
and Star centre
'lozenges' (14)

△ Figure 95
Newgrange – K52
backstone constellation
alignment, Draco, the
Dragon

Figure 96 ▷
*Solar differential cairn
T, Loughcrew.
This little engraving
shows an obvious
solar/planetary
relationship. seemingly
$^{14}/_9$ dots around the
main wheel with the
planet 'W' (World)
engraved on the
lowermost part of the
print-out. Maurice
Cotterell tells us that
the relationship of
P △ E △ W Polar/
Equatorial rotation to
the World is expressed
as $^{42}/_{28}$ – here we have
42 (3×14)/27 (3×9).
Since these early sites
are solar orientated it
seems reasonable to
suggest that SAM had
a distinct knowledge of
the Sun flare cycle*

111

Figure 97
Scottish stone ball:
dodecahedron, an
expression of universal
symmetry (Keith
Critchlow, *Time
Stands Still*)

Chapter X
GREAT POWER SITES

Innishmurray

The main Irish energy line crosses the country through Newgrange. This line proceeds to County Sligo through the side of the Arigna Mountain and across Benbulben to the cashel on Innishmurray Island in Donegal Bay, completing the fourteen size 'B' Star patterns as engraved on the backstone K52 at Newgrange. Innishmurray Island has a Christian history that is recorded from Abbot Molaise in about AD 520. He and his monks had seemingly chosen a Stone Age site directly on the main energy line. SAM had done the same about four millennia before and for the same reason.

The cashel perimeter is an enormous egg-shaped structure with a vast high dry stone wall surround. This was completed probably in Iron Age times, or even added to as an extra defence against the Vikings who attacked here around AD 800. The conformation of the wall follows the original shape of the Stone Age layout, a sort of type II 'ovoid' as defined by Professor Thom, or here a 'winter solstice' layout. The site is situated over a substantial water platform of underground streams that was identified and incorporated into the Christian rebuilding programme when these water points were reconstructed as 'altars'.

It has always been assumed that the only supply of fresh water on the island came from the inland pond area, but directly under the cashel there is an adequate water flow to supply the abbotsbury and provide energy (water spirals) in several different places. To occult these springs or spirals the monks built stone platform structures over them, and called these 'altars'. As we know, a water spiral acts as an energy riser that feeds into the grid and also vibrates the little altars themselves. This intensifies their spiritually so to speak and 'alters' the energy.

In Figure 101 these streams are clearly marked flowing under the main points within the cashel. Low walls are even built over part of the flow which is only about six feet below the surface. The only external well shows this table within its 'house' outside to the south-east corner of the wall.

The Star energy pattern of Innishmurray is positioned so that Stars of three sizes combine to form an integrated expansion of the spiral. There is a Star size 'A' around the cashel and a 1,600-yard Star on 'the site of an ancient altar' inland. Actually the exact centre is five feet to the east of the altar point but clearly substantiates that the Christian monks knew about the Earth Star energies and plotted them for use in their work. These three Stars form together to give another example of an energy beat that has a vibration within the heart of the cashel of 365^{100}, a point of great power, now dormant.

As the main energy line hits the cashel wall it is split and refracted, on the same principle as Newgrange, with the negative proceeding around the outer perimeter of the wall and the positive around the inner perimeter. The main positive flow also passes in and across the corner of the chapel to enter the passageway of the monks' quarters. Here it deflects to the left (clockwise) and is circled into a 'beehive' cell which acts like the oval and hut structures at Newgrange to accelerate and capacitate the flow. The very shape of these early 'beehive' cells suggests a perfect form for the purpose – just like a generator; a fire was lit in the cell to heat up the walls and a stone shelf 'bed' was built for the monks to lie on.

*Figure 98
The cashel of
Innishmurray*

N

◁ *Figure 99*
The altar and DNA
cross at Innishmurray

▽ *Figure 100*
Innishmurray Island,
Sligo: Earth Star layout

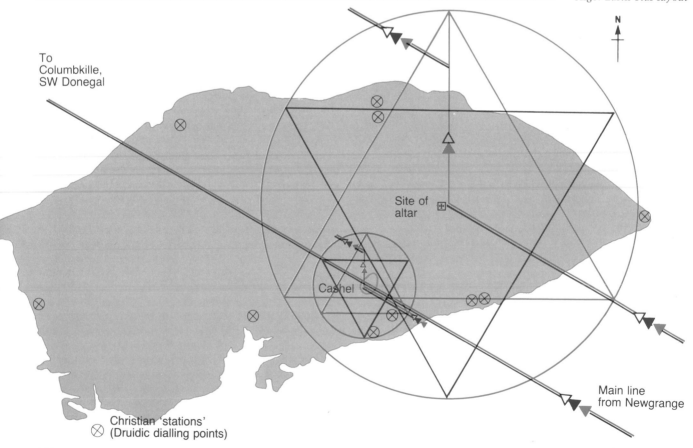

To
Columbkille,
SW Donegal

N

Site of
altar

Cashel

Main line
from Newgrange

⊗ Christian 'stations'
(Druidic dialling points)

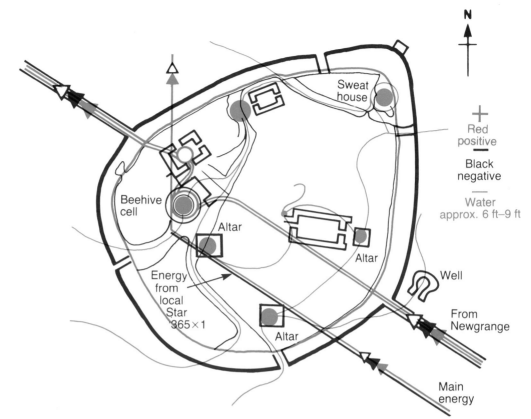

N

+ Red
positive
— Black
negative
— Water
approx. 6 ft–9 ft

Sweat house

Beehive cell

Altar

Altar

Energy from local Star 365 × 1

Altar

Well

From Newgrange

Main energy

▷ *Figure 101*
The cashel on
Innishmurray Island

▽ *Figure 102*
Christian over-
engraving on standing
stone

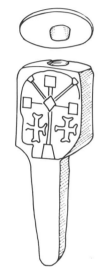

3-D centre stone
engraved with a cross
compass

Wedge-shaped 'stand'
stone with circular
cross stone (on top), a
turning compass dial

Then the energy flows to the inner chapel where it reverses before it leaves through the cutaway portion in the outer cashel wall to rejoin the grid. It has, therefore, gone through a pair of positive/negative poles on its journey, building up the forces of the cashel. There are no natural deposits of crystals on Innishmurray to heat up and enhance this energy flow, so the monks heated stones with fire within the so-called sweathouse to expand water by heat into steam. A sweathouse, therefore, was not just for cleansing but was also part of the energy enhancing system performing in much the same way as heating or expanding quartz. The aim was to build up the shape of the cashel into a geometric spiral, the ϕ shape of the cashel once again dictated by the solar movements; the windows of the beehive probably being aligned to the winter solstice sunset.

The artefacts in the cashel are interesting as they give us an understanding of how SAM or his later Bronze Age children symbolised their beliefs.

On the main water energy point or altar, there are about forty beach stones, known as 'the cursing stones', amongst which is a curious wedge-shaped pillar with a hollow in its top on which a stone 'cap' fits.

This is a Bronze Age pivotal stone which performs like the stand of any sighting instrument. It is heavy and pointed so it can be carried around and positioned as necessary. The cap fits snugly in the top and can be turned to orientate any marking on its top surface to line up with the required observation. Therefore it acts like a crude theodolite in the hands of an astronomer priest. The original engraving is thus: $\curlyvee$ which represents the well-known Druid greeting to the Sun, i.e. man with his arms raised, suggesting the Golden Mean proportion. Later the Christians over-engraved it with the Cross of Calvary.

On the altars are many round stones taken from the seashore of the island. Some have been engraved with a cross, within a circle round the perimeter. This is the Sun cross or compass (N S E W). We will see a similar gold cross in the next chapter to verify that this was used for Sun and Moon calculations. These stones were placed on the stone stand for dialling purposes. The altars are sited over a water table that has not been disrupted by electricity or modern machinery so the vibrations are still in balance and symmetry. If a pendulum is suspended over the centre of any of the altars it will start to swing, settling down to five beats true north/south, then five circles clockwise followed by five beats east/west and then five beats clockwise, repeating this performance of five, five, five continuously. As already stated five is the creative symmetry of water (H_2O) and the equivalent in the Earth of blood in our veins. We are a water planet. These 'cursing stones' as they are known locally were originally aligned N S E W true on the altars in conjunction with

117

the water spiral just explained. If a person of ill-intent wished to disrupt or curse someone, it was simple to invoke their name and speak the curse at the same time as turning the stones anti-clockwise out of balance and symmetry, thereby sending a disruptive force out through the grid (or ether) to that unsuspecting individual, *but* of course it only really works if the perpetrator of the evil is clairvoyant and knows how to work those energies on a psychic level. The same principle applies to individuals who disrupt (archaeologists beware) the symmetry and balance of such structures as fairy forts and rings, cairns, standing stones, etc. They are said to fall ill and die soon after their 'folly'. Look what happened to the people who opened and despoiled the tomb of Tutankhamun. The

'altars' were therefore deliberately sited to change the energy from day to night to day (+ − +) to sanctify the sacrament – the bread and the wine.

Engraved headstones. The inside of the cashel has been filled up as Christians buried their dead. So there are several early representations of the cross or crucifix carved on local stone, presumably as memorial headstones. Amongst these there is one particular stone that is from a much earlier period as it is pentagonal. It is engraved with the true Celtic cross incorporating four 'dots' within its arms. This is a representation of Sun geometry.

Tara

Although the main Irish energy line crosses the country at Newgrange there are obviously

Figure 103
Pentagonal cross stone

Figure 104
Tara from the air,
Bronze Age structures.
Note similarity to corn
circles near Silbury
Hill, Wiltshire (UK).
Summer 1990 (photo:
George Wingfield)

N

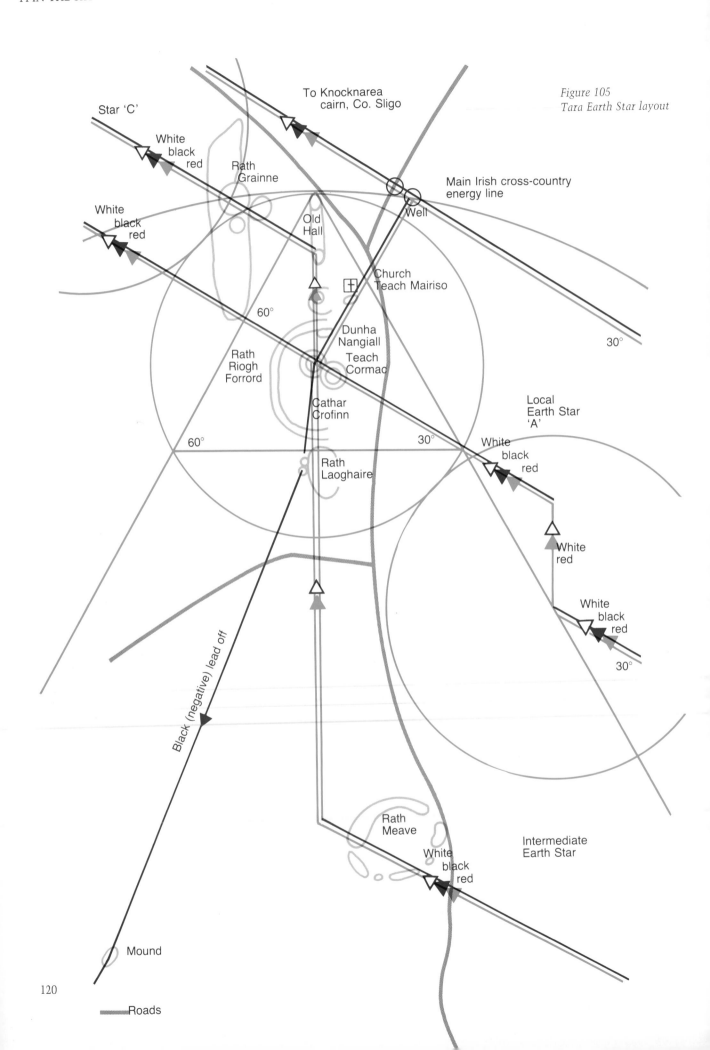

Figure 105
Tara Earth Star layout

Star 'C'

To Knocknarea
cairn, Co. Sligo

White
black
red

Rath
Grainne

White
black
red

Old
Hall

Main Irish cross-country
energy line

Well

Church
Teach Mairiso

60°

Dunha
Nangiall
Teach
Cormac

Rath
Riogh
Forrord

Cathar
Crofinn

Local
Earth Star
'A'

60°

30°

White
black
red

Rath
Laoghaire

White
red

White
black
red

Black (negative) lead off

30°

Rath
Meave

White
black
red

Intermediate
Earth Star

Mound

Roads

many lesser but parallel lines proceeding at the same angle incorporating size 'B' type Stars. The line that runs through Tara, the ancient Bronze Age capital of Ireland, follows its north-westward course and passes through Loughcrew and then the Carrowmore dolmen area and touches the great cairn on top of Knocknarea Hill in County Sligo.

Tara was the capital of the four realms of old Ireland, Ulster, Munster, Leinster and Connaught. Here the late Bronze Age Bards, Ovates, Druids – the scientist priests – assembled every year for the major festivals before the kings of the late centuries of the first millennium BC and on into the Iron Age. Most of the mythology of ancient Ireland comes from this period, but once again we are concerned with the layout and workings in the energy grid. There are several Stone Age structures at Tara, the best known being the Mound of the Hostages, a cairn of usual form, as at Carrowkeel and from the same period. The artefacts found within it prove this as they are the typical pendulums, chalk balls and bone pins we associate with the third and second millennia BC. Later Bronze Age gold instruments were found nearby that we will discuss in the next chapter.

There is quite a muddle of earth works thrown up at Tara, but once we plot the occulted triangulation of the Earth Stars, their conformation will fall clearly into our understanding and their interlock will be obvious.

This main line passes by the hill top of Tara at the expected 30° just near the present-day crossroads. Tara was chosen as the capital as it is a hill that, although not very high, commands an uninterrupted view around 360° for many miles. It is a perfect dialling viewpoint within the mid-east coastland area and is roughly centred in the province from north to south. The energy line is deflected off at a right angle south-west, by the original construction of a well or water point. Water has the property of acting as a liquid crystal and can refract energy if set up correctly. This water point is discernible with a pendulum still, but the original structure is missing or filled in. The lead off line at 90° passes through the churchyard, not through the modern Church of Ireland building, but through the original chapel known as Teach Mairiso whose foundations, dating probably to around AD 550, are still to be seen on an older mound. Once again the Christians had taken over and used the earlier knowledge in their 'new' religion.

We read in our history books about 'the cursing of Tara' and how an early Christian priest was so incensed by the misuse of power by the then King of Tara that he put out the ritual fires of Tara for 1,500 years. The ritual fire of Tara was the psychic fires of the Earth energies flow that activated the whole of the Tara layout. As stated, the flow came into the structures from the well area, so in order to 'cut off' Tara from its energy 'the curse' took the form of a Christian stone being raised at the corner of the tiny original Christian church within the present graveyard and right over the inflow energy.

By doing this the priest effectively put in a barrier; just as if we put a large boulder in the middle of a stream, the water is disrupted and has to part and flow around it. Tara was

Figure 106
Author at the energy-blocking stone at Tara

therefore effectively immobilised as a sacred site and after that its effectiveness as a place of magical power was lost. This was a deliberate act of energy manipulation performed with full knowledge of the effects and the history of Ireland has been predictable since, as the country has suffered ever after.

The line crossed in front of the entrance to the Mound of the Hostages (Dunha Nangiall) and centred on the main positive mound of Cathar Crofinn. Here there is a modern statue and an old standing stone, known as the Stone of Fal. Both are placed in the wrong position and are not on the actual energy centre of the structure. The companion mound touching this centre mound is built over a negative water spiral about fourteen feet below its surface. This spiral is very strong and feeds into the grid on the connective line that proceeds from the local size 'A' Stars. There is a larger Star centring by the Iron Age rath several hundred yards due south. The positive central red and white energy line of this Star runs through to the rath Riogh Forrord which is its break-off point. The break-off point of the smaller Star is at the southern tip of the 'Old Hall of Tara'.

You can readily see from Figure 105 how the Earth energies are precisely aligned due north and interlocked to allow the structures placed within them to draw maximum power and energy from the grid and return maximum energy and power back into the grid. Once again the energy beat spirals up to 365^{100} at the centre of Teach Cormac to create another massive lift point for the use of the priesthood. The surface dimensions of all the different structures reflect the dimensions of the underground water energies.

Ceremonial axe heads. Several polished stone 'hammer' heads have been found near Tara and are now in the museum in Dublin. Their shape is significant, as obviously they were not used to bash out brains, but were ceremonial in that they were used to deliver the ritual blow to the forehead to open the perceptions of the third eye. A similar ceremony is still conducted today in the rituals of Freemasonry and its initiations. SAM built in geometric and mathematical dimensions and wedge-shaped examples were used as dividers of a circle.

Knocknarea and Carrowmore

This dolmen area is the largest and most important outside Carnac in Brittany.

The Tara line at the Atlantic coast of Sligo passes through the much reported but little understood dolmen cairn area of Carrowmore,

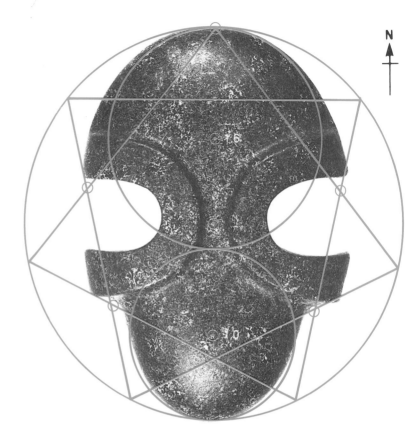

a very extensive Stone Age site. There were many structures on this fertile plain but as Sligo town has expanded over the last hundred years local farmers and landowners have inevitably misused and destroyed many of these circles. Even Sligo County Council was recently debating whether to allow the construction of the new corporation rubbish tip in the centre of this area. If we accept this is a cemetery, surely such acts must be vandalism. The early Christian structures of AD 400 to 800 were placed on many of SAM's 'points' purposely to enjoy the energy of the Earth Mother 'Mary' herself*, and to sanctify the buildings. We should protect these early places with due reverence.

Knocknarea

The line from Tara crosses through Carrowmore and passes just to the south of the great cairn on the top of the hill of Knocknarea. This is a vast stone cairn built of carboniferous limestone that glows deep purple and white to 'sight'. SAM built this cairn as his western marker but from the Atlantic (Atlantean)

*For further reading see Hamish Miller and Paul Broadhurst, *The Sun and the Serpent*, Pendragon Press, Launceston, Cornwall.

Figure 107
The Clonmore Castle stone battle-axe (National Museum of Ireland). *This 'battle-axe' was found in Ireland at Clonmore Castle, County Carlow, under a large stone with a small bronze axe and a bronze pin. Applying the principles of sacred geometry, we can discern, built into this enigmatic shape, that it is an elliptical gauge, an instrument that unfolds the secrets of seven-fold symmetry and the Golden Mean proportion. It was used to lay out elliptical or egg-shaped structures – a perfect example of which can be seen at Le Menec, at the end of the alignments at Carnac, in Brittany (see Chapter XII)*

viewpoint, this was the *eastern* marker to the energies of Ireland. It can be seen for many miles around as a great sentinel of the light. Later, a somewhat disreputable Iron Age queen known as Maeve gave her name to it and used it as a symbol of her power, but surely she had no understanding of its real uses. Thankfully this structure, like the Heapstown cairn, has not been defiled since its entrance was closed way back in early times. For it was the later priests that ordered these 'pagan' structures to be closed for all time as they superimposed their law on the distracted communities of the later Iron Age. To them these cairns were symbols of the old religion then seen to be in chaos and disarray long after the genuine priesthood of SAM's time and even the Bronze Age had fallen apart. The religious practices of the Iron Age were founded on power of arms and the power of iron might. Their laws were not the laws of justice and truth, but often of black magic and witchcraft, the spell of fear and death which stood behind every rock of the hillside, or tree of the forest. The later Celts were the warring warriors of this time, tough, cruel and imperative – they were not the kind, gentle giants or the heroic knights of mythology. Unfortunately we always choose to romanticise conquests in the past for that is usually the only way we can accept history and live with the results, for history is written by the winning side!

So this great cairn remains closed up with its entrance hidden away from prying eyes. At least we know that these structures are not places full of gold, jewels and treasures or they would have been sacked long ago, nor were they places of sacrifice. If ever Knocknarea cairn or Heapstown are to be opened up, let us do everything possible to stop the authorities turning them into some Stone Age Disneyland. Let us try to persuade those directors in the world of glass cases that the understanding of SAM's world can only be appreciated with the combined disciplines and intuition of physicists and psychics, astronomers and architects amongst the ranks of the pragmatic archaeologists.

So here at Knocknarea, at last, is a huge unopened cairn of grandeur for all to see. The Stone Age energy plot is again quite clear and concise, the cairn forming the apex of a large Star within the higher chakras of an Earth energy landscape system. The cairn is, if you like, the brow point of this Star with all the necessary forces flowing through it to give it the expansion and multiplication of the spirals to allow the auric body to actuate from the platform of this great hill.

Down on the sands of the bay below lies an old circle built by SAM several millennia before the little church that now stands, sadly depleted, on its mound. This is the church of Killspugbrone built, we are told, by Bishop Brone around AD 512. He was supposedly ordained by Patrick and he placed his church within the sacred confines of a much earlier Stone Age site, for the energy of this site is closely connected to Knocknarea. We can now realise how the early Christian monks built up their churches. We have always thought they went to the extremities of the Western world to escape the chaos of the Dark Ages; to build their little beehive cell 'accelerators' far away from marauders. But did they? Surely they built at Killspugbrone, Innishmurray and Columbkille (Donegal), later at Iona, to take over the earlier sites of SAM and the Bronze Age priests. They could not have built their churches on worthless empty sites that had no significance; if that had been the case they would have chosen any area seemingly convenient to the community – just as we build today anywhere in our towns. The true early Irish Christians were unsullied by materialism and power emanating from the hangover of the Roman Empire. They were the reincarnation of earlier priests of the light, living holy, simple, dedicated lives of prayer and service as dictated by the example of the Master himself. They began to understand and use the energy of the spirals in meditation and began to accept the gifts of 'out-of-body experience' as part of the gifts of the Holy Spirit. Little did they realise (or did they?) that they were recreating and perpetuating SAM's knowledge. They even rearranged the old festivals into their calendar to allow the people the freedom of the Druidic understanding of the seasons. So, of course, Rome looked askance at this blooming flower of pure love growing up miles away from its dogmatic power centre. The temporal hierarchy finally said 'enough' and sent emissaries to bring those magical abbots and monks throughout the British Isles to heel. This early period had been the purest in the history of Christian mysticism.

We unhappy materialists today are living at the end of another great age and have already passed the point of no return. The changes that are coming will lift humanity through the higher vibration of ultra-violet light to the start of another age.

We have now crossed Ireland from east to west, from the portals of Newgrange to the cairn at Knocknarea, the final extremity of the west coast, but not quite, for now an airport

Figure 108
Knocknarea 'pyramid
cairn' (photo: Steve
Rogers)

N

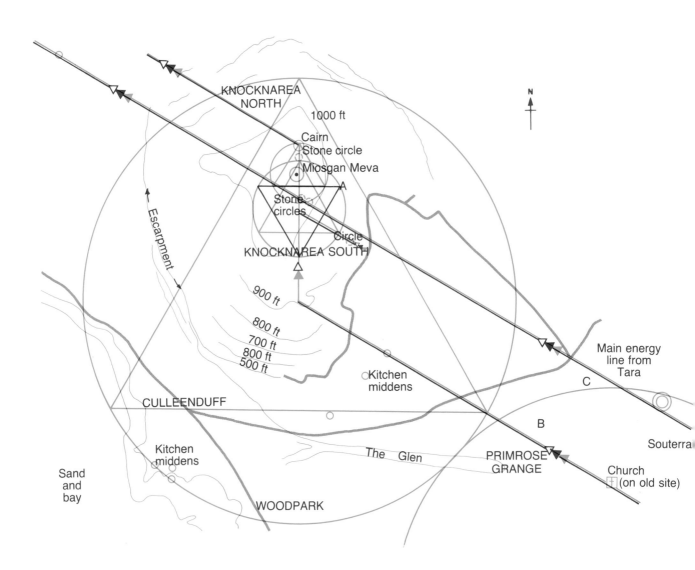

KNOCKNAREA
NORTH

1000 ft

Cairn
Stone circle
Miosgan Meva

A

Stone
circles

Circle
KNOCKNAREA SOUTH

900 ft

800 ft
700 ft
800 ft
500 ft

Escarpment

Kitchen
middens

CULLEENDUFF

Kitchen
middens

Sand
and
bay

The   Glen

WOODPARK

Main energy
line from
Tara

C

B

Souterra

PRIMROSE
GRANGE

Church
(on old site)

N

*Figure 109
Knocknarea Earth Star
layout*

has been built below Knocknarea and the mound at Killspugbrone – the landing strip going right across this great energy line.

Ogham and the Early Monks

An Irish monk's 'board game' (calculator). The early monks are often thought of as rollicking gamesters from boards and engraved stone dice, but this little wooden board game pierced with 49 holes (7 × 7) and bounded by 4 × 3 divisions (Figure 110) is a simple weekly-monthly × 3, 4, 5, 6, 7, 8, 9, 10, 12 calculator – the pegs are missing but were probably of seal or walrus ivory. However, the two little handles shaped as 'heads' centred at either side of the square give us a clue to other uses. If we draw two circles around the inner and outer squares and check the Golden Mean proportion we find the heads exactly fall on the larger and smaller arcs. We know that the Golden Mean proportion is an expression of the solar

energy/wind. Now let us look at the American Indian 'Sun dance' as depicted on the traditional weaving of cloaks and tepees and even in rock carvings of indefinite age (Figure 111).

Here we immediately recognise the two small heads of the board showing a slightly different layout from the 7 × 7 holes of the wooden board. Here is an idea of the zig-zags we have already seen on SAM's lintels! The flares of the Sun are clearly marked at the sides. Could it be that the American Indians and the people of the era of this board game c. AD 700 really did correlate and travel between cultures?

So let us try and relate the Irish secret language of this period (about AD 400–700), the pictographic Ogham, to mystical solar activity and the tripal spiral.

Ogham – Ireland's secret language. Ogham is generally accepted as a form of writing from ancient Ireland, a secret language of unknown

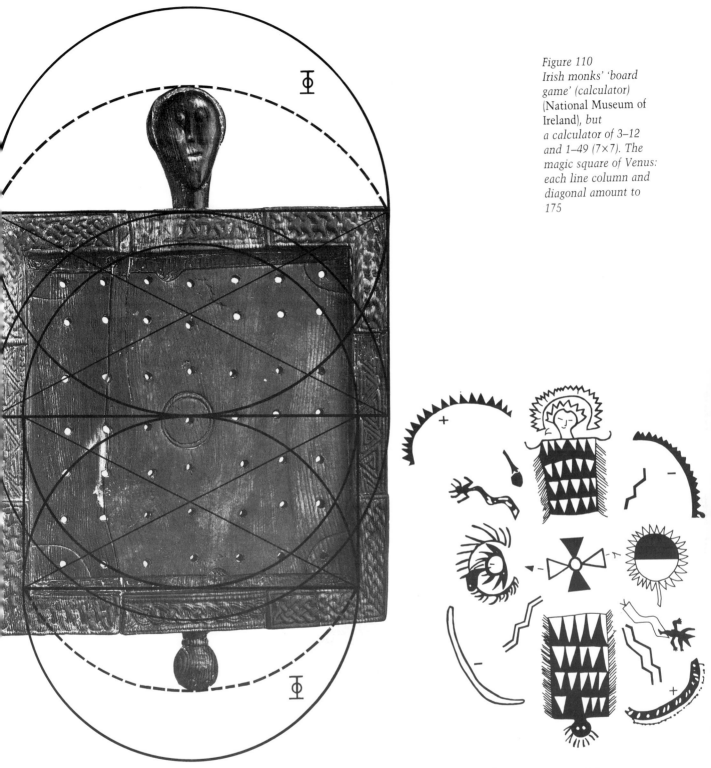

Figure 110
Irish monks' 'board
game' (calculator)
(National Museum of
Ireland), but
a calculator of 3–12
and 1–49 (7×7). The
magic square of Venus:
each line column and
diagonal amount to
175

Figure 111
The North American
cloak Sun dance
calculator, similar to
Portuguese slate
calculators

origin usually found engraved on stone pillars. These small 'standing stones' are commemorative, referring to a family or tribe, and are also sometimes thought to have been used as boundry markers. The interpretation of Ogham script is usually taken from the Book of Ballymote (c. AD 1300) but many similar interpretations have been put forward. The engraved letters or signs are always carved on the hard edge of the standing stone, up and down, so that the edge acts as a centre line.

Ogham is pronounced 'Ohm', the same sound as the 'OM' or 'AUM' universally known in Eastern religions; and if you accept this, then one of the secrets of this hidden language is revealed, for OM or AUM is written ॐ. It is a representation of the cosmic sound of the universe that pervades everything, and 'OM' is the signature of Hinduism, extolling Brahma, the creator of all. In Ireland

Figure 112
Ogham script and engraved stone
(National Museum of Ireland)

at Newgrange in the chamber of the Great Cairn, the same symbol is engraved in the central chamber as the triple spiral 🌀 . As has been explained, the triple spiral depicts the joining of the forces of the Sun (fire) working through earth, water and air to create new life. So here is a perfect clue to Ogham, a secret language that somehow reflects the energy of the creative force we choose to call 'God'.

As far as we know, SAM, and many peoples after the Stone Age, did not have a written language and spoken language has been so mixed up through migrations that the form even of old Irish is still very difficult to decipher. The reason is that the ancient peoples did not chatter away all the time as we do today. Mostly they lived in silence and close proximity to the natural forces. Talk was expressed by the use of hands and facial expressions. Today, we have a very adequate sign language which is used all over the world by people who are deaf and dumb, expressed with arms, hands and fingers, and sometimes in conjunction with lip reading. Ogham was equivalent to that language, a vocabulary of silence used from earliest times but not engraved until around AD 400.

The monks often took vows of silence, maybe for specific periods, even for life depending upon the local abbot. This silence did not preclude communication as the brothers had to tell each other what to do, their daily, weekly, annual tasks, etc., so they talked with their hands expressing Ogham, a language of five groups of five letters or signs with their five fingers, left or right hand as necessary, up and down, and beside a central line – the central line of the body. Today in this time of rapidly expanding interest in alternative medicine and natural physics, there are many techniques that recognise and work with the meridians of the body. These force lines, five on each side including the centre line, flow up the legs and arms from the five toes and five fingers, all meeting at the crown (or cairn) at the crown-chakra point. This is the apex of the human standing stone where the mind can intuit these subtle nervous impulses. Remember the beat of five at the 'altars' of Innishmurray, the creative water beat of Mother (Mary) Earth.

Fountain International is one of many organisations giving healing energy to Planet Earth. Around the world groups of dedicated people dowse the gravity grid or auric body of the planet, in order to repair areas of disruption and chaos. To identify the disrupted areas, many members use their hands as pendulums to determine with their extended fingers, left

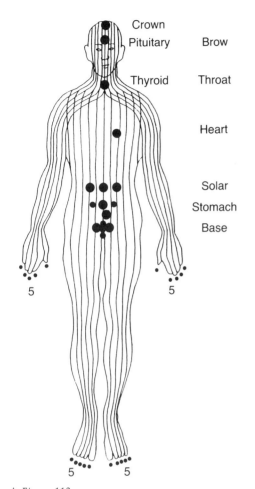

Crown
Pituitary   Brow

Thyroid   Throat

Heart

Solar
Stomach
Base

5   5

5   5

△ *Figure 113*
Meridians of the
human body: the OM
or Ogham of wo-man

everyday life in the form of Ogham.

That is not quite the end of the Ogham story, for we know that without light we live in darkness. Four years ago in Ireland an early chalice and paten were dug up from a 9th-century monastic site at Derrynaflan. The chalice is only the second 'bell' chalice found (after the Ardagh chalice); but the magnificent paten is the first of its type recorded in Ireland. These two artefacts together with an attendant strainer spoon were the astronomical and astrological instruments of the monks. The early monks were the mathematicians, astrologers and alchemists of the known world. They had taken over within the Christian religion the magical practices of the Druids whose knowledge and intuitive gifts spanned the millennia back to SAM. By placing the

▽ *Figure 114*
German silver-gilt
chalice 'dial', 16th
century AD (British Museum). *Note the centred gnomon pin in the bowl which threw a shadow on the inner surface*

or right hand, the shape and force of the natural energies that are active in any particular area.

To see a peson dowsing with his or her hands certainly appears strange, as the individual seems to have a far away look in the eyes, with the hands shaking up and down each side of their body's meridian line. The dowser or diviner is intuiting the dis-ease of gravity in a specific part of the grid. The Ogham script originated in this way.

We have discussed the extraordinary energy of underground water flows and the power that emanates from blind springs – altars – and how, when the force is restructured into balance, it reforms to five concentric circles above the central point. This is Nature's way of divulging the same energy as we have in our bodies, either chaotic and diseased, or healthy and shining. The early people and certainly the monastic monks experienced these seemingly divine forces and put them to use in their

Figure 115
*Derrynaflan chalice.
Note: chalice and
paten are not to
relative scale* (National
Museum of Ireland)

strainer spoon in the chalice or on the surface of the paten, so that it became a gnomon, they were able to determine the path of the Sun, the Moon and the stars.

The use of 'chalice dials' is very obscure and was certainly kept secret since, if the holy vessels were known outside the academic Church to be both scientific and practical instruments, then their sacred association of wine and bread would have become debased.

The early bell-shaped chalices were used in much the same way as the later (German) chalice dials having a fixed central pin, or gnomon. The difference was that the strainer spoon was moved around the face of the dial,

Figure 116
Derrynaflan paten
(National Museum of
Ireland)

with its *crystal* boss at the end of the handle representing the Moon or Sun.

The paten was used the same way. Around the top of the rim there are twenty-four bosses which tell the hours: a twenty-four-hour clock being used from sunrise to sunset to sunrise. The upper vertical rim of the paten has twelve bosses whilst the lower stand of the paten has eight bosses. It is possible that the top half of the paten was originally turned on its stand to allow differential dialling of the Sun's magnetic fields and of the equinoxes, solstices and quarter days, i.e. the 'pattern' of the Druidic year.

The paten's polished silver surface is also a reflector and was used as a heliograph (mirror/sun-reflector) for passing messages over long distances to transmit Ogham from one settlement to another. It was the Morse code of light and flashed either side of a central sight line between the two structures. This was the same principle as the beacons lit in ancient times along the coasts to warn of possible invasion, or from church spire to church spire. How strange it is that in the Ogham script, there is a circle around the vertical line φ to depict the phonetic of 'oi' when today if we wish to catch someone's attention we shout 'oi' at them or as the town cryer says 'oyez' ('hear' in Old French). Has anything changed?

Once again we have seen how the knowledge of the natural sciences has been used secretly by the intelligentsia of that age. Whilst today, still using the same vessels in Christian services, neither the clergy nor laymen seem to have any idea of their alternative scientific purposes.

Lincoln Cathedral

The tiny early Christian churches of the 6th and 7th centuries were always sited over underground water courses, and the altars placed over 'risers' or blind springs. There are still many of these structures in good repair along the western seaboard of Ireland. We have discussed the monastic settlement in the cashel of Innishmurray. This is a classic example, following the principles of layout of much earlier cairns in SAM's day. As the Church increased in power and wealth, so its building programme became more ambitious until in England, particularly after the Norman Conquest, some great cathedrals were started. They all followed the same principles.

First a suitable site was chosen, preferably on a hill top to be visible to the general populace. Secondly, the underground water courses had to flow through the earth providing a series of lines of force and conjunctions to fulfil the general conformation of the cross.

The thread of knowledge direct from SAM, of the use of the pendulum and plumb-bob, and the use of sacred geometry, was held secretly and jealously by the Freemasons – the master builders, who built these wonderful structures encapsulating sacred space, to be filled with angelic voices of the great choirs, exalting God.

Lincoln Cathedral is such a building. Started in AD 1072, the first building was completed in 1092, subsequently destroyed and rebuilt after an earthquake in 1185.

In the underground water map (see page 132), note how the entrance and nave are centred over the main flow, coursing west to east – how the font is in its correct place at the rear of the body of the church, the base chakra or birth place. The transept conforms to a general cross-flow incorporating 6 spirals, 3 north, 3 south, of the centre line, later to be little side chapels, and how the original church had its altar over the great spiral in the middle of the present choir. When the church was rebuilt in the 12th century this spiral was then hidden away from the body of the church by the Rood Screen, thereby debarring the unordained from the mystery of that spiral. A new spiral was chosen further up the underground flow away from the general public and is the site of the present high altar. Note how the many side chapels, doorways and special rooms were sited to conform to the flow throughout the building, all coming together to produce a structure of grace and power.

Here SAM's programmes have been faithfully followed producing exactly the same ideas of the eternal opportunity for the passage of the soul, to and from God. The bishops were even 'entombed' over the flows and spirals. How sad it is that today these wonderful buildings are nearly empty, and unacknowledged as places of real divinity set up by psychic dowsers to fulfil the lore of natural physics – the mainstream thread of esoteric knowledge that is our birthright. Lincoln Cathedral, as our other cathedrals, is recognised as a landscape temple, incorporating a perfect chakra system from sacral centre, the doorway and font (baptism), through to the solar plexus, transept, through the throat chakra, the choir, to the altar (alter) rail of the brow (initiation of communion), to the high altar, the very crown itself.

Understanding these sacred secrets could revitalise the ailing, lost and divided Christian communion in a magical way, but it requires an archbishop of spiritual awareness and courage to state that divining is not pagan and of the devil, for a start!

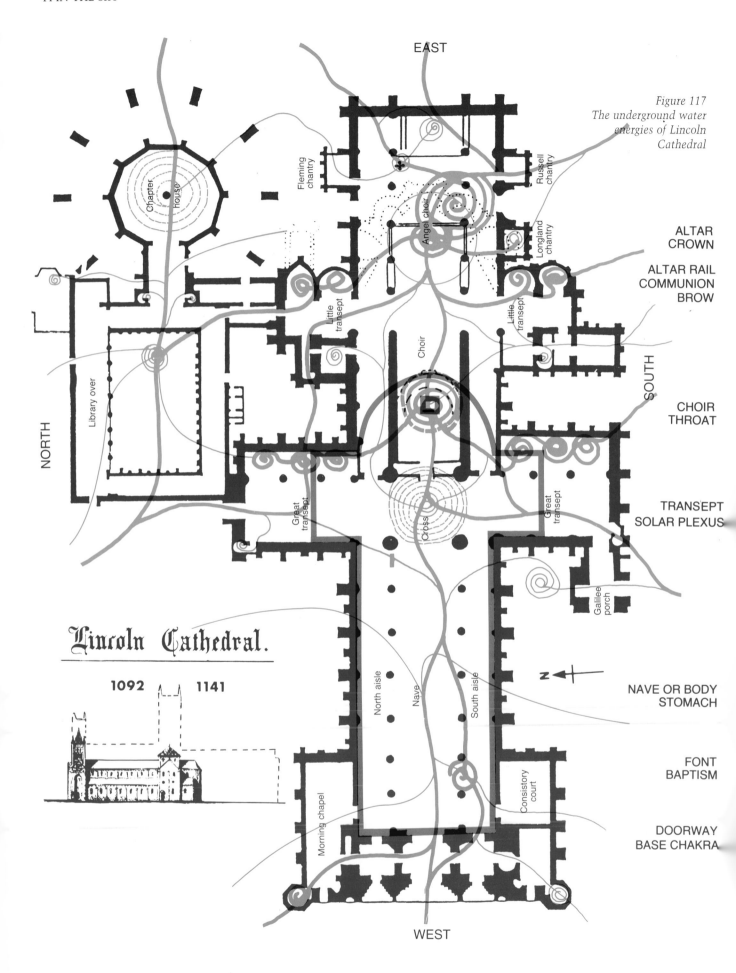

EAST

Figure 117
The underground water
energies of Lincoln
Cathedral

Chapter house

Fleming chantry

Russell chantry

ALTAR
CROWN

ALTAR RAIL
COMMUNION
BROW

Angel choir

Longland chantry

Little transept

Little transept

SOUTH

Choir

CHOIR
THROAT

Library over

NORTH

TRANSEPT
SOLAR PLEXUS

Great transept

Great transept

Cross

Galilee porch

Lincoln Cathedral.

1092   1141

NAVE OR BODY
STOMACH

North aisle

Nave

South aisle

FONT
BAPTISM

Morning chapel

Consistory court

DOORWAY
BASE CHAKRA

WEST

Chapter XI
THE IRISH GOLD AGE

An enormous question mark hangs over the long transitional period between the end of the Stone Age and the beginning of the Bronze Age with the general introduction and use of metal artefacts heralding the tide of immigrant peoples from Western Europe into Ireland. Also along with this new metal, an amalgam of copper and tin, came the supposed sudden discovery in Ireland of large deposits of seam and alluvial gold mainly centred on the Wicklow Hills. Really we should call this period the 'Gold Age'. The people had lived through a period of stability, an untroubled age enjoying peace and timelessness. This was from approximately 7000 BC to the beginnings of the Bronze Age, generally accepted to be around 2000 BC. The expansion of trade and craftsmanship that had begun in the eastern Mediterranean had permeated through the Iberian Peninsula along the Atlantic seaboard and finally reached Ireland.

Rare small gold objects from Portuguese dolmens have been dated as early as 2400 BC, whereas we are told that the enormous quantities of early Irish goldwork extant, and mainly in the National Museum in Dublin, date only from about 1800 BC. To try and put dates to this transitional period is virtually impossible, but it would be intriguing to know when the priesthood of Carrowkeel, with their cairns depicting planetary movements, were able to start using miniaturised instruments held in the hand. Before this statement can be understood, it is essential to realise that the use attributed to these enigmatic gold objects has nothing to do with adornment, jewellery or personal wealth. Dr George Eogan of University College, Dublin, states that:

Early Irish gold objects have not been found in burials or in connection with human remains, so the use of these beautiful objects must be for ritual or other purposes.

Gold is the Sun metal, it does not tarnish or rot and its softness allows it to be easily worked and cast. Another interesting point is that when these gold artefacts have been found they have been located in what are euphemistically called 'hoards' which suggests a materialistic connotation. But often the gold is folded or bent into shapes to make it smaller so these 'hoards' were actually hiding places chosen in haste for secrecy. Many of the gold lunulae are heavily ribbed from being folded up like little concertinas.

'Lunulae'
Perhaps the lunula is one of the best known of the early Irish gold styles as its shape does suggest the new Moon. Over 100 have been found so far; approximately 80 known in Ireland, the rest from southwest England and France. The disc was made to show from its centres the movement of the Sun/Moon and the planets around its perimeter. If we look again at the disc we see it has an inner circumference marked off with the tiny zigzags we already associate with energy and movement day to day. There are two definite centres within its form, in a proportion of approximately two (inner) to three (outer) circumferences, although they vary from disc to disc both in proportion and sophistication. If you will accept first of all this is an Earth-centred calculator showing the movement of

the planets around us, you will have accepted half the inherent truth of the knowledge the disc projects. Draw a series of circles around the plate of the disc with your compass point at the centre of the outer perimeter and another with your compass point at the centre of the circle made by the inner perimeter. The larger circumference is centred on Planet Earth and the smaller circumference on the Sun, the centre of our solar system. If we now draw schematically the orbits of the planets in order of their appearance outwards from these two centres, we will find that they seem to interlock.

To suggest that these 'primitive' Stone Age people knew that the Earth went around the Sun with the other planets is indeed radical since this knowledge supposedly only came to us in the Renaissance, but we know that for dialling convenience and seemingly for explaining the seasons to the people it was accepted that the Sun went around the Earth (see back to Chapter I).

The lunula is often thought of as a pectoral ornament, i.e. something to go around the throat like a necklace, but it would be impractical to wear it thus as the continual movement of the metal would lead to distortion. However, it is obvious that the flanges at each end had some purpose. This was twofold, primarily when in use a fine braided hair cord attached to a pin would have been used as a 'compass' point around the perimeter and secondly, ritually, it might have been worn in the hair and depicted to the people as the halo or head aura of the priest, just as we see depicted in Renaissance painting and, with psychic sight, around the head chakra.

The idea of gold of that time was as the God of Light enfolding nature. The communication between man and the spiritual deities began to diminish with the incursions of the Celtic migrations from all over Central Europe into Ireland in the late Bronze Age, and with the advent of iron (8th–9th centuries BC). It was natural that the incoming powerful chieftains should wish to acquire the extraordinary magic held by the priests and the Sun people but they could not do so using persuasion or threats, and they could not understand the deep spiritual impulse that the inhabitants of the western Atlantic seaboard had been given with their age-old Atlantean consciousness. So they tried to acquire it by force. The priests were killed because they were unable to divulge the magical mysteries just as the Spanish conquistadors killed the Inca Sun priests for their gold. (See the recent BBC film on 'The Koji Tribe' of the Sierra Nevada,

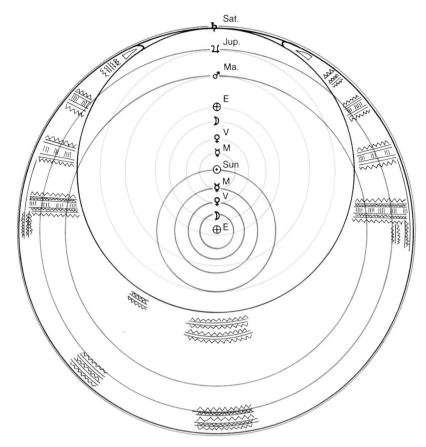

Colombia.) As the priests were increasingly threatened so their ritual objects were hidden and the old stone structures fell into disuse and became places of superstition and fear. At first the new leaders of the Iron Age attempted to acquire the old powers by offering the blood sacrifice of animals, but when this was seen to be ineffective in attracting the attention of the gods they sacrificed first their captives and then their own people. Finally they said 'if we offer our own sons and daughters is this not the ultimate sacrifice that we can perform and surely the magic will be given to us'. So the ritual of evil and negative black magic began to pervade the planet. It happened in Ireland and England and it happened in the Americas; and the awfulness of it is still with us today. But the original purpose of the cairns was *not for sacrifice* as is stated by the Church.

The thread of SAM's pure knowledge, however, was carried forward through the dark periods of the early Iron Age and was already part of the 'mysteries' held safely by the Druid priests. When the teachings of Jesus were brought to England (and Ireland) by Joseph of Arimathea and the remnants of the lost Disciples in AD 36 – the first travelling Universal Christians – 'the word' was accepted as completely relevant and natural as it retaught everything already known from the 'light'

△ *Figure 118*
Overlay of Ross gold lunula Sun-centred solar system and Earth-centred solar system. Note the original lunula is distorted

Figure 119
Ross Lunula (National Museum of Ireland)

schools. But later, in the 7th century the doctrinal expressions of the expanding Roman Catholic power base could not allow man free religious thought, so once again the mysteries became occulted and deliberately hidden. It is only now that, with an understanding of the spiritual energy of light, these mysteries are again surfacing as man realises he is not a fallen sinful creature, but a part of the living Christ and the Sun and eternal.

Here is an understanding of how the lunula was used astronomically. Set out around the outlying edges of the Ross Lunula are the rises and sets of the Sun and maximum and minimum Moon phases. These are calculated for the latitude of Tara at 2000 BC and are as follows:

(Az = Azimuth)

Date	Az of Sun	Max rise	Min rise
20 March	88.2°	80.4°	97.8°
3 May	60.0°	50.9°	70.1°
21 June	45.4°	34.6°	56.9°
2 Nov.	117.0°	127.8°	108.8°
20 Dec.	131.7°	144.7°	122.7°

NB. Sun and Moon *set* positions are similar, of course, on the left half of the disc.

Now that we know the azimuth of the rises and sets we can calculate the height of the arc of Sun and Moon as they travel round the sky from morning to evening. Only a few of these arcs are shown; to put them all onto the diagram would obscure and confuse the illustration. For example, the Sun's path at 21st June, the summer solstice, when it is at its most northerly point on our horizon, can be calculated:

Time of sunrise	Elevation	Azimuth
0415 (am)	0°	45.4°
0600 (am)	19°	75.0°
0800 (am)	37°	99.0°
1000 (am)	53°	131.0°
1200 (noon)	60°	180.0°
		(due south)

We can calculate the various seasonal arcs for both the Sun and the Moon and then superimpose them onto the disc to see what happens. The obvious way to do this is to align the diagram with the disc in the normal position, i.e. with the 'horns' or flanges in the north and the bulge of the larger circle in the south. We see immediately that the various

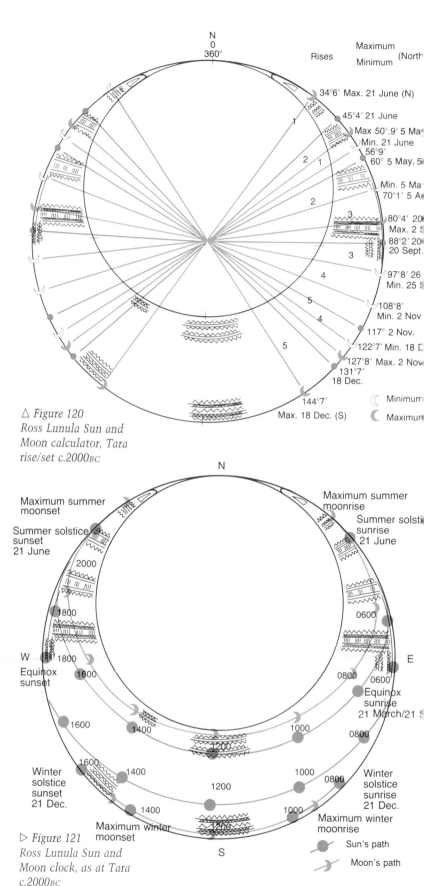

△ Figure 120
Ross Lunula Sun and
Moon calculator, Tara
rise/set c.2000BC

▷ Figure 121
Ross Lunula Sun and
Moon clock, as at Tara
c.2000BC

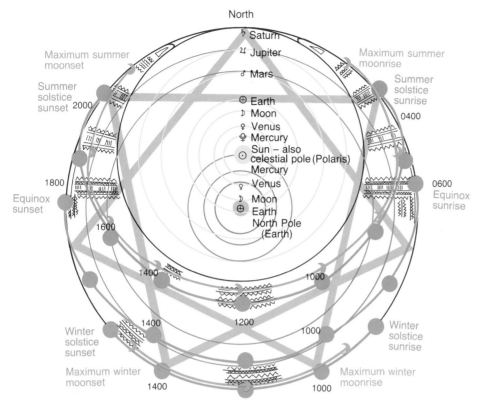

North
Saturn
Jupiter
Mars

Maximum summer moonset

Maximum summer moonrise

Summer solstice sunset 2000

Summer solstice sunrise
0400

⊕ Earth
☽ Moon
♀ Venus
☿ Mercury
⊙ Sun – also celestial pole (Polaris)
Mercury
♀ Venus
☽ Moon
⊕ Earth
North Pole (Earth)

1800

0600
Equinox sunrise

Equinox sunset

1600

1400   1000

1400   1200   1000

Winter solstice sunset

Winter solstice sunrise

Maximum winter moonset
1400

Maximum winter moonrise
1000

Noon 12 o'clock
South

Figure 122
Ross Lunula seven-fold symmetry

rising and setting points have significant equivalent markers on the disc. With the disc this way up we can therefore easily plot the Sun and Moon rises in the *summer* months of the year – from spring equinox, even to the hours of the day; so we have a clock.

However, because we have always assumed that this disc is 'jewellery' or adornment we have always depicted it only one way up. Reverse the disc so that the horns or flanges are pointing due south and envisage the template over the engravings the other way up and the secret of the dialling is simply revealed. Suddenly the paths of the Sun and Moon during the winter months are also disclosed by the graduated engraving on the 'horns'. It is an easy model to construct out of cardboard.

The engravings on the lunula are possibly a key to the dialling, the lateral engravings referring to the intervals of days/weeks during the year and also on the circular perimeter.

From the path of the Sun and Moon around the calculator we can now understand how SAM laid out his beautifully geometric circles and ellipses. Professor Thom, who is quoted in every book on megalithic art, has 'deciphered' many circles with a geometric progression that he has labelled as type 'A' and type 'B' flattened circles and type I and II egg-shaped circles, ovoids, etc. But here on the disc calculator are all the flattened circles and ovoids SAM needed. All SAM had to do was to

follow the path of the Sun and Moon around the ecliptic three-dimensionally and 'lay' that arc flat on the ground to give him, for instance, the flattened winter solstice perimeter of Newgrange. If we now plot the actual rising and setting points along the horizon of Newgrange, the position of the outer standing stones and the curb itself will conform to a winter solar orbit; and a 'disc' or 'lunula' duly flattened for that structure will evolve. No wonder the discovery of gold, the Sun metal, in Ireland was greeted so joyously as the large old structures could from then on be miniaturised on to those handsome instruments. The 'lunula' is actually an astronomical 'pocket' calculator, the origin of modern 11th–19th-century instruments – astrolabes and universal equinoctial calculators. These rising and setting points may be understood as aspects of the seven-fold symmetry of the light of the Sun (the seven vibrations of white light). Now we superimpose the geometric figure of seven onto the lunula and the markings become most clear as solar and lunar rising and setting points.

So what happened to this knowledge? A modern planisphere showing a map of the heavens gives another answer to the use of the lunula. It enables the observer to calculate the date, the day and the time of the year exactly by the position of the stars according to his accurate knowledge of the seasons. The Druidic wheel is the seasonal cycle from the

137

Figure 123
Ross Lunula
superimposed on a
Philip's Planisphere
(George Philip & Son)

birth of the age, year, month and day to the very hour. The Church still perpetuates the 4 × 6 hour cycle intoning the angelus bell at midday, twelve o'clock, and 6 pm. After 6 pm the 'clock' moves towards seven o'clock, i.e. its 'sevening' or 'the evening' – towards sundown.

The planisphere is used by turning the disc against the correct seasonal day time of the nature cycle then facing the required direction of observation. Hold the disc over your head looking up through the inner perimeter (the zenith) with your eye and with the midnight point due north. The stars showing will coincide with the natural time of the year.

SAM used it the other way round. By knowing where the stars and planets were he was then able to calculate the date of the season.

Illustrated are three more 'lunulae' in the form of an English jet necklace marked out with the same solar engravings on the separators; an Egyptian lunula 'calculator', also constructed as a necklace (note that instead of flanges at the ends, it has the sky-hawk's heads, i.e. Horus = hours = time); and a tiny Portuguese 'earring' which is really a miniature, single, pendant, lunula calculator. Ancient artefacts as (ritual) calculators are the origins of modern jewellery, pendants, necklaces, crowns, tiaras, rings, etc.

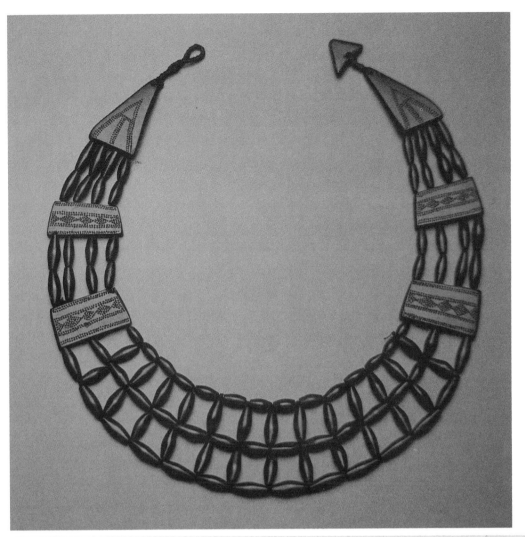

*Figure 124
English Yorkshire jet
necklace (lunula)*

*Figure 125
Egyptian winged collar
(lunula)*

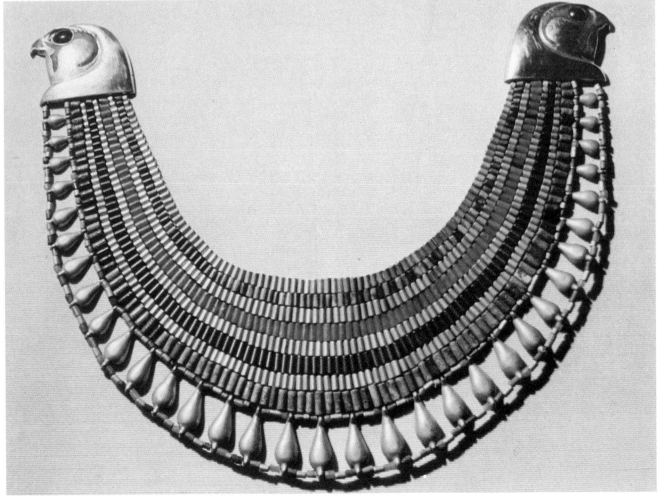

Figure 126
Portuguese 'earring'
(calculator)

Actual size

In Chapter I we saw how P/E *the Sun fraction* was arrived at by the polar rotation of thirty-seven days over the equatorial rotation of twenty-six days. However, if we include the movement of the Earth 'W' in this calculation, the fraction changes as the Earth's movement adds drag to the calculation which becomes

$$\frac{42}{28} \text{ or } \frac{6 \times 7}{4 \times 7} \text{ or } \frac{3}{2} = \frac{1.5}{1}$$

Remember the Sun's energy changes the Earth's polarity from plus to minus every seven days. Here, therefore, we have a solar calculator or rather what is now called a biorhythm calculator. As already mentioned, the actual proportion of the lunulae generally seems to be

$$\frac{3}{2} \text{ or } \frac{1.5}{1}$$

A pair of circular repoussé gold discs in the musuem collection in Dublin are thought to have been sewn on a dress, but once again examination shows they are carefully constructed calculators. They are very similar, and the two central pinholes were probably for securing them to either a leather or a wooden backing. There are two circles of zig-zags, repeating the proportion of two (inner) and three (outer) circumferences. As will be seen from the figure the outer zig-zags depict the twenty-eight day calendar. If you will accept

this, it is not a big step to see that the solstices and equinoxes, and no doubt the movement of the planets and stars, can be foreseen. The number of punched dots within the geometric patterns also have a mathematical significance. The imprint of the zig-zags is a much more sensible way of showing the rise and fall of a celestrial body rather than the clock-face method that we normally use – for seemingly the Moon rises and sets as does the Sun ∧∧ .

'Dress Fasteners' and Bracelets
Many so-called 'dress fasteners' have been found dating to the Bronze Age and from their shape there is no reason why they should not at least have been used to adorn a wrist, yet again they have never been found in conjunction with a corpse, so we must assume they had other uses. The flanged and flared ends of the object shown in Figure 128 suggest that it could have been attached as a handle to a large vessel, but nothing like this has ever been discovered. If we now go back to the illustration of the large stone balls found at Loughcrew and elsewhere (Figures 91–93) and the explanation of their use as geometric calculators we can now link them to these gold 'handles'. If we hold this object in our hand with an outstretched arm and with our clairvoyant sight picture a sphere sitting snugly on the two flanges, then from within its shape we

▷ *Figure 127*
Gold Sun disc
(National Museum of Ireland)

Half size

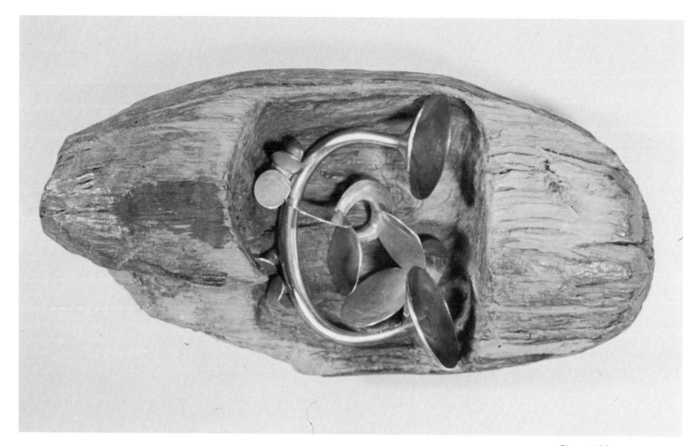

Figure 128
Gold 'dress fasteners'
in original keepsafe
(National Museum of
Ireland)

can 'see' the pentagonal form we recognise in sacred geometry. By moving our arm closer to or further from our eye, just as an artist does with his pencil to get perspectives, we can then project this geometry three-dimensionally onto any given piece of landscape.

The illustration shows a 'dress fastener' from the collection of the National Museum which was found in a bog, carefully hidden in its own wooden case, showing how the priesthood of the Bronze Age had treasured it and kept it safe.

Figure 129
Geometry of Irish
'dress fasteners'
(calculators)

This gold dress fastener was found in the accompanying wooden box in the early 19th century. The box is made of alder and is of very simple construction being carved from a single piece of wood. The recesses in the bottom of the box are made to receive the terminals of the dress fasteners.

Gold dress fasteners were made from solid bar gold in circular cross-section. There are several recorded examples of gold objects found in rather crude wooden boxes including a lunula from Crossdoney, County Cavan, and a gold dress fastener and three gold bracelets from Kilmoyley North, County Kerry.

(National Museum of Ireland,
Treasures of Ireland)

*Figure 130
Gold torc (measuring rod or coils – origin unknown)*

Torcs

The museums have suggested that these are waist torcs – like stiff metal belts, since they have mainly been found curled in a wide circle and fastened by bending the end flanges together, but really they are quite impractical for this purpose and would be extremely uncomfortable to wear. In this shape they are easy to carry however, but this seems inconclusive as where would they be carried to if they were an integral part of a 'ritual' of an important centre such as Tara? Also they were not a form of currency.

The first possible use is that they were the priest's measuring rod. In the New Testament of the Bible we find in *Relevations* Chapter 21:15 'and he who talked with me had a measuring rod of golden reed to measure the city and its gates and its walls'.

The careful twisting of the flanged gold would give an accurate measurement along its length if the 'belt' was straightened out. The rod, or 'Tara torc', in the National Museum of Ireland has an extension on one end of the body which looks remarkably like the core or centre for a straight wooden handle; then it really would have been a rod. What are the

Figure 131
Bronze box and gold
torc (National Museum
of Ireland)

different lengths of the torcs that have been found? It is not possible to get this information as they have not been meausred and, of course, no museum is going to take the responsibility of unrolling or straightening a torc to gauge it.

Alternatively we know that gold is a brilliant conductor of electricity, a holder of energy. The torc has been found in other forms – literally coiled as if around a space or central core, the ends being the 'terminals'.

Such a coil, flanged as it is along its own length, and then coiled with terminals at each end, suggests the centre of some energy attracting device. We know from the passage stones at Newgrange how the life force energy is coiled around the length of the passage as part of that great generator. Could it be that these gold torcs were a miniaturisation of this whole passage system and became the new tool of the scientists of the age? Once again none of these early Irish gold objects has been found in conjunction with a burial or a corpse – they have all been located separately. If the torcs – the extensive ones – were to do with the major structures then the smaller torcs may also have had another scientific purpose far removed from adorning the neck, yet surely to do with the Sun.

Figure 131 shows the bronze circular box in which a smaller torc was found. Look carefully at the lid of the box and note the engraved concentric circles that are offset to the entwined expanding coils – this is repoussé decoration, i.e. pushed up three-dimensionally from

behind. It suggests the amplification of sound, maybe the solar wind. Inside there is a twisted, flanged gold torc and three studs which are for holding and securing something within – could this have been a piece of quartz or crystal? Perhaps we are back to the resonating earphone and the cat's whisker of the crystal set such as we had as boys fifty years ago.

If we take another look at the cairns themselves perhaps they begin to take another 'shape or purpose'. With only earth, air, fire and water SAM had placed his structures carefully to attract maximum energy from both the planet and the Sun. Were not the cairns within this vibrant grid receivers of all the frequencies and energies we now know as ultra-violet/X-rays and radio waves, and if so, who was communicating with whom? If you can accept that there are extra-terrestrial 'travellers' in space moving superluminarily through the solar system then 'why on Earth' should not some early priests have come from amongst them, to teach and help on our planet and communicate?

Latchet Brooches

The latchet brooches of Ireland are also enigmatic little bronze pieces thought to be 'fasteners' yet if the geometry is drawn out it is easy to see how they project four quarters which, with the 14 (7 × 2) spirals in the centre and the engraved zig-zags on the open arm, immediately tell us that they are seven-day Sun calculators, or 'biorhythmic' calculators.

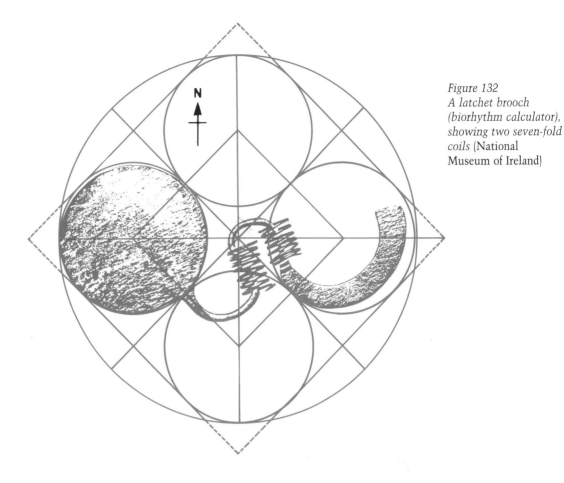

Figure 132
A latchet brooch
(biorhythm calculator),
showing two seven-fold
coils (National
Museum of Ireland)

The Tara Brooch

The most famous of all Irish artefacts is the beautiful early Christian equinoctial ring calculator mistakenly called a 'penannular *brooch*'. This piece was found in the mid-19th century at Bettystown on the seashore of County Meath and ended up in the hands of a jeweller in Dublin who copied it and exhibited facsimiles at the Great Exhibition in London in 1851.

The official description of this 'brooch' is as follows:

> *made of cast silver-gilt with gold fili-gree, amber and polychrome glass orn-aments. Diameter of ring 8.7cm, maximum width of terminal plate 4.55cm, length of pin 32cm, weight 224.36gms.*

Actually this is a comparatively small example alongside some of the enormous ones in the museum, and although this is just small enough to wear in a plaid shawl thrown across the shoulders it is really quite impractical. So it has been called a 'brooch' for want of any understanding of its true purposes. You will note it even has a carrying strap of plaited silver-gilt wire from its side. The National Museum

states that the name 'Tara Brooch' was given it by the jewellers and no-one in modern times, seemingly, has seen its close connection to the royal site or its inherent geometry.

However, in Egyptian history we read of Akhnaton, the pharaoh, who killed his father and married his mother by whom he had a daughter. His mother was Queen Ti. The modern name Tara is derived from Teamur – Tea-Mur, the wall of the Queen of Egypt. Wall can be translated as 'earthern bank' in Irish.

In the following verse translated from the poem 'Temark II' from the *Dun Senchas*, Book of Leinster version, we read:

> *Brega Tea – the teeming home*
> *Is famed because Ti was a noble dame*
> *The funeral mound under which is the*
> *   great one of the standards –*
> *The burying ground which was never*
> *   rifled –*
> *The daughter of Pharaoh with tale of*
> *   warriors*
> *Tephi the bright who used cross, the hill*
> *   –*
>
> *Slope framed a stronghold (handy the*
> *   labourer)*
> *WITH HER STAFF AND WITH HER*
> *BROOCH SHE TRACED IT*

Figure 133
The Tara Brooch
(National Museum of
Ireland)

Before we can understand the use of the calculator (for that is exactly what it is), we must unravel the basic geometry of the piece step-by-step. Here Peter Dawkins stepped in with his expertise as an architect and draughtsman.

Let's take the geometry step-by-step. In the first diagram you will find the basic geometry of the six-pointed star, drawn as the first circle and then the six other circles drawn round it which divide the circle into six. Then, from one of the arms of that star the first triangle can be drawn as shown. This is the fundamental of all geometry. In the second diagram you can see added in the big triangle that forms one half of the great six-pointed star that fills the initial circle. I have also drawn in two other lines that derive directly from the bigger star figure, which we will need in finding out the centre of the circle.

1

2

3a

3b

4

5

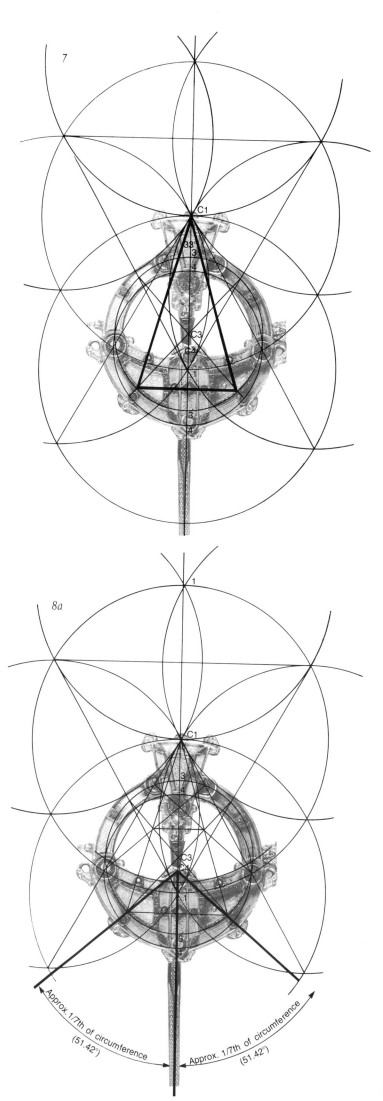

Diagrams 3(a) and 3(b) will show you how the centre of circle 4 is found. It is in the mid-point of the base of the smaller triangle whose apex is the centre of circle. 1. Diagram 4 gives you the next horizontal line needed for finding the centre of circle 3. Diagram 5 completes the geometric lines to give you the centre of circle 3 and I have shown both circles 4 and 3 drawn on this.

These two circles, circles 3 and 4, are slightly different sizes and they are offset by that small amount that you can see. This is a critical offset and allows the geometers to derive some amazing geometric solutions. I have not come across this before until I looked at the Tara Brooch and it is really quite wonderful. It eventually gives us a way to divide a circle up into sevenths.

Diagram 6 begins to show how the next figure of importance is found, namely the 33° triangle; Diagram 7 goes on to show you this triangle drawn out. The angle of the apex is the 33° one and this is highly significant as you know. Again, it is not normally very easy to find a geometric way to draw a 33° triangle, but here it is. Magnificent!

Diagram 8 shows the whole lot,

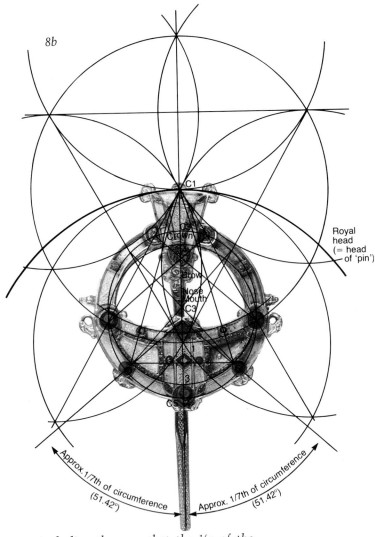

8b

Royal
head
(= head
of 'pin')

Approx. 1/7th of circumference
(51.42°)

Approx. 1/7th of circumference
(51.42°)

because of the age of the brooch and the way the photography has been made of it, but at least it is near enough to show you that this geometry is really intended and that the design of the brooch is derived from it.

In Diagram 8(a) you can also see how the centre of the crown chakra of the 'king' is found. This disc is coloured yellow on the brooch head. The centre of it is not found exactly by the two lines drawn in. On Diagram 8(b) those two lines are as if marking the centre of this crown chakra. In actual fact, when you look at the photograph of the brooch this is not quite so. However, this is the best geometric arrangement that gets anywhere near marking this crown chakra. Surely it was meant because it gave rise to a little triangle which delineated the eyes and the brow and top of the head of the man, and this is a very important triangle indeed. The horizontal base of that triangle goes right through the bridge of the nose. As the whole face is a summary of the whole body of man himself – that is to say, it shows the whole law in the face, just as the whole body shows the whole law of God – so the bridge of the nose actually marks the heart centre in terms of the face. By 'bridge' is meant the point just a little below the eyes. The two eyes of the face of the man lie just above this triangle base and the apex of the triangle delineates the actual brain, of which the two hemispheres are showing beautifully as the two coils (or as shown in other traditions, as two ram's horns). The mouth and nostrils lie lower down below the base of this small triangle, as you can see, and the mouth, again, has been found already by one of the geometric lines that helped us find the centre of circle 3.

From the head of this illuminated man the crown rises us beautifully with the golden disc marking the crown chakra itself and (Diagram 9) the great crown resembling a very big version of a pharaoh's crown. The arc of the top of this huge crown is formed as being on the arc of a fifth circle whose centre is right down at the bottom of the brooch (as shown marked) and in this way they have joined root with the crown in a rather amazing way – or perhaps I should say, sacral with crown, because if we count the bosses going up the

including the way that the 1/7s of the circle are found and clearly this was one of the functions of the brooch, because if you know where the centre of circle 4 is, which is actually easier to find on the brooch once you know its whereabouts, then the two smaller bosses on the outer circle of the brooch will give you the sitings for dividing the circles into sevenths (including the main axis). The 33° is delineated by the other two small bosses which are coloured in green, that fall on the two lines of the 33° triangle; and so the owner of the brooch, knowing where circle 1 is at the top of the pin, would soon be able to construct his 33° triangle from the centre of 1 down to the two smaller bosses that are coloured green. The designers of the brooch have in this way occulted the actual geometry that gives rise to that triangle. As you can see, it is very clever indeed.

You can see that in places the geometric lines do not pass exactly through the centre of the circles. This is probably

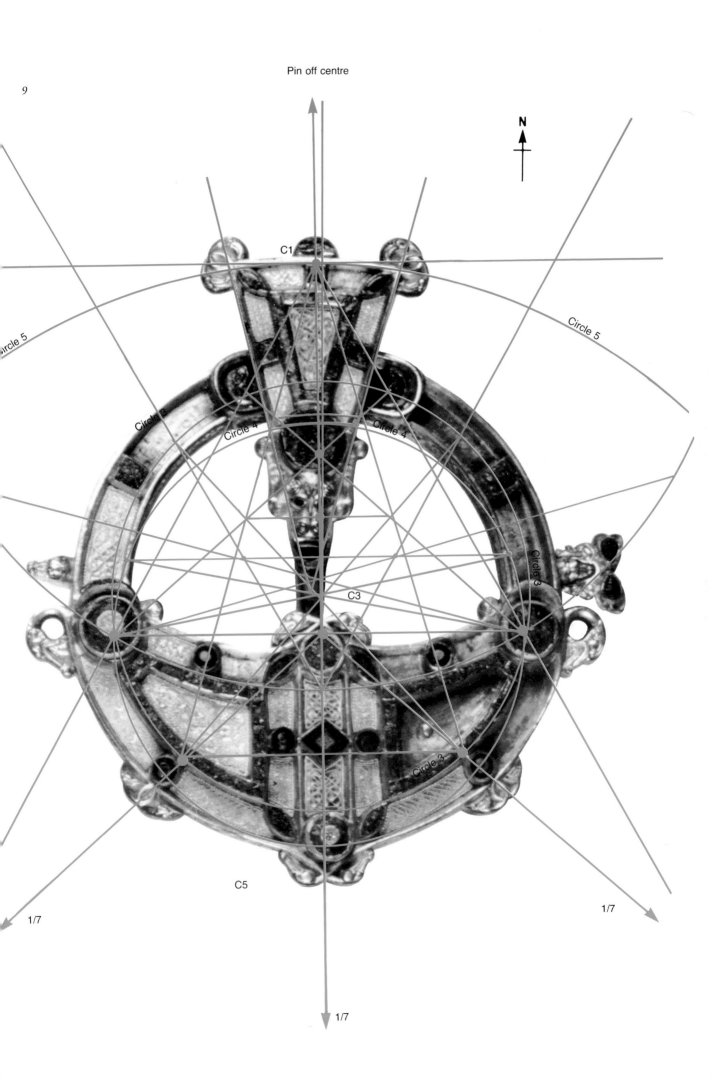

Pin off centre

9

N

C1

Circle 5

Circle 5

Circle 3

Circle 4

Circle 4

Circle 3

C3

Circle 3

C5

1/7

1/7

1/7

brooch we find the lower boss could represent the sacral chakra. The next boss (which is diamond-shaped) could represent the solar plexus. The next boss, I am almost certain, represents the heart (and this is associated with the centre of circle 4). The next boss (i.e. the centre of circle 3) is not marked by a boss but lies on the pin of the brooch, midway between the heart boss and the mouth of the face on the head of the pin. This centre, I think, marks the throat chakra. It is strange how it is occulted but perhaps this has great significance. The next chakra is marked by the centre point between the eyes on the face of the

head of the pin, which, of course, is marked by the final circular boss above the head.

The two big bosses on the left- and right-hand side of the brooch indicate the left and right arms and hands, and from those hands rises up the rainbow or arc which is the Ark of the Covenant. The complete arc, or arch, is actually a whole circle and so the circle carries down below the hands, and in this case down the sacral chakra, or what would appear to be the sacral chakra, which is cabbalistically the principle called Yessod, or Foundation, the place where all things are generated or procreated. I

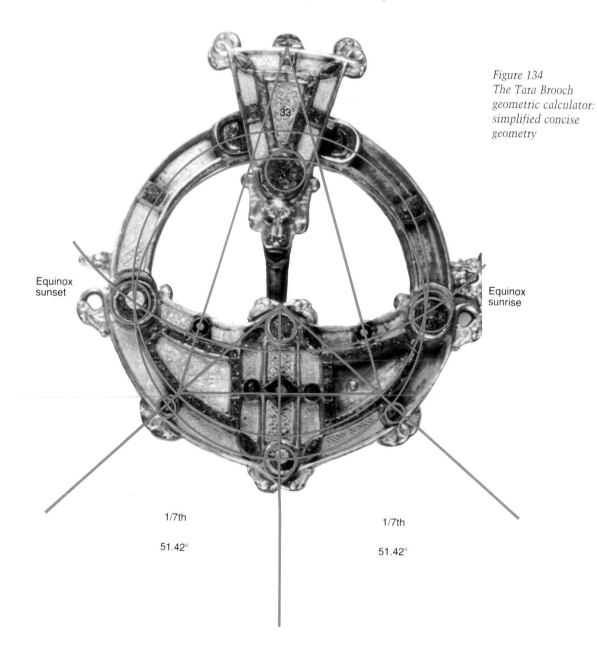

Figure 134
The Tara Brooch
geometric calculator:
simplified concise
geometry

33°

Equinox
sunset

Equinox
sunrise

1/7th

51.42°

1/7th

51.42°

think the root chakra must be intended by the actual ground itself into which the pin of the brooch is stuck – because in this brooch is the whole temple complete and beautifully drawn.

The Tara Brooch is complicated geometry but it is very wonderful. Every geometric figure had a particular meaning. What is so marvellous is that the whole thing begins from the basis of the six-pointed star which is the greater universe, then the brooch itself is one part of that universe, i.e. at one point of the six-pointed star like a planet revolving around its Sun. Then, furthermore, out of the brooch itself comes the head of the king or illuminated man with his great crown upon his head and this is, of course, as it should be, the head of the so-called pin of the brooch itself. It is a fabulous head, especially as the geometry defines the features of that beautiful head and the carving on the face itself delineates different energies of that face. The face is a great key because the face reveals divinity, it is the 'countenance of the Lord'. Yet it is also (and quite rightly so) this head of man which controls the directions that the brooch can give. The arm of the pin is the axis/spine of that man and this is what can be swung in different directions; or indeed, actually spiked into the ground and the arc of the brooch swung around to coincide with the arc of the horizon and of the rising stars, etc. From this, sitings can be made and the geometry drawn out on the ground ready for the building of the temples and the working of the energies.

(Peter Dawkins, The Gatekeeper Trust)

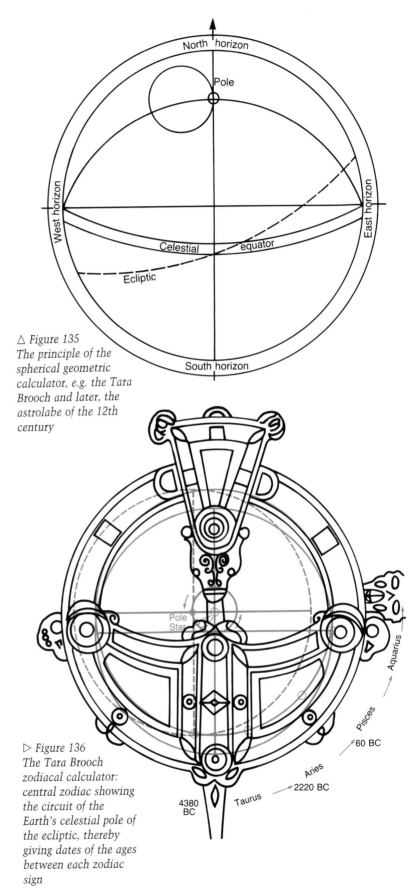

△ Figure 135
The principle of the spherical geometric calculator, e.g. the Tara Brooch and later, the astrolabe of the 12th century

After all these hundreds of years since the Tara 'Brooch' was discarded on the shore at Bettystown, probably by some fleeing Viking robber, its secrets are being unfurled again.

From this geometry several other possibilities arise. What, for instance, is the meaning of the two interlocking circles occulted within its frame and why should the pin or spike travel around its frame? Here are shown the movements of Planet Earth from one great age to the next.

As the Earth turns around its pole it is, at the same time, spiralling through space around its central solar father, the Sun, and once again, as with the lunula, we can depict this duality of the Earth/Sun/Earth centres.

▷ Figure 136
The Tara Brooch zodiacal calculator: central zodiac showing the circuit of the Earth's celestial pole of the ecliptic, thereby giving dates of the ages between each zodiac sign

153

The dimensions of the Earth in relation to the Moon have always held a fascinaton as we are told that the Great Pyramid – Pi-Ra-Mid – has these proportions built into it. This is beautifully shown on the Tara Brooch in the relationship between the main frame and the pin-head since half the frame represents the radius (Ra-Di[Day]-Us) of the Earth to half the pin-head representing the radius of the Moon in proportion.

Since this book is really about the dimensions and actuality of light or seven-fold symmetry it is lovely to realise that the sum total of the radius of Earth and Moon, 3,960 miles and 1,080 miles, equals 5,040 which, broken down, gives the simple multiplication of $1 \times 2 \times 3 \times 4 \times 5 \times 6 \times 7 = 5,040$ – the fulfilment of light – and this also gives us the Pyramid angle of 51.42°, the division of the circle into one-sevenths.

For what reason is it do you think that the British Isles have always been held very sacred in all mythology, as the islands of Hyperborea? The Pyramid angle gives us the clue of 51.42°

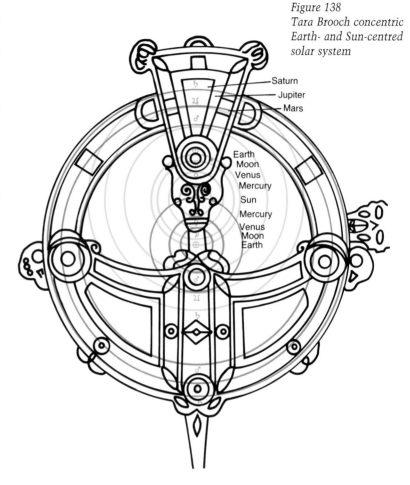

Figure 138
Tara Brooch concentric Earth- and Sun-centred solar system

Saturn
Jupiter
Mars

Earth
Moon
Venus
Mercury
Sun
Mercury
Venus
Moon
Earth

Figure 137
19th-century universal equinoctial calculator

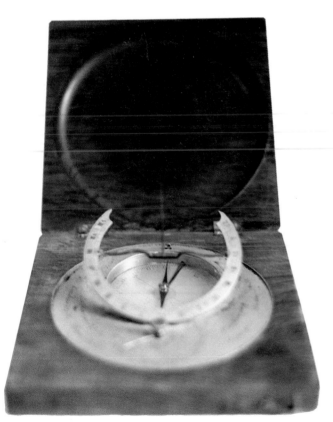

– for we subtend that angle here at our latitude from the centre of the Earth. Here is also the magical point of the Sun's arc (ark) at the summer solice mid-day point over our islands, for it is the arc of the summer Sun that gives us the Ark of the Covenant or the arc of the Golden Mean proportion – the most sacred proportion of all geometry.

Once again, if we now plot the arc of the Sun and Moon around the frame of the Tara Brooch we can easily use it as a clock from the solstice summer and winter points and the Moon's more complicated but similar paths, rise and set points. So far the Tara Brooch has given us predictable information just as a hand-held calculator but why is it that no-one has ever

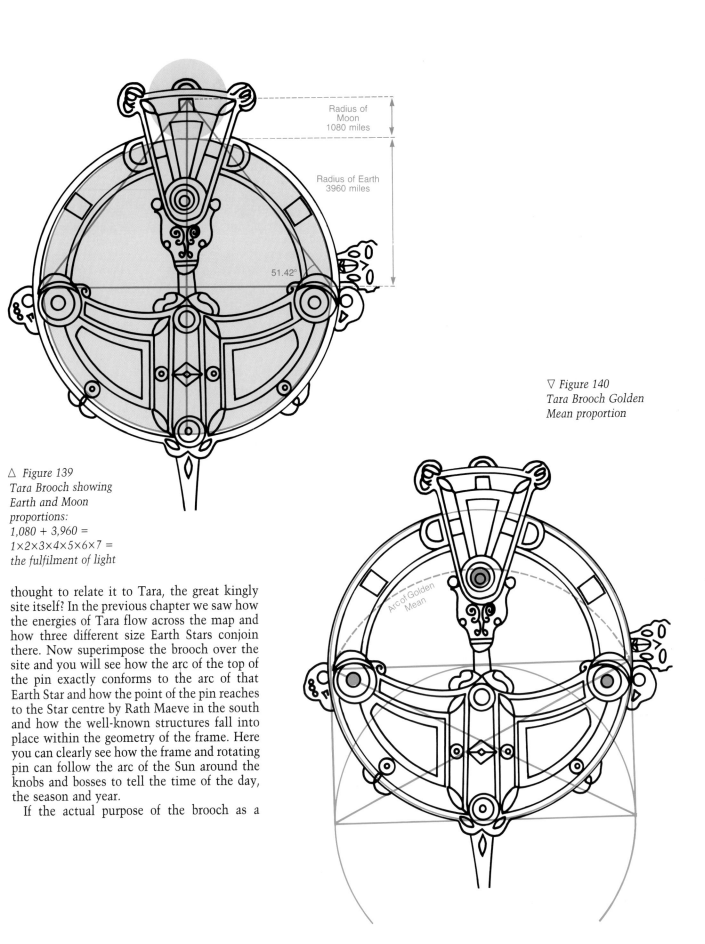

Radius of
Moon
1080 miles

Radius of Earth
3960 miles

51.42°

△ Figure 139
Tara Brooch showing
Earth and Moon
proportions:
1,080 + 3,960 =
1×2×3×4×5×6×7 =
the fulfilment of light

▽ Figure 140
Tara Brooch Golden
Mean proportion

Arc of Golden
Mean

thought to relate it to Tara, the great kingly site itself? In the previous chapter we saw how the energies of Tara flow across the map and how three different size Earth Stars conjoin there. Now superimpose the brooch over the site and you will see how the arc of the top of the pin exactly conforms to the arc of that Earth Star and how the point of the pin reaches to the Star centre by Rath Maeve in the south and how the well-known structures fall into place within the geometry of the frame. Here you can clearly see how the frame and rotating pin can follow the arc of the Sun around the knobs and bosses to tell the time of the day, the season and year.

If the actual purpose of the brooch as a

temple calculator seems remarkable, there is more to come. Now reverse the brooch and place the pin-head at the southern point with the pin pointing due north and here the 'Hall of Tara' fits into the crescent of the lower part of the frame and the brooch is seen also to fit exactly the other way up, i.e. south to north. But surely that is impossible! But is it? Apparently from early records, certainly in South America's Inca/Mexican/Aztec civilisations, it is suggested that around AD 500 the Earth's magnetic field turned completely on its axis and magnetic north became south. Perhaps this incredible instrument shows this too.

▽ *Figure 141*
The Tara Brooch on the structures of Tara, Co. Meath (north/south)

▽ *Figure 142*
The Tara Brooch on the structures of Tara, Co. Meath (south/north)

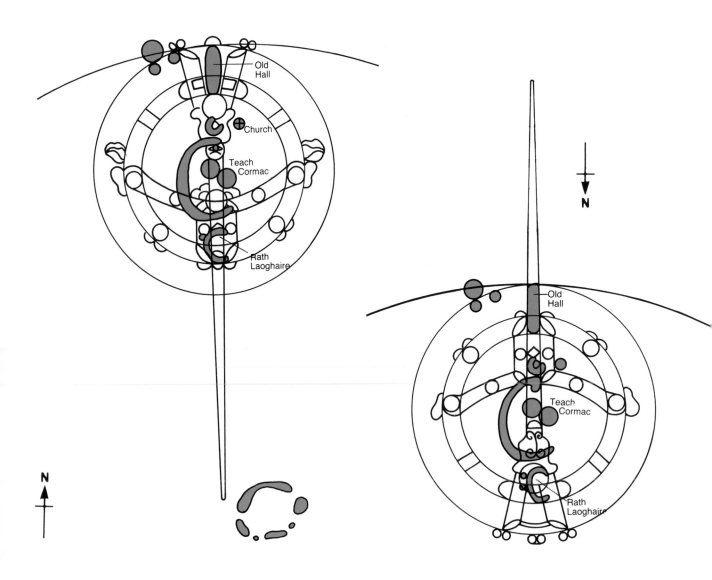

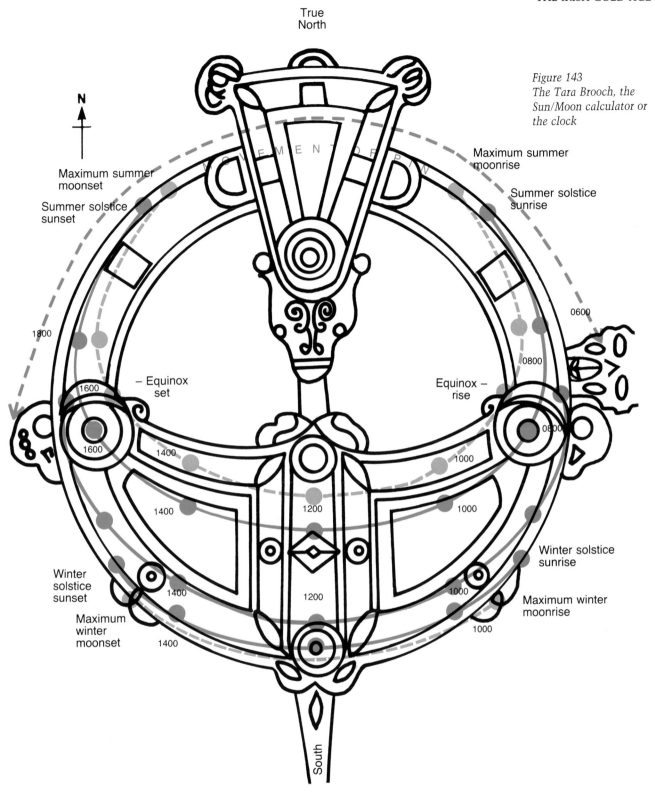

True
North

N
↑

Figure 143
The Tara Brooch, the
Sun/Moon calculator or
the clock

Maximum summer
moonset

Maximum summer
moonrise

Summer solstice
sunset

Summer solstice
sunrise

0600

1800

0800

– Equinox
set

Equinox –
rise

1600

0800

1600

1400

1000

1400

1200

1000

Winter
solstice
sunset

Winter solstice
sunrise

1400

1200

1000

Maximum
winter
moonset

Maximum winter
moonrise

1400

1000

South

We have already plotted the Sun and Moon rising and setting points on the lunula for Tara in 2000 BC. If we transpose those points onto the Tara Brooch now around the arc of the ecliptic for the different seasons of the year, it is easy to see that the brooch performed as an accurate clock, for the different months of the year and also from day to day (dei to dei) and hour to hour. Note how the summer solstice Sun at twelve noon gives us the arc of the Golden Mean.

There are many calculators similar to the Tara Brooch but generally not as important. It is the royal 'brooch' and comparable to an 18ct gold Rolex Oyster watch – just as the Ross Lunula is an instrument of great sophistication and some of the lesser lunulae are virtually unengraved and look coarse in comparison and are annotated by the archaeologists as provincial.

Now we can begin to look at other artefacts from other countries to see if we can find a thread of similar geometry to substantiate the 'template' of the Tara Brooch. First let us go back to the 'tombs' of the Sun King himself, Tutankhamun of Egypt. In Figure 144 we see the Royal Pectoral Pendant of the Winged Scarab, representing the Sun and topped by the Moon disc. Put the Tara template over this piece and draw on the geometry using the same format and descriptions (Figure 145).

The Sun centre is the scarab and the arc of the Sun's travels around the brooch is clearly shown from equinox to equinox at left and right where there are red carnelians set. There is no need to spend time describing in detail

Figure 144
Tutankhamun's
pendant

Figure 145
The geometry of
Tutankhamun's
pendant

what this picture diagram tells us clearly. So let us move on to a whale-bone plaque, quite a common artefact of Northern Scandinavia. This one is in the Bergen Museum in Norway, dating supposedly to Viking times, and once again we see with lovely simplicity the over-lay of the geometry fitting the design clearly and conforming this knowledge. The design even looks very Egyptian with the stylised horses' heads having palmetts as mouths, yet showing the arcs of the Sun's path reflecting the Golden Mean.

Figure 146
Norwegian whale-bone plaque showing Golden Mean proportion
'Stop press'
A similar Viking whalebone plaque has just been unearthed in the Orkney's, reported December 1991

Figure 147
Norwegian whale-bone
plaque as a calculator

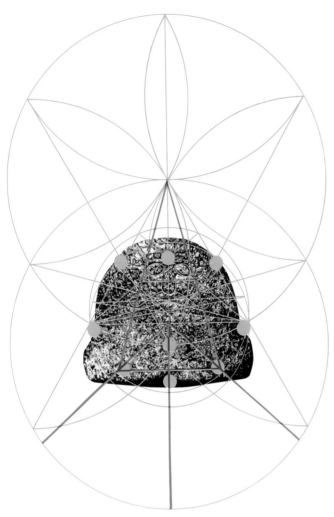

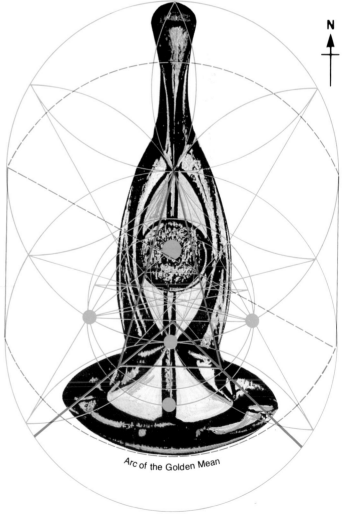

△ *Figure 148*
Danish hearth stone
head and geometry

▽ *Figure 149*
Fibula brooch, La Tène
culture, and geometry

Next let us look at two stone figures, the first from Denmark and called a Viking hearth stone or bellows stone. Clearly the engravings on the stone face mark exactly the same conformation of this seven-fold geometry of light.

Then we can look at the simple little object well known in the Bronze Age here of the *La Tène* culture, called a fibula. Straight away we see how the form suggests a marriage of the female and male sexuality but depicted in six-fold and seven-fold geometry, a perfect marriage of the material Mother Earth meeting the masculine energy of procreation – in this case the mutation of light into matter. The arc of the Golden Mean is even included in the curve around the base.

Figure 150
Irish standing stone
head and geometry.
Note Egyptian-style
face and posture

If we come back to Northern Ireland and County Fermanagh, we can see how a well-known stone figure again gives us the same geometry. This face, with its crossed arms, reminds us of the pharaoh. Surely in all these diagrams we can see that it is the face of man that projects this divine proportion and again we are reminded that man is made in the image of God as the Bible tells us, for the human face from chin to brow and ear to ear conforms to the path of the Sun as it travels around the Earth and as the Earth travels, in turn, around the Sun.

163

It would be possible to show artefact after artefact from museums all over the world that give us the clues to the ancient widsom tradition that is so securely hidden from us by programmed education and religious bigotry, the mistaken idea that everything pre-Christian is 'pagan' and therefore evil. The history of art and mathematics needs to be rewritten and retaught. In the case of so many beautiful objects, often weapons, the symbology of this wisdom tradition has been built in almost as a protection to the user. The greatest surviving artefacts were the property of the rulers – kings, priests and great warriors. So often their knowledge was even put into their weapons for added protection.

Illustrated here is a 'Sun shield'. Count the bosses or dots on it, circle by circle, and they read as follows: from the centre there are *seven* rings with 22/34/44/53/65/73 knobs – this totals, when multiplied together, 8,276,874,320 which happens to be $^2\sqrt{} \times 7$ P/E (Polar Equatorial Sun differential). Since 1.42 is the solar fraction and there are seven vibrations of white light this may be expressed more easily as $^{10}\!\!/\!\!_7{}^{(64)}$, very significant numbers indeed. What greater protection could a warrior need than the shield of light?

Figure 151
Irish Bronze Age
shield, Lough Gur
(National Museum of
Ireland)

Figure 152
An astronomical
observatory, built to
sacred geometry, a
'church' on Inis Mor
(Arran Islands, Galway,
Ireland) 7th century AD

Chapter XII
THE PLANETARY STAR OF HYPERBOREA
The Seven-fold Symmetry of Light in SAM's World

Up to now we have seen how SAM measured and built many of his structures to the symmetry of six with his knowledge of the crystal structures and the equilateral Earth Star patterns. However, in the previous chap-ter, we have also explored some early artefacts that show us how he worked with the seven-fold symmetry of light. Here we will see how the Star of 'seven' is incorporated within the centre of the Earth Star. We can draw the

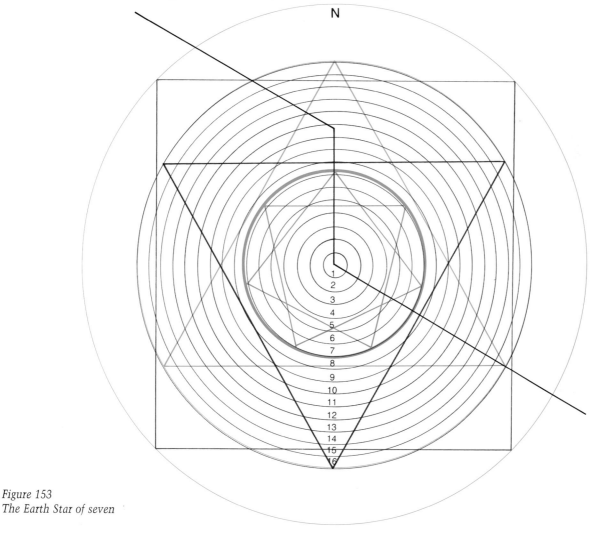

N

S

Figure 153
The Earth Star of seven

centre of the Earth Star (Figure 153) to conform to the seven-pointed light star.

Carnac

One of the most sacred places was undoubtedly Carnac in Brittany, France, where SAM measured and regulated the life force through the medium of the Sun, the Moon and the Earth. Today at Carnac there are still over 1,670 standing stones arranged in eleven rows covering some two miles.

At the top left-hand corner of the map is the Chapelle of St. Laurent. The centre of this quadrant of the grid is in six-fold symmetry laid down from the highest point of the landscape – a spot height of 43 metres (about 150 feet) above sea level, approximately 200 metres to the east of the *chapelle*. From this vantage point the whole area could be seen, all the way down to the sea and out into Carnac Bay – particularly to the man-made tumulus of St. Michael to the east and the tumulus on the natural hill at Kercado to the west.

The alignments are towards the ecliptic Moon/Sun rise and the equinoxes of spring and autumn, allowing the pathway of the stones to project bands of light between stone after stone and row upon row, so that the speed of light might be measured as the Sun was gradually obscured at eclipse. At the east (sunrise) end, the structure at Kerlescan is laid out in the Golden Mean proportion; similarly in the west at Le Menec.

The light starting at Kerlescan travels through Manio II and Kermario and eventually finishes its course at Le Menec in the west. In each of these structures there is a particular stone, later known as the *pierre sacrée* (sacred stone) and in one sense they are just that, because, acting as vast reflectors on the same principle as the basins at Newgrange, they reflect and refract light into the sacred sculptured space of the egg-shape of the Golden Mean 'cromlechs'.

A beautiful stone reflector mirror (sacred stone) lies unrecognised at Kermario, called Les Jumelles (the Twins). It is split in two down the centre. Often in modern times, the Church particularly wished to destroy the magical stones of old sites, and the only way they could achieve this was to heat the stones with charcoal and split them in half, the heat dissipating quickly with cold water, thereby contracting the material, just like putting out a camp fire with a bucket of water and seeing stones crack. Avebury had many of its stones split and removed this way in the last century.

People often wonder why the alignments are not laid out in straight lines instead of the

undulating course the stones take across the landscape. The answer is that they follow the course of the water table which flows close under the surface at Carnac. For it is these water courses, running through old granite only six feet underground, that activate the structure and help accelerate the life force from end to end of that linear generator, from day to night. Here we have a light factory with energy directed along its course from one pole to the other – one symmetry to the other. It is through the egg-shaped curved stone structures of Le Menec and Kerlescan that the energy really builds up, allowing a quantum leap throgh time and space. The solar wind changes the polarity of the Earth energies every seven days from (+) to (−) along the length of the standing stones.

Figure 154
Carnac: 'Les Alignements'
Note: Pierre sacrée mirror/reflector

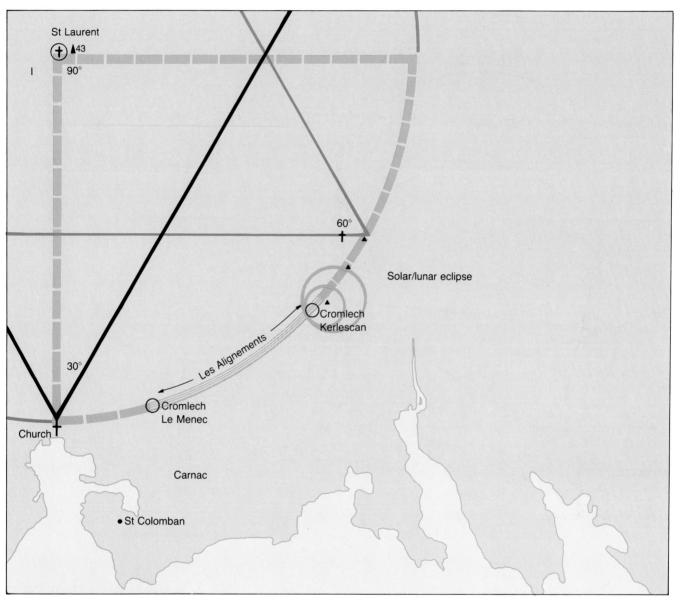

St Laurent

43

90°

60°

Solar/lunar eclipse

Cromlech
Kerlescan

Les Alignements

30°

Cromlech
Le Menec

Church

Carnac

St Colomban

△ Figure 155
The quadrant of Les
Alignements

◁ Figure 156
Pierre sacrée, Le Menec
mirror/reflector

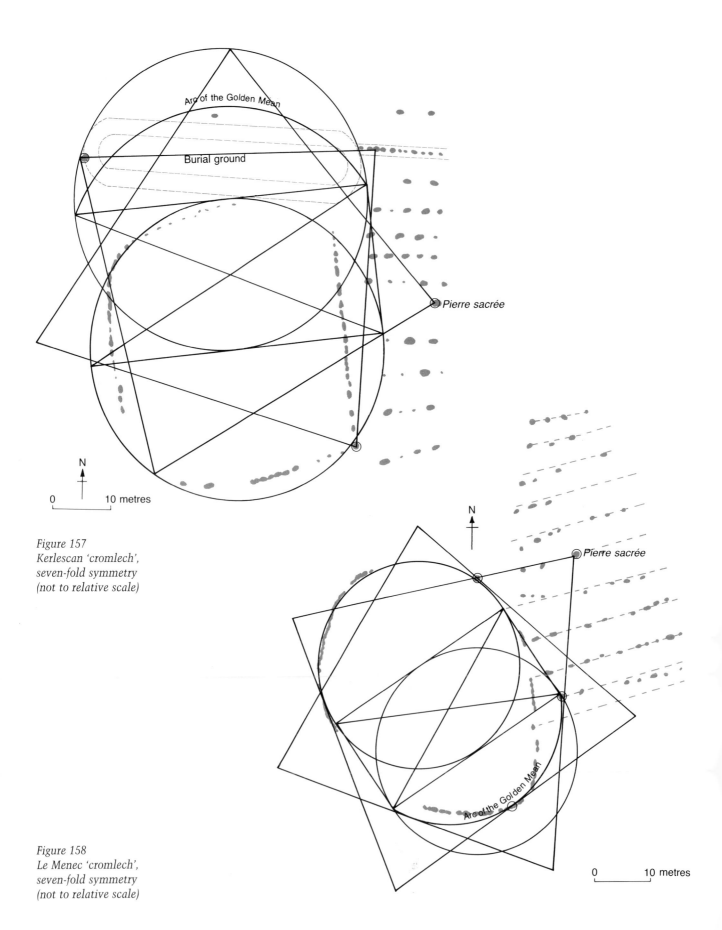

Arc of the Golden Mean

Burial ground

Pierre sacrée

N

0   10 metres

Figure 157
*Kerlescan 'cromlech',
seven-fold symmetry
(not to relative scale)*

N

Pierre sacrée

Arc of the Golden Mean

0   10 metres

Figure 158
*Le Menec 'cromlech',
seven-fold symmetry
(not to relative scale)*

Now look at the artefacts on display in the Carnac Museum and note many beautiful axes and pendulums, also some strange circular serpentine discs. Serpentine is the same basic material as steatite and soapstone and was readily adapted by SAM for his tools. Here SAM has fashioned his ritual objects as a compass and divider of the circle, the basic tools of geometry which together with a pendulum (the museum is full of them, either strung as necklaces or hanging as loom weights) gave him all the tools he needed to lay out these beautiful alignments and circles.

Peridot, the trigger to ancient measurement as we have discussed, is rare indeed and was not generally known other than from St. John's Island, so an alternative must have been available to SAM at Carnac and in the Western world. This material is known as nephrite, a translucent spinach-green crystal of magnesium iron silicate, indeed often known as spinach jade but of quite a different chemical composition from jadeite, the precious form of jade. There is a beautiful nephrite axe-head in the museum.

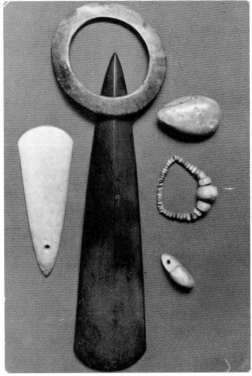

Figure 159
Les Jumelles mirror/ reflector

Figure 160
Axe-head and circle instruments (Collection Société Polymatique, Vannes)

171

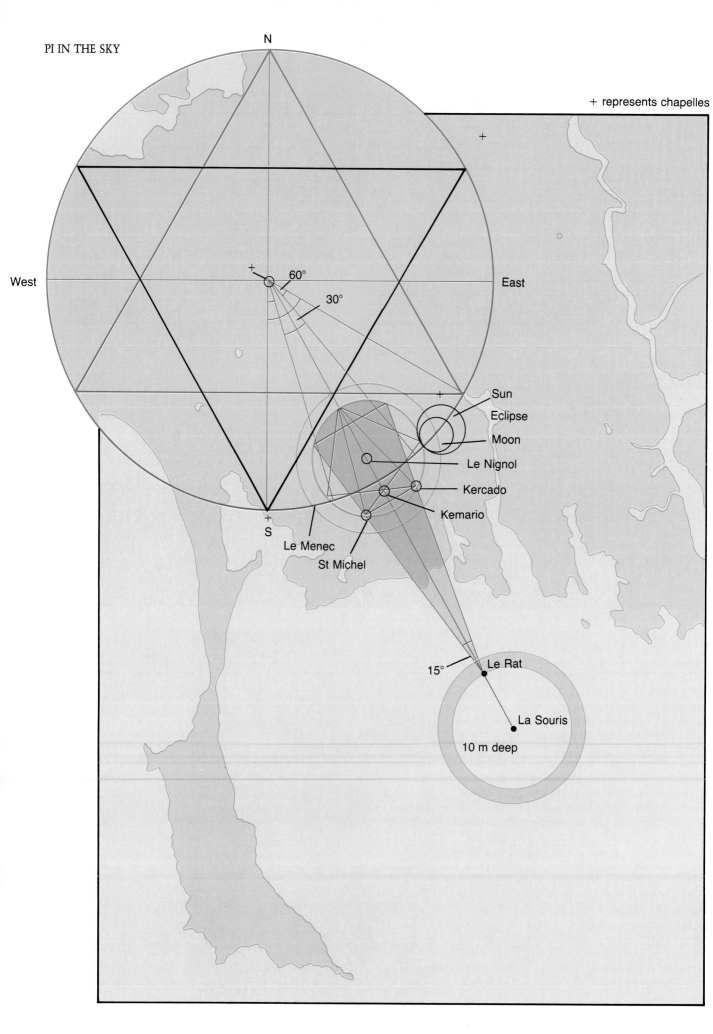

+ represents chapelles

West

N

East

S

60°

30°

15°

Sun

Eclipse

Moon

Le Nignol

Kercado

Kemario

Le Menec

St Michel

Le Rat

La Souris

10 m deep

◁ *Figure 161*
Axe-head and circle π
layout, Carnac
(Karnak)

In Ireland, the equivalent material is called Connemara marble, and is a form of serpentine. Examples of these materials are found as pendulums in the west of Ireland, as Egyptian scarabs, and as prism seals in the kingdom of Minoa (Crete) from the same period.

So these beautiful *ritual* axe-heads are really also the dowsing trigger to Stone Age geometry, while at the same time having a built-in sacred chemical property that actually releases energy into the hands of the user to give us the proportion of Pi (π) and the Earth Star.

Now we dowse Le Rat and La Souris and the axe-head idea of dividing a circle. The alignments form part of a circle centred at Le Nignol inland from the coast and Le Rat and La Souris form another circle in the bay. Between these two circles, using the axe-head shapes, the geometry of the layout of Carnac becomes clear for the proportion of the axe-head to the circles is $^{22}/_7$ or π. Now we dowse the interior of the circle at Le Nignol and around its perimeter. Forming on these structures the pendulum shows a seven-pointed Star.

The waters of Carnac Bay rose to their

▽ *Figure 162*
Cairn at Carnac, now
under water

present levels, we are told by the geologists, in approximately 7000 BC. Therefore, the layout of Carnac must either have taken place prior to that date of the floods were much later, since the archaeologists tell us that the earliest dates at Carnac are around 4000 BC, in line with dates offered by the Swedish dig carried out at Carrowmore in County Sligo. Whatever the answer intriguing questions are raised about ancient history once again.

Within the Carnac layout there are many small churches (*chapelles*) named to the saints of Christianity by the Huguenots in the later 17th century, the great tumulus on the Kercado line being renamed Chapelle St. Michel. Recently John Mitchell rediscovered the great St. Michael line (or alignment) running across southern England from Land's End to Suffolk. Since the Carnac St. Michael tumulus lies on one arm of a seven-pointed Star pattern let us dowse the idea of a seven-pointed Star projecting from Carnac through the British Isles.

The Star of Light – the St. Michael Line and 'Hyperborea'
Carnac is a derivation of Karnac in ancient

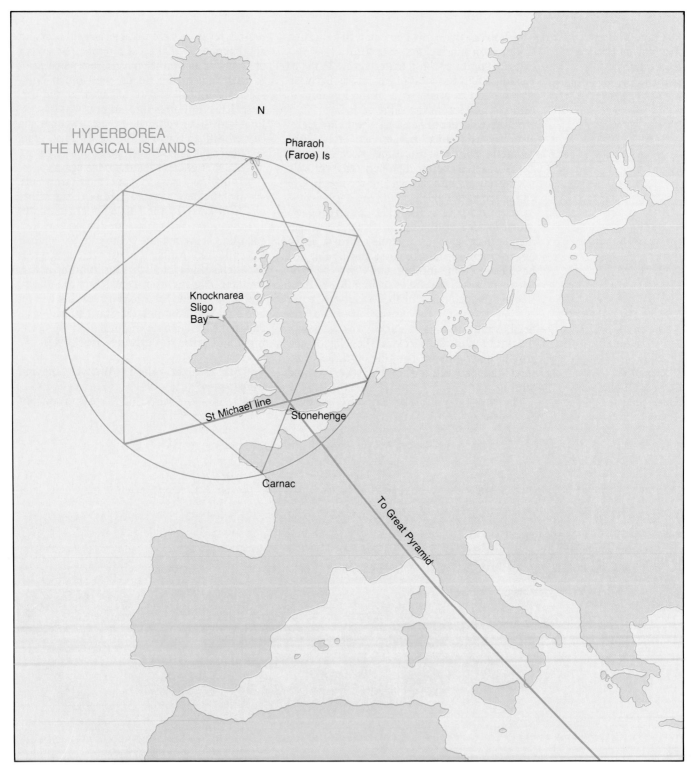

Egypt. The Old Testament tells us that there is a sign laid down in the desert as an aspect of God. We have remarked on St. Michael's tumulus and we are familar with St. Michael's Mount in Cornwall.

If we now dowse the centre line of the Carnac seven-fold Star north-westwards up through Brittany and across the English Chan-nel, it crosses Cornwall by Redruth, 'Carn Brea', across to Ireland and upwards to stop in Sligo Bay in the north-west, perhaps a centre, and we have the St. Michael line running from St. Michael's Mount in the west to Beccles in the east, maybe one line of a seven-pointed Star.

But why should we suppose that it starts in

Figure 163
St. Michael line and 'Hyperborea' (the British Isles) (star drawn not allowing for curvature of the Earth and converging longitude)

Cornwall and stops in Suffolk? When dowsed the line extends both ways, out onto the Atlantic shelf in the west and eastwards into the shallow North Sea off Holland. Once we have found the centre with the pendulum and a perimeter (Carnac, and the St. Michael line) we can draw a circle around the British Isles and disclose the *Hyperborea* of Plato – the legendary islands of magic, geometry and symmetry lost in the mists of timelessness and ages past, suddenly to appear again; the Islands of the Shining Ones, the legendary 'Beings of Light' – the British Isles.

The crossing point of the St. Michael line, the Carnac–North Sea line and the central line from Sligo to Egypt and the Great Pyramid goes exactly through Stonehenge. All seven lines continue outwards both ways beyond the Star around the globe to join up eventually back at the centre point.

In Plato's time of 400 BC, the Star was not really lost at all. We can now begin to trace the lines of the Hyperborean Star around our islands. You may imagine our surprise that the centre of the Star was in Sligo Bay and near Knocknarea, the hill top cairn and the great megalithic dolmen area of Carrowmore; both places intimately connected with the Stone Age capital of Ireland at Doonaveeragh and the passage cairns and temples of Carrowkeel.

The Star configuration becomes alive, covering like a great umbrella these islands of so much history and romance, the Arthurian legends and the grail cup of Glastonbury and Nanteous Abbey.

Now we can see some of the connections within the Star. Part of the Atlantic shelf is

Figure 164
Sites of stone ball calculators in north-east Scotland

included, part of the North Sea and the English Channel. In the area of Aberdeen are found those Stone Age geometric balls of incredibly sophisticated designs, such as tetrahedrals, icosahedrals and dodecahedrals; even one double seven-sided lobed ball.

It is not surprising that the Aberdeen line crosses the Moray Firth by Findhorn and its spiritual community of life and service. The Orkney Islands are just clipped by one line and the northern-most point is the Faroe Islands. Suddenly we think of Egypt and the Pharaohs again!

Figure 165
The Faroe (Pharaoh) Islands (does not allow for the curvature of the Earth and converging longitude)

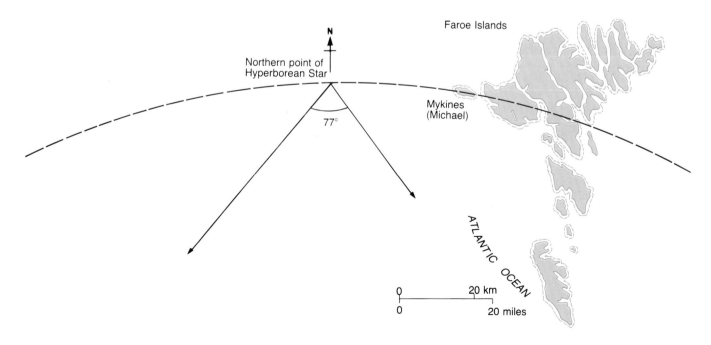

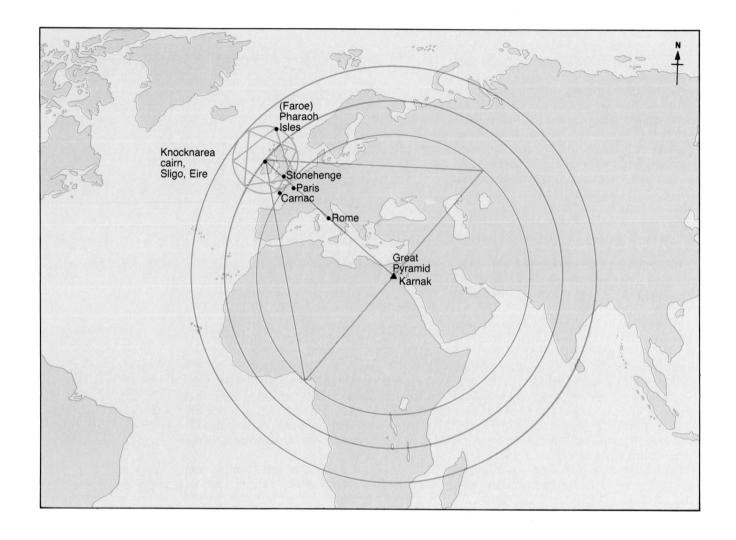

The Egyptian Connection

At last we know how the British Isles' Star is laid out with the 'ley lines' revealed as seven lines of light. The St. Michael line is just part of a much larger Star covering latitudes between 50° and 60°N. But if we are thinking of a seven-fold symmetry, we must be thinking of pyramids, for a pyramid is just another expression of Pi (π), the Sun (Ra) and Mind.

We know that the Great Pyramid of Cheops is constructed in height and dimension as an expression of seven, with side angles of 51.42°, i.e. dividing a circle into seven. Also, the height of a pyramid in relation to its base is seven to twenty-two or Pi (π). If the height is in seven units then four times the base radius is twenty-two units. In the Great Pyramid the height is a reduction in direct proportion of the radius of the Moon (1,080 miles) added to the radius of the Earth (3,960 miles), making a total of 5,040 miles, i.e. $1 \times 2 \times 3 \times 4 \times 5 \times 6 \times 7 = 5,040$ (see Chapter XI).

The Hyperborean connection to Egypt. The radius of the Hyperborean Star represents the proportion of the Moon to the Earth as the distance from the perimeter of this Star to the Great Pyramid, in direct proportion to the Earth's radius, i.e. a proportion of $^{1,080}/_{3,960}$. Hyperborea was the feminine aspect of the then known world through Moon energy. We have always been told that the Pyramids contain the knowledge of Atlantis, the civilisation of the gods of the last evolution of the planet. Perhaps at last we have a key to that knowledge.

The Early Egyptian World

If we accept that Hyperborea existed and was connected to Egypt and the Great Pyramid through such strange structures as Knock-

*Figure 166
'Hyperborea' – the Isles of Light – in seven-fold symmetry*

narea and Carnac and we are told that the Pyramid was not constructed until about 2200 BC, we have, once again, an historical anomaly, for Carnac is dated by the archaeologists to around 4000 BC. Yet we have demonstrated that the (Pi) proportions of Carnac came before the last great world flood.

If Hyperborea is one part of the seven-fold layout of Cheops then it is only a point of a much greater Star pattern emanating from the centre of the ancient world. Let us now draw out that pattern to cover the world of early Egypt. The seven Moons cover all the way across Russia and India down through Africa and back to the British Isles. Maybe it is a fanciful notion but the centre of the Indian Star is near Bombay and perimeter of that Star is near Puttaparthi, the birth place of Sri Sathya Sai 'Baba', the Divine incarnation now on Earth.

This seven-fold plan is the centre of the whole Earth Star plan for if we go back to the pattern of the Earth Stars earlier in the book we can see that this covers circles 1–7 (Figure 153). The remaining circles 7–16–20 to the outer perimeter, therefore, spread outwards to cover the entire Planet Earth. For this planet is just one great Star pattern in itself, in the material crystal world.

From this realisation we can recap and say the Earth really is a crystal structure and so is the solar system we inhabit. How far does this geometry project into the universe and where does the universe end? Within this great crystal structure that is so predictable with SAM's intuitive instruments who and where is the great Creator? Primarily that knowledge of the ancient wisdom tradition lies within us and within the heart of the kingdom, within the heart of man in the image of God, arrayed in his coat of many colours.

Conclusion
The Hypothesis of the Near Future
The Aztec civilization carved a retrospective Sun disc calculator commencing in 3113 BC, 5,104 years ago, that has recently been deciphered. This predicts for us the end of the current age of civilisation, our root-race on

Figure 167
Seven-fold centre of planetary light

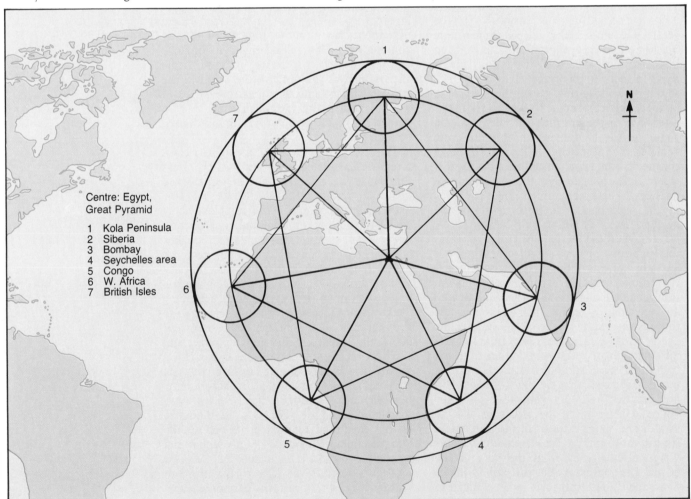

Centre: Egypt,
Great Pyramid

1 Kola Peninsula
2 Siberia
3 Bombay
4 Seychelles area
5 Congo
6 W. Africa
7 British Isles

Planet Earth. The decoded message suggests changes of consciousness and in the ecology will culminate in the year AD 2012 which will herald a New Age of Enlightenment.

We have seen that the priests of the Stone Age used the pendulum and were highly evolved natural scientists with great powers working within a then balanced auric energy grid, our atmosphere. They left us a consistent record of their use of those natural energies clearly engraved on the backstone Kerb 52, or the Great Cairn at Newgrange, County Meath, Ireland.

In Irish mythology we have legends of 'the Shining Ones', the Priests of Light who disappeared at the end of the late neolithic period about 3000 BC by entering the cairns never to be seen again – and how unwary travellers have since wandered into the cairns to emerge many years later to find they have not aged at all, but the world has changed! Could the priests have entered the cairns just prior to 3113 BC knowing that the old age was dying and their work done? The previous great Sun spot cycle was ending prior to a new age about to start.

Can we accept that it is possible to part the accelerated auric body and electro-magnetic life force in/of a cyclotron/cairn to form an unknown substance that materialises into a flying object, at the speed of light, a UFO, spiralling, scintillating, resonating and able to disappear incredibly quickly over the horizon? Then there is perhaps the possibility that crop circles might be the marks of these auric vehicles. The researchers seem only to go to cornfields, but these shapes occur also near stone circles and cairns on the ancient granite hillsides. There they might be seen with psychic sight on the bare rock faces or in the heather. 'Hoax' or not?

One hypothesis is that the crop circles are the imprints of the consciousness of our ancestors, priests of the ancient wisdom tradition who are possibly visiting us again now to teach and help those people of good intent who are prepared to raise their consciousness towards the reality of the New Age to come. These beings are not necessarily from galaxies millions of light years away, but are from our own inner space and our friends. The circles might be seen with the aid of ultra-violet light, not infra-red as is generally used, as clairvoyance seems to be the ability to pick up images and thought forms in the ultra-violet spectrum. Certainly bees orientate on this vibration emanating from the aura of the queen. The increasing Sun spot activity allows more and more ultra-violet to get through to the surface of the planet, affecting the Earth above and below markedly. The interaction of water in earth through air (aura) activated by fire (the Sun) builds up and expands energies within our presently disrupted grid. The obvious work of opening perception is to recreate this grid for our 'friends' to come to us, which seems to be very reassuring and joyful, for that is exactly what many organisations are trying to do.

We have suggested that the mind of the priest was the trigger which implies 'intention', but examples of the material 'cores' of these vehicles lie unrecognised in the National Museum of Ireland, not on display. They are two balls or spheres found in a cairn at Loughcrew. One is of iron ore and the other of granite. We handled these a few years back and as an (unwise) experiment channelled all our energies into first the granite ball and we (our auras) literally expanded superluminarily creating, we were told, a 'white hole'. Then we did the same with the iron ore ball and immediately we were sucked horribly, as though miniaturised, through the floor creating a 'black hole'. Now remember the core of an atomic bomb is a cricket ball-sized sphere of enriched uranium or plutonium that is compressed by a nuclear trigger to implode and then explode the 'bomb'. In SAM's time the trigger was the mind of the priest in the cairn, his intention being to take off and travel at the speed of light through time – or so dematerialise and reappear within our dimension on the planet.

This evolutionary age is drawing to a close after, we calculate, 5,125 years as the great Sun spot cycle completes another differential evolution with Planet Earth. We are now experiencing a vast build-up of solar energy that is disrupting our aura and consequently our weather, oceans, tides, winds, earthquakes and volcanoes, and to come, our tectonic plates. It is suggested that the peak activity will occur in 1998. Consider that the Sun has a periodic rate of combustion such that every 5,000 years it increases vastly in temperature and size and then contracts and cools suddenly, thus pulsating and growing larger and smaller over time. As the Sun expands it grows in size and energy output and Mercury, its consort, increases in temperature accordingly. But Mercury's magnetic field decays with temperature and as it decays so its influence on the equatorial rotation of its parent, the Sun, declines. When the Sun's equatorial rotation slows to the same speed as its polar rotation – thirty-seven days each – the Sun spot cycle *ceases*. Result: the harmonic wavelength on which all our genes, male and female, mutate ceases, so there follows:

1. A drastically falling birth rate, i.e. failing procreation on the planet.
2. Drastic cooling and a subsequent new Ice Age.

So much for the scientific idea of the 'greenhouse effect'. After about a hundred years or four generations, the human population of the planet (animals will also be affected) will have fallen off to a total of, perhaps, one billion – but who can predict that number?

This is one of the reasons that the priests of the Stone Age retreated into their cairns in about 3000 BC. For as the electro-magnetic life force of the planet grew weaker in the auric field, so they manipulated that force with quartz prisms and polarised light. Quartz has a property unique in the whole of the gem world, in that it rotates the polarisation of white light (sunlight) through 45°, thereby striking a new balance and symmetry in the failing solar wind and the shrinking auric field of increasing magnetism. This increase, in turn, helped the priests to 'fly away'. Now the same event is recurring so those ancient priests are returning to help us – again. A second coming indeed!

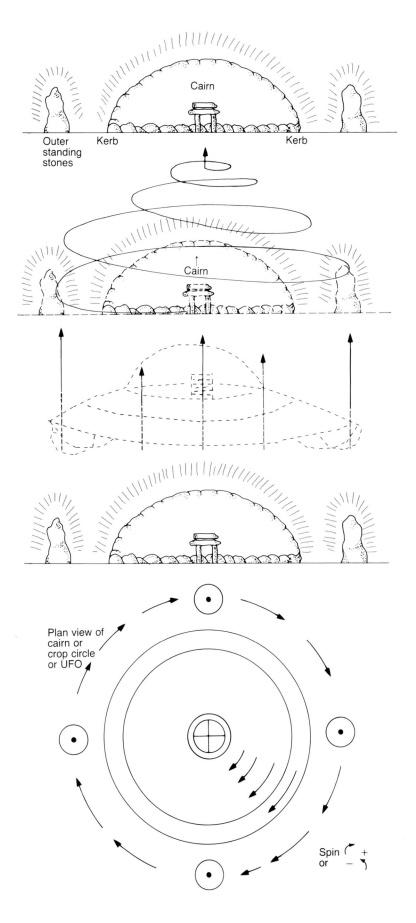

Figure 168
Pi in the sky

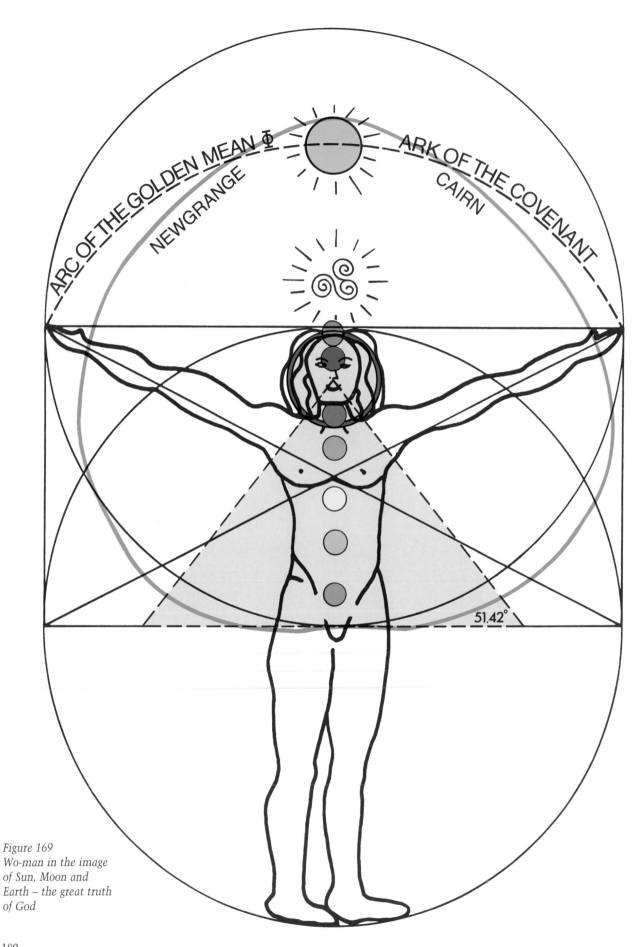

ARC OF THE GOLDEN MEAN Φ

ARK OF THE COVENANT

NEWGRANGE

CAIRN

51.42°

Figure 169
Wo-man in the image
of Sun, Moon and
Earth – the great truth
of God

GLOSSARY
Useful Descriptions and Terminology

Amethyst
A violet or purple variety of quartz thought to be coloured by manganese. Colour will vary markedly under different degrees of heat 400°–500°C. Change will be to brown, yellow or red, even green.

Angstrom
A unit measurement of light wavelength in the shorter vibrations 1 AU = $\frac{1}{10}$ millionth of a millimetre expressed (10^{-7}mm).

Aquamarine
A clear sky/sea blue beryl (of the emerald family) in the hexagonal system of six.

Atma-sphere
The Earth's aura.

Axes of crystals
Imaginary lines passing through the crystal and intersecting at the centre called the 'origin'. Normally parallel to symmetry axes, i.e. basic structures, systems are: 1 cubic; 2 tetragonal; 3 orthorhombic; 4 monoclinic; 5 triclinic; 6 hexagonal; (7 trigonal but similar to hexagonal).

Biaxial crystals
These give two dimensions of refracted light, thereby a double image when looking into the stone; known as 'double refraction'. Uniaxial crystals are single refracting – light being 'bent' between entry and exit of a gem – the amount due to its atomic structure. All gems can be classified by their refractive indices.

Blue John (Bleu Jaune)
A Derbyshire spar, is a form of fluorspar (fluorite), (CaF_2) calcium fluoride.

Calcite ($CaCo_3$)
Calcium carbonate.

Catalyst
A substance which alters the rate at which change takes place but is itself unaltered at the end of the (chemical) reaction.

Centre of symmetry
In crystals, the regular faces are arranged to certain laws of symmetry which classify into 32 mathematically possible classes and into seven crystal systems basically, plane of symmetry, axis of symmetry, centre of symmetry. Once understood the bridge between the microcosm and macrocosm becomes clear.

Chrysocolla
A blue green copper silicate ($CaSiO_32H_2O$) often thought to have been used by the Egyptians in magic and healing – a grounding conductive substance.

Citrine
Yellow quartz wrongly called 'topaz' (which is a different precious crystal mainly from Brazil). Citrine draws its yellow/golden colour from traces of iron in the ferric state (Fe_2O_3).

Clairvoyance or clairaudience	The ability to intuit, see in the mind's eye or hear silently in the ear, vibrations of an unseen/unheard realm of other dimensions, not accepted by science. A knowledge/experiential system as opposed to a belief system. Possibly in the higher ultra-violet spectrum.
Cleavage	A peculiarity in crystals is a tendency to split parallel to certain definite directions as a consequence of the regular arrangement of atoms therein.
Colour	Colour in gemstones is due to trace elements – chromium gives the finest colours of green or red, but iron, cobalt, vanadium, titanium, nickel and copper are also found as 'agents'.
Composite gems	These are 'cheat' stones where different crystals are cut and put together as a sort of sandwich to make the colour or brilliance more attractive. Known as doublets or triplets for obvious reasons.
Diamond	Pure carbon, octahedral, clear gem of purity – a symbol of romantic love.
Dichroism	In double refracting gems, a stone sometimes appears to have a different colour if viewed from different angles due to two rays of light reacting at right angles to each other.
Divining or dowsing	The intuition of unseen energies in the atmosphere and sensed as vibrations in the Earth and the mind.
Earth energy	Vibrations of energy, the interactions of water in earth into air (atmosphere) generated in part by fire (the Sun). Can be picked up by clairvoyant 'sight' and/or the use of rods, twigs and pendulums and annotated as to colour, resonance, direction and purity.
Earth Stars	A pattern of Earth energy that forms into spherical vibrations of the macrocosm, i.e. in the atma-sphere and out into space. These structured spheres are the atoms of the universe that expand in size outwards from our surface. Like all atoms, they are unique to themselves but totally interrelated. The structure of gravity.
Electro-positive and electro-negative (elements)	Elements divide in (+) (−) depending on whether they ionise with a deficiency of electrons + or an excess of electrons −.
Equinox	Day on which the length of time from sunrise to sunset equals that from sunset to sunrise. Spring 21st March, autumn 21st September.
Emerald	In the beryl family, hexagonal system; colour is due to chromium (Cr_2O_3). Chemical composition $Be_3Al_2(SiO_3)_6$. Brilliant green.
Feldspar	$KalSi_3O_8$. Transparent and colourless, sometimes green, orange and yellow and generally known as moonstone. Magical properties grossly overrated as it only affects the lower chakras marginally, with no tangible benefits, yet romantically attractive to the feminine.

Fibonacci scale	$1 + 1 = 2 + 1 = 3 + 2 = 5 + 3 = 8 + 5 = 13 + 8 = 21 \rightarrow$ the gnomonic expansion of the spiral.
Fluroescence and luminescence	The afterglow of a substance following previous exposure to radiation, e.g. sunlight. May be induced by rubbing 2 pieces of quartz together. The American Indians used 'lightning' sets to simulate lightning during rain ceremonies – thunder by beating a drum. Some gemstones luminesce under ultra-violet light.
Fool's gold	Iron pyrites.
Glass	First made by the Egyptians, supposedly glass has a 'former' – usually a silicate (SiO_2). Quartz becomes (SiO_4) in glass mixed with oxides of alkaline metals – lead, etc.: glass does not have crystal symmetry and its excessive use can cause the break-up/down of mental states in high-rise buildings, mirrors, etc.
God	The Great Orb or 'O' of Dei-Deus-Day $\rightarrow$ the Sun.
Golden Mean proportion	The basic sacred geometric pattern and mathematical fraction of the solar harmonic ray frequency. Expressed as $^1/_{1.618}$.
Goldstone	Is a form of aventurine glass – a soda-lime glass coloured with copper oxide, not a crystal or gem.
Granite	This is composed of feldspar quartz (rock crystal) and mica. An igneous rock. The crystallisation of minerals in cooling magma due to volcanic action.
Iolite	Looks like, but is not, sapphire. Be careful especially in India! $(Mg_2Al_4Si_5O_{18})$, also known as dichroite and cordierite.
Iona stone	A form of serpentine found on Iona at the Bay of Portnacarrick. Also known as Connemara marble, soapstone and steatite.
Iridescence	The play of light as seen in opal due to a three-dimensional internal lattice of varying colours.
Jasper	A variety of quartz. Colour, due to iron, is browny-red.
Ley lines (Alfred Watkins orig: 1930s)	A name given to force/energy lines running through the Earth to the surface, on which ancient structures were often built. But also a line imposed in the atma-sphere by projection of thought patterns from a clairvoyant mind. 'Brainwaves'?
Macrocosm	The atma-sphere (atmosphere) spiralling outwards into the solar system and beyond universal space.
Meteorites and tektites	Extra-terrestrial substances, not crystalline in gem terms, but often overstressed quartz such as obsidian-type glass. Considered as coming from exploding stars of other solar systems – cosmic substances. Also consisting of nickel and olivine (peridotite).

Mica	Occurs in granite and is an excellent insulator of energy.
Mica schist	Plates were used by SAM, at Newgrange for instance, to enclose the energy of heated quartz.
Microcosm	The world of sub-atomic physics – the inside of the material world.
Moss agate	Agates are crypto-crystalline quartzes or chalcedony with many different colours – also chrysoprase, cornelian, onyx. Moss agate looks like a flower, fern or tree inclusion forming a pretty picture but is, in fact, a natural inclusion.
Nacre	The secreted juices of an oyster that cover the irritation of a foreign body within its shell eventually becoming a pearl.
Natural glass or obsidian	Formed by the rapid cooling of volcanic lava – too quick to form granite or quartz. Usually black but may have an iridescent sheen due to minute bubbles. It does not have a crystal structure.
Nephrite	Very important to SAM. Often exceptional axe-heads are carved of nephrite and were used as divisors of the circle for laying out Stone Age structures; see Carnac, Chapter XII. $Ca_2(MgFe)_5(OH_2)(Si_4O_{11})_2$. A complicated magnesium iron silicate.
Olivine (peridot)	A green gemstone vitally important in ancient times as the trigger crystal in establishing by divining ancient measurements with the pendulum. A magnesium iron silicate – as is nephrite, and has similar properties. The coarse form of this gem in a lower evolutionary state is steatite, soapstone and serpentine $(MgFe)_2SiO_4$, used in SAM's pendulums.
Onyx	A form of agate (quartz).
Opal	This is an iridescent crystallised 'jelly', a combination of SiO_2 and H_2O. Its unlucky annotation is due to its fragility under extremes of temperature change when it will fracture. Women therefore think it is 'unlucky' to wear this gem.
Padparadscha (sapphire)	Name meaning 'lotus' in Sri Lanka for the golden peach colour, very rarely found in sapphire and highly prized as an emblem of the open brow chakra, and enlightenment.
Pavilion	The facets on the underneath of a brilliant cut gemstone.
Pendulum	Pendants of many substances looking like little plumb-bobs or often annotated by archaeologists as 'jewellery' from SAM's times. Used to gauge (+)(−) energy in the atmasphere when dowsing and divining unseen vibrations.
Plato (c.400 BC)	Greek philosopher who drew attention to Hyperborea, the magical islands of the NW coasts of the then known world, and the attendant Priests of Light, the geometers of the past and from Atlantis.

'Py' or 'Pi' π	The famous fraction that defines a circle from a radius (πR^2). But also the definitive fraction of a spiral S-π-ra-ll. 'Pi' is shown to us in SAM's time as a dolmen structure usually sited on the southern-most point of an Earth Star.
Pyro-electricity and piezo-electricity	Some crystals – tourmaline, quartz – when heated and expanded or contracted and squashed, give off an electrical charge $(+)(-)$ at either end, i.e. from day to night in many of SAM's structures, such as Newgrange.
Pythagoras (c.550 BC)	Greek mathematician who supposedly gave us the circular fraction of π (Pi), but which is here shown as emanating from the solar harmonic and known 4,000 years previously.
Quantum	The electro-magnetic wave theory of the radiant energy of light, of Einstein and Planck. Maxwell and Faraday suggested that these vibrations were due to periodic alterations in the electrical and magnetic conditions of the 'ether'. This is exactly so, but due to solar cycle variations in the harmonic of the solar wind as is explained in this book.
Quarter days	The four 'quarters' of the year between solstices and equinoxes: 1st February, 1st May, 1st August and 1st November.
Quartz (rock crystal)	SiO_2, the main 'gem' used in ancient times due to its unique properties and so readily available around the world. Vein quartz is often gold bearing. Rock crystal is clear quartz.
Ruby and sapphire	Together, because they are both corundum – the same family. Rubies are red but sapphires occur in every colour, from black to white, violet to yellow and pink to green. All have magical properties. A ruby is the most precious of all the gemstones, put at the throat of Aaron by God.
Sard and sardonyx	A form of agate or onyx, in the quartz family.
Spiral	The spiral is the basic expression of three-dimensional energy progression and can be measured with a pendulum $(+)(-)$.
Solstice	The longest and shortest days of the year: 21st June and 21st December (the Christ-Mass).
Tourmaline	Like sapphire has a great range of colours, but a highly complicated chemical structure, and with special electrical properties.
Turquoise	A pale blue, soft, chalky copper-based stone, colour often now simulated by enhancing with dyes. A 'grounding' stone due to the copper. Best examples found in Iran.
Ultra-violet light	Part of the electro-magnetic spectrum harmful to life on the planet but exciting to the intuitive processes of the mind.
Venus hair stone	Rutilated quartz – thin rods of rutile inclusions looking like strands of golden hair in the crystals, which gives a lovely effect.

A Table of Birth Stones

January	Dark red	Garnet
February	Purple	Amethyst
March	Pale blue	Aquamarine
April	White	Diamond
May	Green	Emerald
June	Cream	Pearl
July	Red	Ruby
August	Pale green	Peridot
September	Deep blue	Sapphire
October	Variegated	Opal
November	Yellow	Topaz
December	Sky blue	Turquoise

(Official List of the National Association of Goldsmiths, UK)
There are many lists varying around the world, but the original goes back to the Breastplate of Righteousness and the twelve tribes of Israel, i.e. the zodiac.

Stones in Hindu Mythology Relating to 'Protection' against the Influence of the Planets

Sun	Ruby
Moon	Pearl
Mars	Coral
Mercury	Emerald
Venus	Pink sapphire
Jupiter	Topaz
Saturn	Blue sapphire
Infra-red	(Raju) Catseye
Ultra-violet	(Gomed) Hessonite garnet

Bibliography and Further Reading

Chapter I
Our Solar System

(a) *Amateur Astronomy Sky Guide*, Mark Chartrant III (Newnes Books)
(b) *The Round Art: Astrology of Time and Space*, A.T. Mann (Dragon World Books)
(c) *Astrology*, Warren Kenton (Thames & Hudson)
(d) *Healing Stones*, Julia Lorusso and Joel Glick (Brotherhood of Life Books)
(e) *Beyond the Jupiter Effect*, John Gribbin and Stephen Plagemann (Macdonald)
(f) *Time Stands Still*, Keith Critchlow (Gordon Fraser)
(g) *Astrogenetics*, Maurice Cotterell (Brooks, Hill, Robinson)
(h) *The Theory of Celestial Influence*, Rodney Collin (Robinson & Watkins)

Chapter II
Crystal Earth and the Atmosphere

(a) *Gems*, Robert Webster (Butterworths)
(b) *Illustrated Encyclopaedia of the Mineral Kingdom*, Dr Alan Woolley (Hamlyn)

Chapter III
Crystal Structures

(a) *Gems*, Robert Webster (Butterworths)
(b) *Crystal Consciousness*, Ron Bonewitz (Shambhala)
(c) *Illustrated Encyclopaedia of the Mineral Kingdom*, Dr Alan Woolley (Hamlyn)

Chapter IV
Planetary Geometry

(a) *Time Stands Still*, Keith Critchlow (Gordon Fraser)
(b) *The Round Art: Astrology of Time and Space*, A.T. Mann (Dragon World Books)

Chapter V
Earth Energy Stars

(a) *Irish Passage Graves*, Michael Herity (IUP, Dublin)
(b) *The Sphinx and the Megaliths*, John Ivimy (Abacus)

Chapter VI
The Carrowkeel Star

(a) *Irish Passage Graves*, Michael Herity (IUP, Dublin) 1974

Chapter VII
Ancient Seasons and Festivals and SAM's Lifestyle

(a) *The Path of Initiation*, Peter Dawkins (journals of the Francis Bacon Research Trust)
(b) *The Genius of the Few*, C. and B.J. O'Brien (Turnstone Press)

Chapter VIII
Newgrange

(a) *Newgrange*, Michael O'Kelly (Thames & Hudson)
(b) *Concise Guide to Newgrange*, Clair O'Kelly
(c) *Irish Passage Graves*, Michael Herity (IUP, Dublin)
(d) *The Boyne Valley Vision* and *The Stars and the Stones*, Martin Brennan (Dolmen Press)
(e) *Gem*, Robert Webster (Butterworths)
(f) *Treasures of Ireland*, National Museum of Ireland
(g) *Innishmurray*, Patrick Heraughty (O'Brien Press)
(h) *The Dancing Wu Li Masters*, Gary Zukav (Rider)
(i) *Ponder on This*, Alice Bailey (Lucis Trust)
(j) Christopher Hills, University of the Trees Press, P.O. Box 644, Boulder Creek, CA 95006, USA

Chapter IX **Symbols and Engravings**	(a)	*The Boyne Valley Vision,* Martin Brennan (Dolmen Press)
	(b)	*The Stars and the Stones,* Martin Brennan (Dolmen Press)
	(c)	*Newgrange,* Michael O'Kelly (Thames & Hudson)
	(d)	*Concise Guide to Newgrange,* Clair O'Kelly
	(e)	*Irish Passage Graves,* Michael Herity (IUP, Dublin)
	(f)	*Time Stands Still,* Keith Critchlow (Gordon Fraser)
	(g)	*Archaeology of Carrowmore,* Göran Burnenhuilt (Swedish archaeologist)
	(h)	*The Fairy Faith in Celtic Countries,* Evans Wentz (C. Smythe)
Chapter X **Great Power Sites**	(a)	*Innishmurray,* Patrick Heraughty (O'Brien Press)
	(b)	*The Sun and the Serpent,* Hamish Miller and Paul Broadhurst (Pendragon Press)
	(c)	*Circular Evidence,* Pat Delgado and Colin Andrews (Bloomsbury)
Chapter XI **The Irish Gold Age**	(a)	*Treasures of Ireland,* National Museum of Ireland
	(b)	*Irish Passage Graves,* Michael Herity (IUP, Dublin)
	(c)	*The Drama of the Lost Disciples,* Rev. Jowett (Covenant)
Chapter XII **The Planetary Star of Hyperborea**	(a)	Museum handbook, Carnac

Vibhoothi Manthram

— ● —

**Pramam Pavithram Baabas
Vibhoothim**

**Paramam Vichithram Leelaa
Vibhoothim**

**Paramartha Ishtartha Moksha
Pradhanam**

**Baabaa Vibhoothim Edamahsra
Yaami**

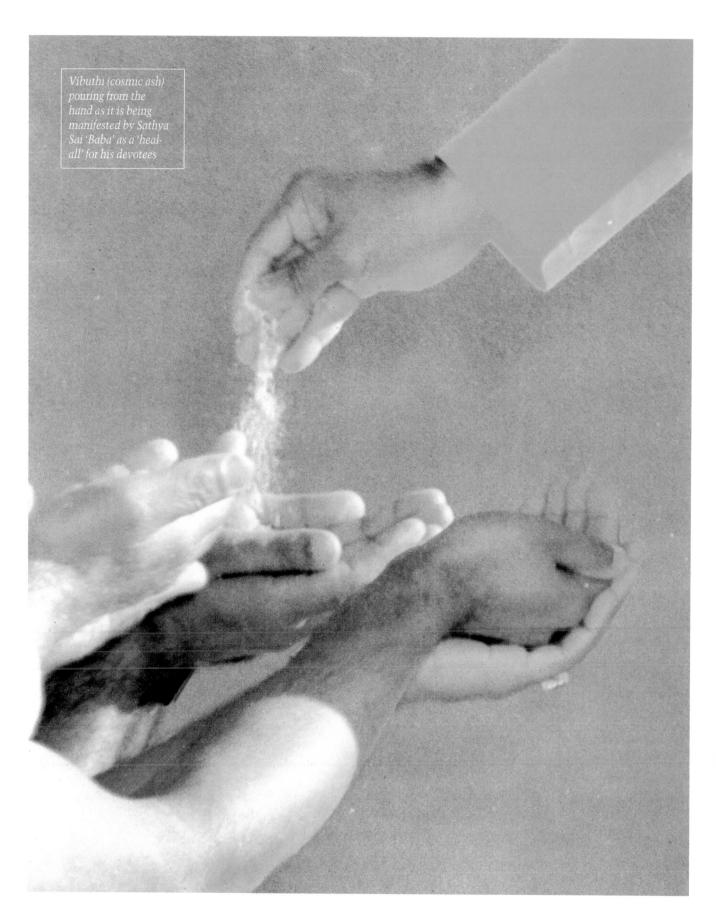

Vibuthi (cosmic ash) pouring from the hand as it is being manifested by Sathya Sai 'Baba' as a 'heal-all' for his devotees

The Future – A Guidance

The future is usually a sight of something
you don't want to happen, and can't control.
If it's happiness you seek or wish to
see it will happen anyway and you'll hasten
it before it's due to arrive by too much
yearning.

The future is NOW as time has no beginning
or end. The past is equally now and therefore
the present is already past and you are
already in the future.

If you can understand this there's no need to
know the future as it will only confuse you
and make you restless and annoyed. You'll go
round all your friends saying, 'Do you know
such and such is going to happen', and when it
does and you've proved yourself right often
enough – then you won't have any friends any
more – you and the future will have become
predictable and therefore boring.